Retrospect

Tom Tottis

Based on a true story,
Retrospect is about human fortitude, chronicling the life of
a Hungarian family, eventually reduced to just mother and
son, their struggle during Nazism in the early 1940s,
followed by tyrannical Communism, the Hungarian
Uprising in 1956, and the aftermath.

Some names have been changed.

Published by New Generation Publishing in 2018

Copyright © Tom Tottis 2018

First Edition

ISBN: 978-1-78719-730-5

www.newgeneration-publishing.com

 New Generation Publishing

To my darling daughter,
Jackie.

I had met the Grim Reaper more than once, have walked side by side with him and observed him at his work. The Reaper's aversion to his task makes him dour and miserable, yet each time our paths have crossed the Grim Reaper smiled at me.

Budapest, 1921

Julia quickened her steps to a half run. The family would be gathering for their regular seven o'clock evening meal and she had another ten minutes' walk ahead of her. Darkness enveloped the streets of Budapest, partly because it was late November, partly due to one of the many ways the government tried to economise. Half the gaslights on all roads, in every town, had to remain unlit.

Although the Great War had ended three years before, it had impoverished the country and its inhabitants. The only benefit was that Hungary was no longer part of Austria and independent once more, but this was paid for in blood and the ensuing grief. In the wake of the war, the economy collapsed. Indirectly this was the cause of Julia being late. To help supplement the family budget she provided tuition to children in mathematics, literature and German, and this evening her young pupil had great difficulty in converting fractions to decimals.

Julia's father, Joseph, was a butcher. His shop was just around the corner from their third-floor apartment in Rottenbiller Street. Shortly after war was declared in 1914, he was called up and over the next three years rose to the rank of sergeant. At the beginning of 1918, just after Julia's eighteenth birthday, he had been dragging an injured comrade back to the trenches when a piece of shrapnel hit him on his elbow. Consequently, his left arm had to be amputated just below his shoulder. Like many other injured veterans he taught himself to be self-reliant, but even though he could perform most of the tasks of his trade they took a lot longer than a butcher would take with both arms and hands. He had no other choice but to hire an assistant, which was a heavy drain on the finances.

Joseph, upon becoming sergeant

As Julia turned at last into Rottenbiller Street, she remembered the one and only time she had been really late. It was in the summer of 1918 and she was at a friend's birthday party. Very few people held parties in those days, so when an invitation arrived no one in their right mind would decline it. Julia truly enjoyed being among friends, entertaining themselves by playing the piano, engaging in conversation, reciting poems or dancing.

And so it happened that by the time she looked at the clock on the mantelpiece it was past ten thirty and she had to say a hasty goodbye to everybody. She thanked her hosts, and the eldest son of the family – a lieutenant on leave from the army – insisted on escorting her home as darkness enveloped the city.

Upon leaving the house the lieutenant offered his arm, and after a moment's hesitation Julia accepted. Walking arm-in-arm with a handsome officer would be quite exciting she thought.

Worried about her lateness, because Julia was habitually very punctual and reliable, Joseph set off to collect his daughter, hoping that no harm had come to her. Dressed in his uniform with three medals pinned to his tunic, he was met by the lieutenant and Julia walking towards him. Joseph stopped and saluted the higher-ranking officer who returned the salute. Julia realised the awkwardness of the situation and introduced her companion.

'This is Lieutenant Bokros, my friend Lizzy's brother. This is my father, Sergeant Láng.'

The young officer took over the conversation, saying how much he enjoyed escorting Julia, and now that the task was complete he hoped there would be another chance to see Julia again on his next leave. He then noticed the empty, folded-up sleeve of the sergeant's uniform.

'I think it is indeed my duty to salute you, Sergeant Láng.'

The lieutenant performed a perfect yet respectful salute, turned on his heels and walked off into the darkness. That was the last time Julia saw Lieutenant Bokros; a month later he was killed in action.

Back home at last, Julia found her younger brothers László and Imre seated around the dining table. Her mother, Hannah, dishing out the food, said she could not keep it warm any longer without wasting more coal to keep the kitchen stove going.

'Don't apologise Mother, it's my fault for being late. My carriage failed to turn up and I had to walk home,' she said with mock indignation.

Julia

The family consumed the meal in total silence, apart from Hannah asking if anyone cared to have more of this or that. Talking during meals, especially with one's mouth full, amounted to bad manners. Finally, as the last knife and fork came to rest on an empty dinner plate, Joseph broke the silence.

'Latzie has found a job.'

'Oh, good,' Julia said, smiling at her nineteen-year-old brother. 'What is it?'

László's face turned into one big smile and for a very good reason. He had passed his exams of a four-year course of commercial studies the year before, yet he had failed to find a job of any sort until now.

'I will be the organiser and bookkeeper at Somosy Removals. The present incumbent is about to retire but he's going to show me the ropes first.'

'I wish I were in your shoes,' fifteen-year-old Imre said. 'I'd love to make money instead of having to go to school.'

1922

A year went by with very little change. Julia was either helping her mother to run their home or assisting her father in the shop and also giving tuition in the evenings. She had more students now because she added piano lessons to her other subjects. Her income was no longer just a supplement to the family budget; her father put half of her earnings aside for her dowry. It was customary for a girl engaged to be married to purchase a valuable present for her future husband.

'Jutzie,' her father said one evening as she was handing over the money, 'right now it is fortunate that you have no suitor because your present dowry would constitute an insult, but isn't it time for you to start looking around? You're in your twenties, a few more years without a boyfriend and you will be considered an oddity.'

The comment was appropriate and Julia herself had pondered about it lately when looking at her reflection in the mirror. She was small in build with a well-proportioned figure, shapely legs and ankles, and an engagingly pretty face with brown eyes and lots of very dark brown, almost black hair.

Young men had asked her out a number of times, but so far none of them made her heart beat faster. 'What am I looking for?' she asked herself frequently, lying awake unable to sleep, but no answer was forthcoming. She did not know. All she knew was that she had not met that special person yet.

László enjoyed working in his first assignment and his employers were happy with his performance. Imre decided, against his father's advice, to finish school at sixteen and enter into an apprenticeship.

Late one evening, in their shared bedroom (the flat had only three bedrooms), Imre asked László for a loan.

'Another loan?' snapped László, 'Imre, you still haven't repaid what I lent you last month! No way will I give you more money until you settle your existing debt.'

Imre implored and begged László to change his mind, but with no effect. Eventually he blurted out that he needed the loan to settle a debt. He had lost money playing cards and it was a matter of honour. László, normally a quiet, placid man shook his young brother by the shoulders.

'Honour! What sort of honour is there losing *my* money and asking *me* to settle your debts again?'

'Keep your voice down,' pleaded Imre. 'If Papa hears about this he'll throw me out.'

'All right, I'll give you the money but this is definitely the last time. Don't bother to ask again and I *do* want it back. All of it, do you understand?' László said angrily. Still fuming at the reckless attitude of his young brother, he went to bed.

Invitations to birthday parties for Julia had ceased completely because after a person's eighteenth birthday it was no longer customary. Birthday celebrations after that took place just within the family. In its place she attended the occasional friendly gatherings arranged by her friends who were better off, theatre outings and christenings of babies born to her friends.

It was at one party when a tall, fair-haired and well-dressed man had caught her eye. The chap noticed her half-averted glance, came over and looked down at her.

'I am Handsome.' He gave emphasis to the last word. 'And you are?'

'I am Julia Láng. Are you sure you are handsome?' Julia responded with gentle sarcasm. 'Wouldn't you also be complacent to some extent?'

'I sincerely hope not,' the man said. 'My name is Handsome. Zoltán Handsome. I cannot help myself pulling this trick on the unsuspecting individual.' They burst out laughing and spent much of the evening in each other's company.

Tucked up in bed that night, Julia was happy. She liked Zoltán Handsome very much. They met again some time later at another gathering but he did not ask her out even though he arrived and left the scene without a girl on his arm. Curious, thought Julia.

1923

'Jutzie,' Joseph said to Julia one evening. 'Your birthday is coming up in a few weeks' time and your mother and I have decided that instead of a present you can give a party for your friends. Our home is yours for the evening; the two of us will go visiting and your brothers will help you set up a buffet or something of that nature. I will cover the cost of it.'

This was a marvellous idea. Julia had attended a number of such gatherings over the years, but had been unable to organise one herself. As invitations of this kind had to be sent out at least a month before the event to avoid the clashing of dates with some other party, Julia set about writing to her friends. She wrote eighteen letters entitling each recipient to bring a friend or partner. Should they all accept and turn up, she thought, the lounge would be tightly packed. She did not mention her birthday it was to be a party like any other.

On the appointed day when everything had been arranged and furniture moved out of the way by Latzie and Imre, the front door was left wide open so that guests could enter without ringing the bell and the host wouldn't have to attend to it each time it rang. They arrived in ones and twos, most of them with a friend, fiancé or fiancée. Few of them were married – couples quickly disappeared from the party circuit, primarily because of their initial joy as newly weds and also due to family gatherings on both sides that could not go unattended. Last but not least, the arrival of the first baby put an end to any socialising.

Suddenly a booming voice silenced the happy chatter. 'May I have your attention, please?'

All eyes turned to the door of the lounge where the tall figure of Zoltán Handsome loomed.

'I have brought a friend I haven't seen for many years, the best friend anyone could have. We were classmates at a Roman Catholic High School and quite by chance we bumped into each other last week. His name is Sándor, Sandy for short.'

Zoltán stepped away from the door, revealing the person standing behind him. The man in the doorway was in his early twenties with light brown hair already receding, brown eyes with a friendly glint in them, a nice straight nose and attractively curved lips. He was of medium height but seemed to have broad shoulders and had a stylish, smart appearance.

Sándor

Julia stepped forward, introduced herself as befitting the hostess and took him around the room making the necessary introductions. She observed that the man had impeccable manners.

The party was a great success. Everyone enjoyed themselves and they kept Julia at the piano by repeated demands to play Schubert and Chopin, the great romantics. Finally, as people began to leave, Sándor complimented Julia on her choice of pieces and the excellence she had demonstrated playing the piano.

'My home is quite a distance from here in Lónyai Street, where I live with my parents,' he said, 'but I hope that we shall meet again.'

As for Zoltán Handsome he did not ask Julia for a date, nor did he ask anyone else.

Later in the year Julia and her cousin Irén had seats booked at the Opera House for the performance of the tragic story of *La Bohéme*. Just as the curtain fell, after the first act and before the lights came on, Julia heard a man seated behind her whisper in her ear.

'If there weren't so many people around I would kiss that lovely neck of yours.' This was audacious talk particularly from a stranger.

Julia spun round, intent on slapping the face of the offender. Fortunately, for both of them, she stopped herself at the last moment when she realised that the culprit was Sándor. He was in the company of his sister and her husband who were quite amused by Sándor's act and Julia's reaction to it. Following introductions all around they chatted for a few minutes, then the curtains went up again and the opera continued. At the end, proceeding slowly to the exit, Sándor asked Julia if he could call and take her out the following Sunday to the City Park for a stroll. Julia hesitated for a moment and then said yes. She would have preferred someone taller but she found Sándor pleasant company and there was no one else.

The stroll in the City Park was most enjoyable. Sándor contentedly listened to anecdotes from Julia and responded to her questions; he was an open, sincere type of person with a great sense of humour. He had a degree in chemistry, and was employed in the laboratories of a company producing toiletries.

'From spring to autumn I spend most Sundays with a group of friends, rowing on the Danube,' he told Julia. 'We start from a boathouse at the northern edge of the city and usually row upriver sometimes as far as the small town of Vác. The skiffs are hired for the day and depending on the number of males and females in the group we go out in the four, six or eight-seater variety. Eight of us men in a skiff could manage to row as far as the town of Vác, with six rowing and two resting in turns. The ladies are passengers, oars for their seats we leave behind in the boathouse.' The aspect of boating on the huge river worried Julia because she could not swim.

Back at the entrance of the apartment block, Sándor asked Julia if he could take her out again. Julia smiled at him. 'That would be nice.'

The first time Julia joined Sándor's group of friends for a boat trip she was terrified but managed to conceal it well. The narrowness of the boat with the water only inches below the sides frightened her, but as the four men began to pull the oars in absolute unison with their girlfriends cheering them on merrily, chanting 'pull... lift... pull... lift... pull... lift...' her confidence in the craft and her new-found companions quickly established itself. They rowed upriver, the oars almost touching the embankment to stay in the slow-running currents and the skiff cutting into the water drawing a narrow wake. Facing the rear of the boat with Sándor seated behind her, the man in front of Julia excited her a little. She had seen men of all shapes and sizes at the swimming baths yet hardly ever one with an attractive physique, and on those rare occasions she only took a glance or two. Watching or staring at men was very unbecoming for a lady – only courtesans and women with loose morals would do that. Now, however, she could not help but watch the fellow in front of her bend forward, dip the oars, and then lean backwards towards her while pulling at them. Then, with a simultaneous movement he raised the oars and twisted them turning the paddles horizontal, sat upright, and skimmed the oars barely above water level in readiness for the next stroke. Sándor's powerful arms and shoulders must be the result of this activity, she thought.

After about an hour or so and well beyond the city's northern perimeter, the boat slid into an area covered by tall vegetation. The men raised the oars so that the paddles pointed to the sky and dropped the handles into the shallow water hitting the bottom, enabling them to propel the craft forward as if it were a punt. Scattering some wild birds, they edged the boat to the grassy embankment where they all disembarked and had a long and pleasant picnic.

The return journey was also very exhilarating with the boat at mid-river where the fast current combined with the effort of four oarsmen produced incredible speed.

Changing in the boathouse with the other girls, Julia reflected on how much she had enjoyed herself. She wondered if she was up to Sándor's expectations, would he invite her again? Would his friends accept her as one of them? For the first time she realised with a slight shock how fond of Sándor she had become over the four months since their stroll in the City Park. What did he think of her? What were his feelings? If his feelings were serious he should introduce her to his parents before too long! There was nothing for her to do but wait.

Unbeknown to her, Sándor, or Sandy as his friends called him, was having similar thoughts but even more so. He was in love with Julia, knowing he had found the girl he wanted to be his wife. Yet, the realisation of that caused him quite a problem.

His father was a prosperous merchant; the large warehouse overlooking the Danube at the southern outskirts of Budapest and bearing his name in huge letters, visible from the other side of the river, bore witness to that. The family was well off but as far as Sándor was concerned that would not cause problems. Sándor preferred being self-reliant, he did not intend to depend on anybody. His father Andor was a quiet, placid person, willing to listen to other people's points of view and he would welcome Julia into the family.

His mother would also accept her, but as for his self-centred sister Ibolya...? She was four years older than Sándor, her pleasant looks and elegance disguising a spiteful, malicious, conceited personality with no scruples. Ibolya could always make Sándor's mother take her side at any argument and the two of them overruled his father without fail. Ibolya had already asked him if he was still taking out 'the butcher's daughter'.

'Surely,' she said, 'you must realise that her social standing will only permit you to have an affair and no more. If you carry on with her, what will people think of us?'

The word 'affair' felt like a stab wound to Sándor. Of course he had had affairs, after all he was twenty-four years old, but his respect for Julia was total and he had not even tried to kiss her so far in fear of rejection.

'When you can play the piano as Julia can, when you can teach mathematics and literature like she does, when you are able to read and understand the basics of the ancient languages of Latin, Greek and Hebrew, then you can compare yourself with Julia.'

Instantly he knew that despite it being appropriate he should not have said that, but it was too late. Ibolya stared at him for a moment, unable to respond and then stormed out of the room slamming the door behind her.

Sándor had no doubt that Julia would never be accepted by Ibolya as part of his family.

1925

'Jutzie,' Joseph called out from the main bedroom one morning, 'would you help me with my shoelaces?'

As Julia entered, Joseph said in a half whisper, 'Close the door behind you. I want a quiet word without being overheard.' Julia was surprised because they had always discussed things openly.

'You've been going out with this young man far longer than anyone else before him, yet Mother and I have not laid eyes upon him. Why don't you bring him home one day?'

Julia blushed. 'Papa, I do like Sandy a lot and he seems to like me but after two years of going out with him he has still not offered to introduce me to his family. As a matter of fact, he doesn't even talk about his family unless he really has to. If I invite him he may get the impression that he was expected to propose and thus be frightened away?'

Joseph sat in silence for a few moments digesting the information.

'I see your point and I understand your fears but I would like you to consider the problems you could be facing. This friendship with no sign of an engagement seems to go on and on and there is no harm in that, except that you are twenty-five years old. Almost all of your friends are married. Some have children. If this friendship is leading nowhere you had better find out before it is too late. A few years from now the only suitors courting you will be widowers, probably with a child or two, and even if they grow to like you, you will still be known as their stepmother.'

Days later, after their evening meal, Julia asked if she could invite Sándor for a Sunday dinner. Her mother Hannah said she was longing to meet him, and Joseph nodded happily. There was no going back; now she had to ask Sándor to be introduced to her family.

The opportunity arose quite unexpectedly. Sándor received an invitation to a school reunion and asked Julia to accompany him. Julia said that she would be happy to go, provided Sándor would also accept her family's invitation to a Sunday dinner. Sándor was silent for a few moments and then looked right into her eyes, making Julia afraid of a refusal.

'I should have introduced you to my family a long time ago but I was hesitant to do so. I was terrified that what you may experience would drive a wedge between us and I cannot imagine the future without you. Now that I have declared how much I love you – would you, Julia Láng, do me the honour of becoming my wife?'

It was Julia's turn to be silent. She was choking, trying to hold back the tears of relief and happiness but it was a futile effort. Sándor did not know what to think or say, seeing the huge tears rolling down her pretty face.

'Hug me please and hold me tight,' Julia said and Sándor held her close. 'I have no idea what you mean about a wedge being driven between us but as long as you would not let that happen, nor would I.'

'Would that be a non-committal *yes* to my question?' asked Sándor gently, drying her tears with his handkerchief.

'Oh no! It is a *definite* yes and yes and *yes again*!'

People walking by raised quite a few eyebrows as the couple embraced and kissed passionately, unaware of their surroundings. One did not expect to see such a display of passion in a public place – it bordered on indecency.

They walked on, arm-in-arm without a word for a long time, probably as the result of the sudden release of passion, uncertainty and love that they had left undeclared for so long. Sándor broke the silence.

'I must ask you not to mention this to anyone until I have had the chance to ask your father for your hand in marriage. I intend to pay him the respect he is entitled to. Following that, I shall introduce you to my family. I would rather say no more about the subject. I am certain you will make your own observations.'

Julia helped Hannah serving the Sunday dinner to the four men sitting at the table. Hannah's cooking was simple but very tasty and mouth-watering to look at. Oxtail soup with small dumplings, slices of veal fried in breadcrumbs and served with new potatoes, runner beans, carrots and peas. She made pancakes for dessert filled with a mixture of cottage cheese and sultanas, three on each plate, served hot from the oven and covered with soured cream and sugar.

Although no one spoke during a course, before they sat down at the table and in between courses the men chatted a lot. They fired questions at Sándor about his family, his job, his hobbies and pastimes, and he replied in his confident, friendly manner typical of people with a clear conscience.

The meal over, Sándor complimented Hannah on her cuisine and then asked the brothers about their chosen trades. László said, full of pride, that he was doing well at Somosy Removals who had recently acquired motorised transport wagons while retaining some of the horse-drawn variety. At the end of the previous year the proprietor, Mr Somosy, asked him into his office where the old man had given him a month's salary as a bonus for his efforts.

Imre had little to say except that he worked in the leather trade with skins, pelts and fur.

When Hannah and Julia had finished clearing the table and having brought the coffee sat down, Sándor looked around the table with his eyes coming to rest on Joseph.

'Unconventional it may be to make such a request with the whole family present but I am asking you, Mr Láng, to permit me to marry your daughter Julia.'

'I will have a bedroom of my own at last!' said Imre, grinning. Hannah and Julia lowered their gaze in embarrassment.

Joseph, with his eyes narrowed and eyebrows drawn together, looked attentively at Sándor. Seconds passed in absolute silence before he spoke. 'Why, may I ask, did you wait so long?'

His supposedly innocent question brought laughter all round. Sándor stood up and proffered his hand across the table which was accepted and gripped hard by the older man's powerful hand. Hannah embraced Sándor, the two brothers shook his hand and congratulated him.

Sándor chose a Sunday afternoon when he knew Ibolya and her husband would be visiting his parents to introduce Julia. His father, Andor, immediately took a liking to her and his wife Isabelle smiled benignly. The heavily pregnant Ibolya who was quite friendly at their first meeting at the Opera House now looked at Julia disdainfully, while her husband Paul displayed a sociable attitude.

The conversation was rather strained. Julia tried to break the ice and smiled at Ibolya. 'When is the baby due?'

Ibolya replied frostily. 'In mid-November if you must know.'

For a few moments silence reigned. Sándor, placing his arm around Julia's shoulders, looked at his parents. 'Mum and Dad, I would like you to know that I have asked Julia's father for her hand in marriage and he consented.'

'Welcome to the family, Julia.' Andor smiled at her.

'How very nice!' said Isabelle.

'Well, I *do hope* your marriage will be a happy one.' That was Ibolya's acerbic comment.

Paul smiled at them. 'You will make a lovely couple.'

Sándor and Julia set about looking for an apartment to rent and furnish before the wedding; the date of that depended on how soon a suitable one might be found and established. Andor had offered to pay for all the furnishings they intended to purchase but Sándor explained that he preferred to do that himself, without help from anyone, and asked his father not to take offence.

How could I be offended by such a healthy attitude, Andor pondered, but if my son declines to take his share of the family's wealth then in time it will revert to Ibolya who deserves it least of all.

1926

Walking home from the cinema on a warm evening in May, showing Charlie Chaplin in *Easy Street,* they kept reminding each other of some scenes to have yet another laugh. They had parted with a lingering kiss under the main entrance of Julia's apartment block. Entering her home Julia found Joseph in the lounge, on his own.

'Papa, why are you up so late? You will have to get up at the crack of dawn.'

Joseph looked at her. He appeared to be gaunt and haggard and Julia noticed that all of a sudden he looked very old.

'What is it Papa? Please tell me!' Julia pleaded.

'I wish I didn't have to, Jutzie. I would give anything for not having to tell you. Sit down please.' A long silence followed. Joseph's struggle with what was on his mind was apparent.

'Imre has lost heavily playing cards and betting on horses. He's lost more than I have money saved. Apart from losing face, if we cannot settle the debt we are in danger of the bailiffs coming in.'

The enormity of the statement was such that Julia needed a few seconds to organise her thoughts.

'Papa, my dowry is there for the taking. I hope it will be sufficient to cover the debt.'

The old man's voice was coarse and Julia realised her father was hurt a lot more than she imagined.

'I had guessed you would say that, and that I would have no other choice but accept your offer.' He remained silent for a while. 'What about your future, your forthcoming marriage?'

'It will make no difference either way Papa, having a scandal or not having a dowry.'

Julia had a vision of Ibolya laughing at her.

'To lose a good man like Sándor due to the irresponsible act of your brother would be an absolute tragedy.' He paused briefly. 'There is one more difficult task for me to do.'

Joseph rose from his chair and entered the bedroom shared by the two brothers. László emerged a few moments later, obviously woken from his sleep.

'What's going on?' he asked his sister.

'It's not for me to say, Latzie, but you will soon learn about it,' replied Julia.

'Imre, give me your key to the front door,' Joseph commanded in a tone he used to employ in his days in the army. Imre got out of bed and produced the key from his coat pocket.

'Your debt will be settled with the help of Jutzi's dowry,' Joseph said. 'Tomorrow you will pack your belongings and move out of here. From now on you are on your own. I doubt that you can comprehend the damage you have caused.'

Having said that, the old man turned around and walked out of the room with his back straight but his heart aching.

Two days later, 31st May, Julia and Sándor met at their pre-arranged rendezvous under the clock at the National Theatre, a favourite meeting place of Budapestians. They intended to inspect an apartment in Rákóczy Road, a very nice area nearby. When Sándor saw Julia he sensed that something was wrong.

'What's the matter, Jutzi?' he asked.

'Could we sit down somewhere before looking at the flat?' asked Julia.

'Of course we could. Let's go to the New York.'

The New York was a very stylish restaurant and cafeteria on the Main Boulevard, a short walk from the National Theatre. The restaurant, with its ornate red marble columns supporting the cafeteria above, was a favourite gathering place of artists, actors, musicians, painters, and the like. Julia would have preferred a more tranquil place but did not say so. It did not matter any more.

The New York Palace Restaurant, built in 1894

'Would you like a slice of cake, a mignon or ice cream?' asked Sándor.

'No thanks, coffee will be more than enough.'

Sándor ordered two coffees with cream and after the waiter had left, he looked at her inquiringly.

'What happened Jutzi? You look shattered.'

Julia explained what had happened at home and revealed that she no longer had a dowry.

Two thoughts emerged simultaneously in Sándor's head: The Dowry, an old-fashioned tradition, had no importance for him at all and also that Ibolya would never let this go, she would keep rubbing it in all the time. It would be; 'I told you so,' for years to come.

'What do you think I desire more – the dowry or having you as my wife?'

'Sandy you are very kind but can't you see that somebody without a dowry is like someone who is not prepared to honour a commitment?'

It was patently obvious that the dowry was a matter of great importance to Julia. Sándor said nothing but he appeared distraught and thoughtful. He looked at Julia. 'We must not forget the people waiting for us at the flat we are going to look at.'

'You mean the flat we *were* going to look at,' Julia said looking at him.

'Jutzie, my dear, we cannot leave them waiting for us to no avail. I'll be back in twenty minutes.' He stood up and he was gone.

Twenty minutes passed, forty and more. Julia ordered another coffee and had a strong premonition that her future had evaporated. Sándor should have been back quite a while ago from the address at Rákóczy Road, Julia was certain of that. Sipping the coffee that was going cold, her mind was in turmoil. To accept that the happiness of three years of courting had vanished like this was very hard to do but she had to face the fact that Sándor had gone for good and deserted her. The temptation to have a good cry was overpowering but being determined and strong-willed she did not let her tears come forth in a public place.

Head down, deep in unhappy thoughts, she did not notice the legs of a chair scraping the floor but then someone sat down and a warm hand settled on top of hers.

The hand was Sándor's and he looked at her with a bright smile.

'Well, that's been resolved. If you have finished your coffee we'll go for a long walk.'

Julia sat there in a daze like someone slowly regaining consciousness.

'Sandy, I didn't expect to see you again.'

Sándor's genial expression turned sombre.

'Let's assume you didn't say that. I'll go and pay the waiter.'

They left the New York arm-in-arm but without talking. Eventually Julia asked where they were going and the reply from Sándor came in one word:

'Home.'

'Home? Whose home?'

'Mine.'

'What are you trying to do?' pleaded Julia. 'Embarrass me even further?'

'Trust me. Only my parents will be there. All you have to do is to look normal and cheerful.'

Julia had a terrible foreboding, but short of refusing to go there was nothing else she could do.

Their unexpected arrival was well received. Sándor said that they had decided to pop in because he had something to discuss.

After some general chit-chat about Ibolya's little son born six months previously, Sándor changed the subject.

'Julia's dowry.'

Julia froze. I must face this come what may, she thought and braced herself. Sándor produced a flat and oblong ebony box from his inside pocket.

'Here it is,' he said and opened it. Nesting on black velvet inside the box was a gold Schaffenhausen fob watch attached to an inch wide and three-inch long braided gold band. An item like this would only be worn on very special occasions.

While Sándor's parents admired the contents of the box Julia's thoughts were racing. So that was where Sandy had been this afternoon, not just to cancel the viewing of the flat. Today being the 31st of May he had been paid, as was customary on the last day of the month. He must have spent all his salary and some more to buy that watch with the gold band! She had to steady herself to hide her surprise and the emotions welling up.

Andor looked at her. 'This is a Dowry the like of which is seldom seen. Apart from the value the choice is superb!'

'Yes, very true,' added Isabelle, nodding.

'Sandy, I don't know what to say,' Julia said after their departure from the home of Sándor's parents. 'You have saved me from disgrace but don't you think we are starting our future under false pretences, that we are cheating?'

'We are not cheating. You had been cheated out of what was rightly yours and that in turn would have cheated me out of having you as my wife. What is more important – a sum of money or our future?'

Later that evening, after dinner at Julia's home with only four members of the Láng family around the table, no one had the courage to ask Julia of Sándor's reaction to the bad news. Joseph realised he must break the silence.

'Jutzie, what happened when Sándor learned that you have no dowry?'

Julia dabbed her eyes with her hankie and disclosed what took place after she had confronted Sándor with the unexpected episode.

Hannah cried silently. Julia also in tears, comforted her mother. Comfort for the misfortune that hit them, for the loss of a young son and brother, and for the gallant act of Sándor.

1927

Early in the year Julia and Sándor's new home was fully furnished and decorated, had electric lights instead of the old-fashioned gaslights and also hot and cold water.

The only cloud on the horizon was the warning from Julia's family doctor. He had asked to see the young couple prior to the wedding.

'I have known you since your childhood, Julia.' The doctor said. 'You always were and still are a picture of health. However, you are very slim and your pelvic structure is very narrow, unsuitable for giving birth. A pregnancy could cost you your life.' He looked at both of them. 'I wouldn't risk it if I were you.'

The wedding, attended by both families and a few selected friends, went without a hitch. The Best Man's speech over, Sándor looked at the guests and said that his bride Julia was lovely, charming, multi-talented, caring, warm-hearted, intelligent, and an excellent cook. Then he turned to Julia with an expression of curiosity, "Was there something else you wanted me to say?"

The laughter of the audience rattled the windows.

The morning after the wedding Andor complained of unusual stomach pains. Isabelle told him that as he was nearing three score years and because he had had more to eat and drink than usual on the previous day it wasn't at all surprising. The pains had gone by the next morning and neither of them gave it a second thought. Yet, unbeknown to them, Andor's cancer was spreading.

Julia and Sándor enjoyed gloriously happy days. Instead of tutoring children, an evening time activity, Julia filled her day and contributed to their income working as an assistant to a milliner. Her day at the shop began at nine thirty which meant that she had to start preparing their evening meal in the morning. At four thirty she dashed home from the shop and cooked the food in readiness for her husband's arrival in the evening. Socially it was also a delightful time; they still went rowing on the Danube on many summer Sundays, found time for theatres and the opera, picnics with friends in the hills of Buda on the other side of the river and, of course, visiting their families.

Ibolya had accepted the fact that Julia was her sister-in-law and her antagonism lessened. Her friendliness on the other hand was superficial. In the company of other people Ibolya had nothing but condemnation for Julia.

1928

A letter arrived at the Láng household in the spring, addressed to Joseph. The contents were rather short:

Dear Papa,

I think you ought to know that I have married a girl called Lilly and that she has just given birth to our son Robert.

I would like to add that I have not played cards or placed a bet since the day I had left home.

I love you all and always will,

Imre.

Joseph read the letter several times and then stared at it for some time. The lesson had been learnt he thought and reflected on the tears and heartache it cost all of them. He walked into the kitchen and passed the letter to his wife. Hannah read it and burst into tears.

'I am a grandmother,' she said between sobs. Joseph hugged her.

'It tends to happen to women at your age you know.'

She laughed through her tears. 'But I did not expect it. Latzie is not even courting and Jutzie cannot bear children. I didn't know if we would ever hear of Imre again and now two things at once! Could we visit them?'

'Of course we could and we will. We shall not mention the events of the past.'

The day of the visit arrived. Imre and his young wife occupied a small dwelling in a rundown area of Kispest. Hannah was troubled to see bits of clothing lying around and furniture that should have been dusted but the baby was beautiful, a healthy bouncing boy. While Hannah and Lilly chatted and played with little Robbie, Joseph inquired about Imre's job and circumstances. Imre insisted his job in the leather trade was secure and assured his father that his earnings were adequate for the needs of his family.

On the way home Joseph and Hannah discussed their misgivings concerning the impression of untidiness Lilly had left them with and the state of the home. Hannah expressed her fears of Lilly not being a good wife. Joseph tried to put her mind at rest.

'They are young, especially Lilly. She can't be more than nineteen years old.'

Shortly afterwards, the Láng family gathered for a reunion and the family treated Imre as if he had never left them. The only one getting hurt again was Julia but at this time not by any act of Imre. Julia held little Robbie in her arms, cuddling him as much as she could, even changing him when he needed it, all through the day. Why, oh why, can't I have a baby when I want one so much? she kept thinking.

1929

The lack of a baby and thought of the future without a child or children played on Julia's mind constantly. She had taken the precautions advised by her doctor to prevent conception, and the obvious terrifying consequences of an abortion. Her greatest fear of an accidental pregnancy was not the operation itself but the thought of getting rid of the baby she so much wanted to have. She still had hopes of having a baby and vague plans started to form in the back of her mind. One was a house with a garden for a child to play and run around in.

Lying side by side one night with their bodies touching she asked Sándor, 'Sandy, what would you do if I did become pregnant?'

'I would be very worried. I could lose you in the process.'

'I know that but what would you actually do?'

'I would take you to your gynaecologist.'

'To do what?'

'To stop your pregnancy of course.'

'You mean you would be prepared to do away with my baby, the baby I want so much?'

'First of all it would be *our* baby not just yours but yes, I would do that to save your life.'

'Why? Doctors are not right every time. Wouldn't you like to have a son?'

'What I would like is beside the point, what I don't want is to lose you and that is my final word.'

This was the nearest they had ever been to an argument in almost two years of married life so Julia did not make any further comment but a plan was taking shape in her head. She made the first move during their summer holiday at Lake Balaton.

'Sandy, do you think we could afford to move out of the city to somewhere in the suburbs and into a house with a garden?'

'Funny you should say that because I had similar thoughts recently. I suppose our present home has served its purpose. It's in a nice area but the sun never shines in and I feel we could do better. I didn't consider the suburbs because one has to commute, but that might not be much of a problem. People travel back and forth every day from the outskirts. If we find the right place I would give it a go.'

At the family gathering at Christmas, Sándor asked his sister if there was something wrong with Andor because he did not look well.

'He isn't exactly young,' Ibolya said with a shrug. 'What do you expect?'

There was no other option but to ask his father himself. The old man admitted that he was not feeling well and was thinking of consulting his doctor. Sándor asked him to arrange the visit so that he could also be present.

On the appointed day and after a thorough investigation the doctor's opinion was that while there was no cause for alarm, he would refer Andor to a hospital for a specialist to have a look at him.

A week later the specialist took some X-rays and carried out a comprehensive examination. While Andor was getting dressed, the doctor said to Sándor, 'I regret having to tell you but your father's cancer is too far spread, it is inoperable. Prepare him and yourself for a hard time. He will suffer a lot but not for long I believe.'

1930

After being semi-conscious for weeks and more and more sedated, Andor passed away in June. To the great surprise of the family he had left no Last Will or any other instructions.

In the autumn Sándor received a letter from his father's solicitors Markos & Barna. He opened the envelope with some concern. What would his father's solicitors want from him?

The letter was very short asking him to make an appointment at the solicitors. That sounded ominous, since Andor died intestate all his property would go to his widow Isabelle. That was the law and that has already been over and done with. What sort of a problem could there be?

The following day Sándor telephoned for an appointment but the office clerk told him that owing to some legal requirement he could not have one until after the weekend. That struck him as being rather odd.

He arrived at the solicitors' office ten minutes ahead of time and was shown into the senior partner's chamber without delay.

'I am indeed sorry we could not grant you an earlier appointment,' said Mr Markos, 'but we received strict instructions not to, until a period of thirty-one days of settlement had passed following the transfer of your late father's estate to your charming mother, Isabelle. That was finalised a month ago so here we are.'

'What is it about?' asked Sándor. 'I am at a loss trying to guess.'

'Quite simple really. I have been instructed to pass this envelope over to you.'

Sándor took hold of the rather large, sealed and slightly bulging envelope, displaying only his name. Before removing the red wax seal from the flap he asked the solicitor, 'Do you know what it contains?'

'Indeed I do. I have had the privilege of arranging the relevant matter from the start.'

Sándor removed the seal and opened the envelope. From the corner of his eye he glimpsed a touch of amusement on the solicitor's face. The envelope contained what seemed to be legal documents and a smaller envelope addressed simply: *Sándor*. It contained a letter from his father, dated July 1926.

My Dear Son,

I cannot put into words how proud I am of you and your attitude of self-reliance, building your future yourself. I am confident that you will succeed and I wish you luck all the way. Your decision of going it alone placed me in a difficult situation of which, I am certain, you are unaware.

Starting with some general stores my Father had left me, I, with the help of God, managed to open more and more, resulting in our present state of wealth. Dividing the business for the purpose of inheritance would not be beneficial and could lead to squabbles within the family.

Leaving you out of my Will to satisfy your wish to go it alone would be unthinkable, unjust, and very cruel to you. So I decided to leave no Will.

As for the contents of this envelope it is up to you who should learn of it, my suggestion would be no one but your wife.

Hoping that your future with Julia will be a long and happy one,

Father.

The envelope contained the Deeds and documents referring to a recently built apartment block and each document was in Sándor's name. The completely unexpected legacy stunned Sándor. He expected nothing from his father's estate and anyway he had intended to create an existence all on his own. Yet he had to admit after reading his father's letter once more that the old man acted very wisely.

Sándor admitted to Julia that he felt guilty for underestimating his father's wisdom and comprehension. She reminded him of the old proverb: *'Slow waters run deep.'*

Sándor said that sometime in the future he would sell the property. Combined with the accumulated revenue he would have a head start in setting up his own company of chemical products from the proceeds.

The search at the outskirts for a property to their liking proved to be a lengthy business, far longer than anticipated. When the property was right, the approach to it or that of public transport proved to be inconvenient. When the commuting aspect was acceptable the house was either too small, too large or in a poor state of repair. At times they got fed up looking any further. It seemed that the type of home they would have liked never came onto the market because their owners liked them too much.

Eventually they settled for a corner property with the right size of garden in the suburb of Rákosszentmihály – 'Szentmihály for short. The railway station serving the Western Rail Terminal in central Budapest, referred to as 'The Western' by everyone, was within a short walking distance. Ten minutes' walk in another direction would take them to the local stop of the Suburban Tram Service, green in colour to differentiate it from the yellow inner city tramways. This service started from and ran back to the Eastern Rail Terminal in Budapest.

1932

Sándor and Julia moved into their new home in April in the sixth year of their marriage and accomplished the first step in Julia's plan. During the following months they invited and entertained either family or friends almost every Sunday. They received both praise and approval on their choice of property and sitting under the huge cherry tree in the garden some visitors expressed their envy. There was a large walnut tree as well at the west-facing side with flowerbeds around it. The only adverse comment came from Ibolya, following her visit with her family.

'They call that *an address?* I knew from the start that she would drag my brother down to her level! I can only hope that none of our friends will ever find out Sándor has moved to the suburbs.'

Their lives had settled to a familiar pattern. Sándor left early in the morning, coming home after six in the evening, while Julia busied herself with their home and garden. She had also found time to play the piano and do some crochet work; one by one her handiwork started to appear below vases and other decorative objects. Even so, she experienced more and more the emptiness of a home without a child. She had achieved the first step of her plan, the garden, but there was no child running around or playing in a sandpit. Indoors the stillness would not go away even when she had the radio switched on. Worst of all, her arms were aching for holding a baby to her bosom.

As autumn approached she put the next part of her plan into action and discontinued taking the precautions the family doctor advised her to take. The die was cast.

On a dreary mid-November afternoon somebody rang the bell at the apartment in Rottenbiller Street. Opening the door, Hannah found Lilly standing there with four-year-old Robbie hanging on to her skirt. Hannah sensed that something was wrong and ushered them into the lounge. Before she could ask or say anything Lilly burst into a frantic tirade.

'I told Imre he was working too hard, very long hours. He wouldn't listen to me! Then he started to have dizzy spells and digestive problems. He had passed out the other evening at home yet went to work the following morning as if nothing had happened. Today his boss came to our home saying Imre had collapsed while he was checking a consignment of cowhide and was taken to the Rókus Hospital.'

'Please calm down, Lilly. Being upset doesn't help, it only frightens your little boy,' Joseph said.

'Oh, him.' Lilly threw a glance at the boy. 'I'd be better off without having the bother!'

'We'll pretend not to have heard that remark for everyone's sake.' Joseph said, with eyes revealing anger and hurt.

Lilly burst into tears. It was not clear for what or for whom the tears were coming forth.

Next day Joseph and Hannah visited Imre at the Rókus. The young man looked pallid and seemed to have lost weight. He assured his parents that apart from nausea and a feeling of being unwell he was not in pain. The doctor treating him admitted he had no idea as yet of the nature of the illness.

They made a detour on the way home to tell László, at Somosy Removals, the bad news because he had moved into rented rooms the previous year.

'There is no need to tell Jutzie just yet. Hopefully this will be over in a week or so, Imre is in good spirits,' Joseph said.

Yet, after a week and then a fortnight had passed Imre's condition did not improve. He had problems holding food down and lost weight rapidly. His doctors did not know how to treat him because they had never been confronted with symptoms like his. He did not respond to any form of medication, making the doctors both confused and embarrassed.

Julia and Sándor duly turned up on their customary visit on a Sunday in December and Joseph informed them of Imre's state of health. Shortly after lunch they set off for the Rókus.

When Julia saw the pallid, greyish face of her brother with the cheekbones clearly outlined she thought, God is punishing you. Immediately she felt intense guilt for the thought.

The specialist now in charge of Imre had sent the symptoms of his illness and the treatments already tried to other hospitals, requesting information or any record of such cases. Very few replied and nothing from any of them proved to be of any use. He then wrote to some institutes abroad he had dealt with in the past or knew of as experts in tropical diseases.

As Christmas was only days away Julia thought the best present for her would be a missing period. Despite abandoning precautions so far nothing had happened.

The family visited Imre on Christmas Eve expecting Lilly and little Robbie to show up. They did not. Joseph asked when Lilly had visited last. Imre clenched his teeth and swallowed,

'Twelve days ago.'

'I am sorry son, I really am sorry, you did not deserve this.'

Out of the hospital Joseph asked László to see if Lilly was all right or if she was in need of anything.

Next morning, Christmas Day, László set off to Kispest, hoping that whatever was ailing Imre did not strike Lilly and the little boy. He knocked on the door and got no response. He looked at his watch: 10.52. They could have gone out he thought, but he tried again anyway. A few seconds later the door was opened by a man in pyjamas. László was taken aback but comprehending the situation he apologised, pretending of being at the wrong address.

He walked away feeling hurt and offended that Lilly would act like this, cheating on his seriously ill brother in hospital.

To his parents he reported finding no one at home.

1933

One of the replies the specialist at the Rókus received from abroad came from Switzerland:

9 January 1933

Dear Dr Vassváry,

The symptoms you described in your letter I had come across twice in the last 18 years.

At the first instance I had no idea of the cause, I was in a similar situation to yours. Many years later, faced with another patient with the same symptoms, I referred to my notes of the previous case. I noticed that the common denominator between them was their trade or occupation working with animal pelts and leather. Our researchers have investigated the cause of this disease by taking tissue samples from the patient and from all kinds of animal skins. Our findings suggest that when the process of preserving hides or pelts is not carried out efficiently and thoroughly, a microscopic fungal growth develops on some but not on all. We do not know yet why this is, just as we do not know why most people in the leather trade are totally immune to the fungus when some are apparently not.

I regret to inform you that if your patient is the victim of this type of infection there is no cure for it yet. The disease does not appear to be contagious and it will not affect your staff or other patients.

I trust the above is of interest,

Prof. Wernher Schrenker.

Imre was laid to rest on a cold, frosty day, with snow covering the cemetery and the tops of headstones. Three weeks later Lilly deposited four-year-old Robbie at an orphanage. She told no one in the family about it. Next day Lilly moved out of the rented flat she had occupied with Imre, taking all her belongings and leaving no forwarding address.

Julia was in despair. Eight months had passed without protection and still nothing. The possibility of being barren kept coming up in her mind. Sándor noticed her preoccupations and worried looks, but when he asked her what was wrong she replied she could not stop worrying about the political events in Germany.

'This man Hitler and his Nazi Party has come to power in Germany and immediately Nazi officials are in charge of all local government across the country. That amounts to a dictatorship!'

Sándor agreed. He was also concerned. The news on the radio and articles in the newspapers largely applauded the German economic revival but they carried critical comments as well about the nature and direction of the new regime.

On a bright sunny day in the spring, Julia visited the open market on the main square for groceries. She was familiar with most of the traders as they occupied the same spot every time. Even so, in the last row of stalls she came across a new one selling canaries, goldfish and other pets.

A large wicker basket on the ground contained a handful of puppies with brown and black patches on their white coats. Their eyes already open they kept climbing over each other in a playful manner, making them look very sweet. At that moment Julia realised how much she needed the company of a living creature, now that her hopes for a baby were fading. Instantly, she spotted the one she knew she must have – the pup that was completely white; it reminded her of a ball of cotton. The trader told her that the bitch was a pedigree

Spitz, hence the white coat, and which to the embarrassment of her owners committed an unspeakable act with a beau of unknown origin. Consequently, the pups had not been retained.

Julia bought the pup and she was cuddling the little creature in her arms when Sándor arrived home. The puppy's appearance amused Sándor.

'You are right, just like a ball of cotton with three black spots, two eyes and a nose. What is it, male or female?'

Julia looked perplexed. In her excitement she had neither asked the trader nor checked herself. Sándor picked up the little bundle and laughed. 'He is a dog! He won't have puppies thank God. What are you going to call him?'

Julia replied that so far she couldn't think of a suitable name. She wanted something different from the usual names given to dogs.

'All right,' said Sándor, 'what do you think of "Bobby"?'

As he pronounced the word Bobby the puppy pricked up its ears. They looked at each other.

'Bobby it is,' Julia said.

'I must mend the fencing at the weekend,' Sándor said. 'There are small gaps in it all round.'

They trained the puppy in the following weeks to empty its system at only one place, behind the old wooden shed in a corner of the garden. He also had to learn that apart from the kitchen where bedding was placed for him under a corner shelf, he must not enter any other room, to prevent him from gnawing furniture while teething or later in life. They were pleased to see that the little creature was a very fast learner. By the time he was five months old his fluffy hair changed into a smooth white coat and his tail curled up in a circle. The only problem he presented was that he dug holes under the fence with incredible speed and disappeared, although he always returned, the latest by the evening for his food. As soon as Sándor had filled in the hole, even with bricks, the dog made another one or re-dug the same one. There was no way of stopping him except by tethering and that Julia found unacceptable.

Sándor in the meantime had set his plan into action. He sold the apartment block and acquired a suitable two-storey factory building for his project in an industrial area on the outskirts of Budapest. He purchased equipment to produce soap, shampoos, hand cream and other similar commodities. He also rented premises for his head office in a prominent location, Alkotmány Street in central Budapest, registered the company as Technokémia and began looking for industrial chemists and other employees. It was too early to employ anyone except a secretary/shorthand typist for the office who would also deal with telephone inquiries while he was visiting prospective clients and building up the business.

June came and went with glorious weather and an added bonus: Julia missed her period. She tried not to be too optimistic as it had happened before although very seldom. When she missed the next one her spirits rose.

By the end of August she had no doubt about being pregnant and it was time to tell Sandy that he was going to be a father.

The news that his wife was expecting a baby genuinely surprised Sándor. After seven years of married life he took it for granted that this sort of thing was not going to happen at all. The unexpected news astonished him.

'How did that happen?'

'I find it strange that you cannot remember that,' Julia said, laughing.

'When did you find out?'

'I wasn't sure until recently and I didn't want to create a false alarm before that.'

'We had better make an appointment with your gynaecologist, Dr Hegyes,' Sándor said.

'Sandy, you are not going to insist on an abortion, are you?'

'That depends on what Dr Hegyes advises. I am going to ring him tomorrow.'

Three days later, Sándor sat deep in thought in the gynaecologist's waiting room. He was utterly bewildered. Should he insist on an abortion? Julia would never forgive him and anyway it was not a decision he wished to make. Yet, on the other hand, Julia's chances of giving birth were virtually nil. She could die in the process and the baby with her. Heads or tails, I could lose both ways he concluded. The only way out of this situation would be a natural miscarriage, he thought.

The door of the consulting room opened and Dr Hegyes invited him in, pointing to the chair beside Julia who sat there with her face aglow. Sándor sat down and Julia gripped his hand.

Dr Hegyes returned to his comfortable chair behind his desk. 'Well, I am pleased to tell you that your wife is in an advanced state of pregnancy. The time of birth I calculate to be toward the very end of March next year. She is in excellent shape, could not be better, but there may be complications at the birth requiring Caesarean section because she is very slightly built.'

Sándor felt relieved. The decision was no longer his to make. From now on they would have to rely on God's will. So be it.

Julia could not be happier. Her plan had worked and the future would have to take care of itself. Sándor immediately arranged for a telephone to be connected in their home.

László was waiting under the clock at the National Theatre for his present girlfriend, a recent 'acquisition'. So far he had managed to dodge Cupid's arrows. His ability to beguile and walk off with the prettiest girl at any party was well known among his friends, most probably because he considered their girlfriends taboo, out of bounds for himself. Making plans for the evening ahead, his attention focused on a couple walking in his direction, Lilly and the man who had opened the door in his pyjamas.

Following the disappearance of Lilly and little Robbie, Joseph and Hannah suffered anguish and grief at the loss of their lovely grandson. They had made inquiries through friends and acquaintances trying to find out where Lilly had moved to, but to no avail. Lilly's landlord had no idea where she had moved to. In effect, Lilly and the boy disappeared from the face of the Earth. The possibility that Lilly, a young mother, would abandon her child had not crossed their minds.

László did not hesitate. He confronted the couple. Lilly was visibly petrified.

'Hello Lilly, how are you?' asked László in his most pleasant manner.

The man cut in. 'Never mind how she is, who are you and what do you want?'

'I am sorry for the intrusion but I happen to be Lilly's brother-in-law and I would like to know the whereabouts of my little nephew to enable his grandparents to see him.'

A flash of recognition appeared on the man's face. 'I think I remember you. You were knocking on our door on Christmas Day last year, haven't you?'

'I will have to correct you on one point,' László replied. 'That particular morning I was knocking on the door of my brother, who was seriously ill in hospital. I needed to find out why his wife and his little boy had stopped visiting him. Seeing you there, I decided to withdraw as there was no point in creating a scene or getting involved in an argument. Presently, I would like to know where young Robbie is.'

The man was distinctly embarrassed. 'I am sorry. I had only met Lilly the week before and I was unaware of her circumstances and background.'

Head bowed, staring at the ground, Lilly admitted that she had left Robbie at an orphanage.

The grandparents visited the orphanage. Robbie was in good health and clean, although his clothes had left a lot to be desired. The garments were badly worn, frayed, ill-fitting and hadn't been recently washed.

'We are too old to adopt him,' said Joseph on the way home. 'But we must visit him regularly so he will know he has a family.'

'For a while we shall but how long for?' Hannah was thinking aloud. 'Neither of us is getting any younger and he is only five years old.'

Sándor paid a visit to the orphanage on a late December afternoon and signed a document taking responsibility for the boy, taking him home for Christmas as Julia had suggested.

Robbie was a bit of a handful. After nine months in the orphanage where regimentation applied only at mealtimes, bedtime and such, he lacked manners. He explored the house, looked into every nook and cranny, opened cabinets and drawers, climbed upon furniture and ran in and out leaving doors open behind him. The only thing he kept his distance from was Bobby. As time passed with Julia talking to him, reading books and playing games, he settled down and began to concentrate on the activity at hand.

When Sándor returned home after taking Robbie back to the orphanage, he was concerned, 'It must have been awful for that little boy to go back to that forbidding place after having such a happy time with us. I wonder if we did the right thing having him here and yet if we did not we would quite rightly feel guilty about it. Adopting him would be the proper thing to do but just now it is out of the question.'

Julia was also having trouble with her conscience. Recently, when she feared being barren, she had been thinking of taking Robbie out of the orphanage and adopting the boy. But she became mindful immediately that young Robbie would be a compromise. Not her own child but sort of a substitute.

Right now she was looking forward to having her baby so much that she could not find room in her heart for someone else's child.

1934

Apart from getting bigger and bigger Julia's pregnancy caused her very few problems and she was a picture of health. Her face developed radiance and her happiness was there for all to see.

Photography was one of Sándor's hobbies and he took several pictures of her glowing looks. As her time was approaching he kept telephoning several times a day to make sure she was all right. When he phoned on the last day of March and heard that nothing was happening he said, 'I'll bet it will be tomorrow, April Fool's Day.'

'I wouldn't mind that,' replied Julia. 'The sooner the better, he keeps kicking me non-stop.'

'How do you know it's a boy?'

'The power of his legs. A girl would be more gentle.'

Shortly after going to bed one evening in April Julia received a kick from the baby, making her curl up in pain.

'What is it?' Sándor was ready to jump out of bed.

'I don't know. No need to panic yet.'

'The baby is overdue. I'd rather have you taken to hospital ahead of time, the weather outside is awful.' Instead of a reply Julia cried out from the effect of her first contraction. Sándor leapt out of bed in such a hurry that the rug at the side of the bed slipped and he finished up on the floorboards on his back with a loud bang. Julia had to laugh in spite of the pain.

'Watch it,' she said, 'or we shall finish up in hospital in adjacent beds.'

Sándor telephoned for an ambulance and called Dr Hegyes who assured him that he would alert the maternity ward of Julia's expected arrival. There was nothing to do but wait.

The ambulance arrived shortly before midnight in pouring rain, thunder and lightning. By the time Julia and Sándor boarded the vehicle the thunder was moving away but the rain was getting heavier, so much so that the driver could hardly see the road ahead.

They reached the hospital after one o'clock, a journey that should have been made in thirty minutes. Everything was prepared and ready for them. At the labour ward Dr Hegyes examined Julia immediately. Back in his office the doctor told Sándor that so far there were no problems. He opened a small cabinet and poured out a large measure of apricot brandy.

'Drink this, doctor's order.'

Sándor sat in the waiting room all on his own. He wandered out after a while and asked the Matron if she would allow him to stay with his wife during labour.

'I am sorry Sir, but we do not allow fathers being present because they tend to become over-anxious and get underfoot. Caring for a woman in labour should be left to the professional staff.'

That was that, the Matron's verdict was final.

Returning to the waiting room, Sándor tried reading books and magazines left on the table but he was unable to concentrate. Like many other fathers before him, he started walking up and down the length of the waiting room. This physical act, almost automatic, renders waiting time easier to bear. Time passed very slowly. On the instructions of Dr Hegyes he was not informed of Julia being taken to the operating theatre. The gynaecologist took the precaution of having a surgeon by his side because he was convinced that the baby could not be delivered in the conventional manner. He had tried nevertheless but found the passage too narrow for the baby's head.

'Forceps,' he barked and the theatre nurse snapped the shiny pair of grips into his hands. He inserted the grips gently, trying to feel the baby's head through them and then tried to grip and draw the baby out. He could not. I will have to grip harder he thought, hopefully I won't cause any damage to the skull. The tighter grip on the handles did not help and the doctor was unsuccessful in his effort to pull the infant out.

'Hold everything for a few minutes please,' he said and turned to his colleague. 'Gábor, get ready for the Caesarean. I'll talk to the husband.'

Ripping off his gloves and gown he dashed out of the theatre. At the door of the waiting room he stopped, composed himself and opened the door with an air of nonchalance.

'Ah, there you are,' he said to Sándor. 'I need a word with you. We have encountered a slight problem, not unexpected. The baby cannot be delivered in the normal manner so I am asking your permission to perform a Caesarean section.'

Sándor was fully aware of the seriousness of the situation. Without the operation Julia and baby would be doomed, with the Caesarean the risks were slightly less. He became conscious of cold sweat running down his sides.

'Dr Hegyes, do what you can to save my wife, she means everything to me.'

'Rest assured we shall do our best I promise you that. It will not take long.'

Sándor was an optimist by nature but at that moment he was deeply concerned. I was looking forward to having a child, he pondered, but I will gladly settle for the survival of my wife. What would the future be like without her? Whom would I strive for when she is no longer there? Suddenly a different fear struck him: what if the baby survived and Julia did not? He would certainly not place his child in an orphanage but who would look after the baby while he was at work? His sister would be the worst kind of stepmother!

Shortly after six o'clock as the morning sun was trying to break through the clouds, Dr Hegyes walked into the room.

'I have excellent news,' he said cheerfully. 'Julia has come through the operation and she is all right but under sedation. You will not be able to see her before the afternoon. I have had her placed in a single room for peace and quiet. You also have a son weighing almost three kilograms. I suggest you go home now, there is nothing here for you to do.'

Sándor could hardly speak, he just about managed to thank the doctor. Dr Hegyes understood, his own wife had had to undergo a Caesarean section in 1927 but their baby had not survived.

The haze in Julia's brain was clearing slowly. She remembered the painful and failed attempt of giving birth and the need for a Caesarean. Moments later there had been blackness. Right now her eyelids were heavy and she was conscious of searing pain.

'Nurse,' she called out, but her voice was hardly audible and nobody heard it. She dozed off again.

Some interminable time later, she became aware of somebody checking her pulse. She opened her eyes, and her mind was quite fresh. 'Have I got a baby?' The question was a desperate shout. The nurse gave a broad smile.

'Yes you have, a lovely little boy. You will be able to hold him in a few moments.'

She helped Julia to sit up, placing pillows behind her back and handed her the baby.

Julia noticed that her little boy was well developed with lots of dark hair. Her eyes misted over at the sight.

I have a baby, a son at last. Thank you, Lord! Then she spotted the purple birthmark above the outer corner of the right eye stretching over to the temple. In area, if not in width, it was the size of a plum. Never mind, she thought, I will comb his hair over it. It will be hardly visible.

When the nurse returned the baby to the cot at the foot of the bed, Julia asked for a mirror and a comb. Sándor would not be long arriving. She was right. Half an hour later she heard a knock – the door opened and a huge bouquet of red roses appeared in the opening ostensibly standing on two legs. Then Sándor's face appeared above the bouquet beaming with happiness. The bouquet of roses had a small envelope attached them. Julia opened it and removed a card from inside that had three simple words written on it: '*I adore you.*'

Informed of Sándor's arrival, Dr Hegyes gave the couple a few minutes to share their joy and then knocked on the door and entered.

'Hello, how is my favourite patient?'

Julia assured him that she could not be happier despite the huge birthmark on the baby's head.

'Oh, that,' said the doctor cheerfully. 'It happens sometimes when forceps are used. It will be gone in seven or eight days.' He pulled up a chair and sat down.

'There is something I must discuss with you.'

Julia and Sándor exchanged quick, worried glances and looked at the gynaecologist with foreboding.

'Nothing to worry about as such,' said the doctor. 'But there are times during an operation when one must make instant decisions, there is no time for delay. Using forceps tends to damage the uterus and accordingly we have decided to remove it. I am afraid you will not bear any more children, Julia. I am really sorry but there was no other option.' He put his chair back in the corner. 'I think I'd better leave you. I'll see you tomorrow Julia. Goodbye for now.'

Dr Hegyes was not quite truthful about the removal of the uterus. A damaged uterus can be repaired in most cases. He asked his colleague to remove it in the knowledge that it was unlikely that Julia would survive another pregnancy.

Throughout Julia's recuperation in hospital, the happy couple wondered how Bobby would react to the new arrival.

'It's fortunate that we had trained him not to enter the house,' Sándor said.

'Yes, but he was no bother when we had Robbie staying.'

They needn't have worried. When Julia returned home carrying the baby in her arms the dog greeted her with such wild tail-wagging that his body bent in the middle.

Shortly afterwards, Julia noticed that every time she returned home from visiting or shopping Bobby ran to the pram, stood on his hind legs and with his front paws on the side, looked inside. Julia wondered what would happen if Bobby did not find the baby in the pram and so, after visiting friends one Sunday, Sándor stayed outside the garden gate holding the baby. Julia pushed the pram to its usual place just outside the kitchen door and watched from inside. Bobby was at the pram within seconds and finding it empty started barking furiously. Julia stroked the dog's head, trying to calm him down to no avail. Only when Sándor turned up with the baby in his arms did he stop barking and then his tail started wagging.

A month later the baby was christened Tamás Andor Tottis at the local Roman Catholic Church.

Both families and some close friends attended the event. Later on at the party at home, among the many subjects discussed in conversation, the one most topical, was the rapid rise of Adolf Hitler. There was no doubt about it, the events in Germany looked more and more sinister.

Without any sign of illness Joseph died in his sleep in June. The shock was too much for Hannah, and Julia suggested that she should come and stay with her and Sándor for a while. Hannah gladly accepted the offer. Living with them and baby Tommy helped her overcome her grief.

In the first few weeks of pushing the pram around Julia had met another young woman who had had her first baby, a girl called Judy, five months before Tommy's arrival. The two mothers befriended each other and the children were to become almost inseparable as they grew up.

1935

Hannah returned to her home in Rottenbiller Street and her sister Helen, who had lost her husband two years previously, had moved in with her.

Sándor's business was doing well and the need arose for more employees. Several people turned up in response to the jobs advertised. One of them, a plain-looking pleasant but rather shy young woman, twenty years old and neatly dressed, had answered questions without hesitation. Sándor assigned her to Packing and Dispatch.

Although a capable manager was running the works Sándor dropped in two or three times a week. At one of his visits some months later he asked the manager, Péter, about Klára Szabó the recently employed girl in Packing and Dispatch and received a good report. He suggested to Péter to try her out in administration at the first opportunity.

Shortly after supper one evening, someone rang the doorbell three times in a row. Sándor went to open the door and found an irate man there who, without any form of introduction, had threatened to kill Bobby. Sándor was certain Bobby did not attack anyone, it was not in his nature. He asked the man in, calmed him down, and inquired about the problem.

What transpired was that the man and his family lived about half a mile away and had a pedigree black spaniel bitch. The man was annoyed because for the second year running the spaniel had a litter of black and white pups.

At one of his customary visits to the factory towards the end of summer Sándor inquired about the progress of Klára Szabó. The manager gave a glowing account. The young woman was conscientious, punctual, reliable, and had not missed a day since she started her employment over six months before. Sándor said he would like to have a look at her handwriting. Péter fetched some shipping files, asking Sándor what he had in mind.

'She appears to me as a person with unutilised, hidden capacity and capability. Someone who would appreciate encouragement and repay such a gesture with interest. May I borrow your office? I would like to have a word with her.'

Péter brought Klára to the office and departed. The young woman was visibly scared.

'Have I done something wrong Mr Tottis?'

'On the contrary Miss Szabó, you have done very well indeed. Please sit down.'

Klára let out a sigh and sat down but it was obvious that she was still very apprehensive.

'Your handwriting is very neat,' Sándor said. 'And your spelling is perfect. What sort of education have you had?'

'State school only.'

'Are you married or do you live with your parents?'

'No, I am not married.' She paused before continuing. 'I live in a rented room. I have no parents.'

'I am sorry to hear that.' Sándor apologised. 'I did not expect a young person like you to have lost both.'

She cast her eyes down and said very quietly, 'I don't know my parents. I was abandoned at birth and grew up in an orphanage.' She seemed very uncomfortable about that.

It was Sándor's turn to stay silent. He had no wish to embarrass the young woman but he needed to know something about her background. He looked at her serene youthful face.

'Miss Szabó, would you like to go on a secretarial course – on full pay?'

Klára's eyes lit up but only for a moment and then she looked uncertain and doubtful.

'What am I expected to do in return?'

Leaning back in his chair Sándor let out a hearty laugh.

'Nothing of that nature Miss Szabó! You have my word that I will never make demands of that sort. Besides, I am still in love with my wife.'

A year later, Sándor's secretary at the Alkotmány Street head office gained an assistant, Klára Szabó. Two years on, after the secretary had left to start a family, she took over the running of the office aided by a shorthand typist. During all this time she had carried on living on her own in a rented room and never had a boyfriend.

1938

Isabelle's birthday, 31st of March, was her sixtieth. The party arranged by Ibolya was lavish by any standard. Regardless of the occasion, the guests mostly discussed and argued about the political situation. People hardly talked about anything else lately.

'I'll bet that by this time next year we are going to be allied to Germany,' someone said.

'Not while Regent Horthy is in charge.'

'I'll second that. Miklós Horthy is a decent, moderate man.'

'He may well be so, but his government is contaminated with Nazi sympathisers.'

'Come on now, he has just thrown one out for trying to implement restrictions on Jews – the sort put in force by some countries around us.'

'If that isn't bad enough look at the pogroms in Germany!'

'Hitler is building up his armaments. The rest of Europe, sick of the memory of the last war a mere twenty years ago, is totally unprepared.'

'We are not going to be involved. What would Germany want from us?'

'Are you blind? We are in the centre of Europe between The Channel and the Ural Mountain Range. If he starts something he will not go West, he'll go East!'

And so the debate had continued non-stop.

Tommy had caught a cold that quickly turned into tonsillitis. On the fourth day of staying in bed in his room next to the kitchen, Bobby was scratching at the door – something he had never done before. Julia, doing the ironing, glanced at Tommy in his bed and went to the door to see what the dog was up to. As she opened the door a fraction the dog rushed in, put his front paws up on the bed and his nose against Tommy's face. Before Julia could utter a word he darted out of the room. Young Judy was the only other visitor coming to play almost every day for an hour or so.

At one of their visits to Hannah and her sister Helen, László turned up unexpectedly with a very attractive redhead on his arm. Her name was Magda and they were obviously in love.

'Seems to me as a case of the rabbit catching the poacher,' Sándor said on their way home, laughing.

'This summer we ought to have Robbie here during the school holidays don't you think?' Julia suggested. Sándor agreed. They had not seen the boy for years.

When he picked the boy up at the orphanage Sándor noticed the change. Robbie was ten years old and while he smiled at Sándor politely, there was some hardness in his expression to the point of contempt or disregard. Maybe I am imagining it, Sándor thought.

Robbie stayed with them for three weeks. He was no problem but he was quiet, not speaking unless spoken to. The age difference between him and Tommy was too great and even though he enjoyed the change of scenery and the lack of regimentation, he missed his friends.

'Could you build a large fenced-off area by the shed, about a metre high?' Julia asked one evening.

'I expect I could. What do you have in mind?'

'I would like to try keeping chickens and have fresh eggs. If we fancied chicken for dinner I won't have to trudge to the market for one.'

'Fine, you can't really go wrong. I'll get hold of some posts and chicken wire.'

So, it was not long before Sandor had built a hen-house, and one day Julia entered the chicken enclosure carefully closing the small gate behind her. Lifting up the hens sitting on their nests to collect eggs, despite their pecking at her in protest, she didn't notice Tommy following her and leaving the gate slightly open. One young hen was instantly through the opening and out in the garden, flapping her wings. Julia spun around just in time to see Bobby leaping to his feet from his slumber and running in a semicircle. He charged at the hen from the side, grabbed hold of its head, shook it vigorously and then let it go. The hen was dead, its neck broken. Bobby walked away from the scene, he had no more interest in the matter.

'By the way, you'll be pleased to know,' Julia said one day, 'our son knows every letter in the alphabet.'

'You must be joking, he's only four years old.'

'I'm not joking. Some months ago I noticed his interest in the newspapers while I was reading them. At first I thought it was the pictures but then he asked me the names of letters. Now he knows all of them.'

'You'd better not tell my sister about that. Her son Dávid is having problems at school although he is not without brains.'

'I'm not surprised. I have never seen a child as spoilt as he is. I'm certain he only does his homework when he wants to. He's thirteen this year, isn't he?'

'That's right. I shudder to think what sort of a person he's going to grow into.'

By Christmas time Tommy was reading fluently. His presents were mainly books for children. He was generally well behaved but also quite headstrong and occasionally defiant. When placed in this type of confrontation with her little boy, Julia had no other choice but to smack his bottom. On each occasion, following the punishment received, Tommy consoled himself by cuddling Bobby and telling him all the hurt and pain in his young heart.

The main event in the spring was the wedding of László and Magda. He was thirty-six, she was ten years younger. They were a strikingly lovely couple and their happiness was self-evident. Magda worked as a hairdresser and beautician, László had the position of general manager at Somosy International Hauliers. Their future looked bright and promising.

'I am thinking of moving house again,' Sándor said as they were having a lie-in one Sunday morning in their adjoining beds. The rain pouring down outside rendered getting out of bed early rather pointless.

'Oh, really, where to?'

'Somewhere in the hills of Buda. We can afford a better property and I wouldn't have to travel to-and-fro' so much. Eventually, if all goes well I intend to buy a car.'

'Ambitious thoughts,' said Julia. 'Do you realise you are going to tear Tommy and Judy apart?'

'Yes I do, but children are very resilient they'll make other friends.'

They pondered in silence. Sándor smiled at her. 'You look irresistible. I am coming over to your bed.'

They were kissing and touching each other when quite unexpectedly the bedroom door flew open and Tommy hopped in. Seeing his father in his mother's bed, he frowned.

'Daddy, what are you doing in my mummy's bed?'

Sándor had to gather his wits. 'I am keeping her warm Tommy.'

'Oh, that's all right. May I join you and help keeping her warm?' Not waiting for permission Tommy slid under the blanket in between his parents with a happy grin on his face.

With Austria already under German command, the mood in Hungary was one of trepidation. Even admirers of the German economic recovery appeared dismayed at the actions of the German government but a minority of the population had openly supported Nazi ideology.

In the autumn of 1939 the German Army occupied Czechoslovakia and shortly afterwards brutally invaded Poland.

Bound by an agreement, Great Britain declared war on Germany. The danger was on the doorstep because both of the occupied countries bordered onto Hungary.

Hitler then requested the stationing of German battalions on Hungarian soil. The Regent of Hungary, Miklós Horthy, refused.

1940

Early in the New Year Tommy contracted tonsillitis again and had to be kept indoors. His consolation this time was a portable typewriter Sándor kept at home. With the aid of the machine he was teaching himself to write in print. At this rate, Julia contemplated, Tommy will get bored at school.

'I'll be back in half an hour or so,' László said to his secretary and walked out of his office. He was meticulously smart in appearance and needed some new shirts and ties.

Walking along fashionable Váci Street he stopped at a man's outfitters and scrutinised the wares displayed in the shop window. The bell attached to the door pinged as he entered, alerting the assistant who appeared almost instantly from the rear.

'Can I help you S...' the man stopped in mid-sentence. László also recognised him, Lilly's boyfriend.

'Hello! I didn't know you worked here,' László said.

'I've been here for almost twelve years, Sir. I assume someone else on your previous visit must have served you while I was on holiday perhaps.'

'As a matter of fact I haven't been here before. Anyway, how are you and how is Lilly?'

'I am well thank you. As for Lilly she left me four years ago for a friend of mine I had introduced her to. Two years later she left him too. I haven't heard from her since.'

'Sorry to hear that. I didn't mean to pry.'

'Sir, there is no need to be sorry. I think I am better off. I had my doubts about her soon after our chance meeting at the National Theatre. She did not visit her young son in the orphanage, not once.'

László made his purchases and left. There was an uneasy realisation in his mind. He had also ignored the existence of his young nephew.

1941

Sándor found a telegram in the letterbox on a Sunday evening when they arrived home from a day out at the Zoo and beautiful Margit Island on the Danube. Péter, the manager at his factory had sent it.

TRIED TO PHONE NO REPLY STOP BROKE MY LEFT LEG STOP SORRY FOR INCONVENIENCE STOP PÉTER STOP

Telegraphic machines having no punctuation marks made the message sound funny but the content was not. Péter would be away for at least six weeks. It was hard going for Sándor when Péter went on holiday, six weeks or more on the trot would be no child's play. He telephoned Péter, asking him how he was and did his best to put the man's mind at rest. Péter was a capable and trustworthy manager and person.

Sándor spent a great lot of time at work, seldom arriving home before eight o'clock in the evening. He supervised the running of the factory every morning and after visiting clients and suppliers returned there late in the afternoon to catch up with the administrative tasks. After the employees had left the premises he could concentrate on the paperwork without interruption.

As he was locking up the factory one evening in August he decided to make a long detour to the main office at Alkotmány Street to pick up paperwork he needed next day. Upon arrival he detected the rattle of a typewriter in the back room and found Klára there, startled by his unexpected appearance.

'Klára, it's long past seven o'clock. What are you doing here?'

'I'm a bit behind with the work Mr Tottis. I'm trying to catch up.'

Sándor was astounded by her devotion but not really surprised. She had demonstrated her loyalty to the business several times in the past. He blamed himself for not anticipating that his spending less time at the main office would increase her workload. 'Finish the page Klára. That will be it for the day. Next time you are overloaded don't hesitate to ask for help.'

Tommy returned from Judy's home at one o'clock as he was told to do.

'What's for lunch Mum?'

'Come and see.'

Julia placed the plate of roast beef, potatoes and cabbage in front of him.

Tommy did not like cabbage. He consumed the meat and the potatoes and then he announced he did not want the rest despite Julia persuading him.

Having failed to make Tommy eat the cabbage, Julia removed the plate and placed it on a shelf.

'Can I have some pudding, please?'

'No Tommy, you can't.'

'Can I have some preserves?'

'No, you cannot.'

'Why can't I?'

'Because you haven't finished your meal. If you are still hungry it is there for you to eat.'

'I don't like cabbage. You know I don't!' the boy exclaimed.

'Cabbage is good for you and that is all you will get. Nothing else until you finish it off.'

'I won't! Not ever!' Tommy shouted and slid off the chair.

He came in from the garden later in the afternoon and asked for biscuits.

'Sorry Tommy, no biscuits or anything else.'

Julia was in the process of preparing the evening meal around seven, expecting Sándor to arrive home in an hour or so. The smell of cooking wafting out resulted in Tommy's appearance at the kitchen door. He said not a word, just stood there. Julia pretended not to have noticed for some time and then asked if he wanted something. The boy responded in a hushed voice. 'May I have the cabbage please, Mum?'

'Of course you may. Just let me warm it up for you.'

A message from Klára awaited Sándor one afternoon as he arrived at the factory. Allied Chemicals had asked to see some proposals he wished to make, the next day if possible. He telephoned the main office.

'Klára, regarding your message about Allied Chemicals. Our proposals are in the top left-hand drawer of my desk in a brown envelope. I would rather avoid making a detour tonight to pick them up. Do you think you could shut shop early and bring them here?'

'Of course I could,' she replied cheerfully.

Buried in paperwork Sándor looked at his watch, 5.38. She should arrive any moment he thought. With six o'clock approaching, Sándor became concerned. He stood up, stretched his arms and his back and walked over to the window. Standing there he had a clear view of the long street leading to his factory. At the top end was the main road where he could see vehicles going either way. He rubbed his eyes to improve the focus. The street busy during daytime looked deserted now. Not a soul, he observed. He was about to leave the window when a woman turned the corner from the main road into the street walking briskly. She looked very attractive wearing a white blouse, light blue skirt and blue sandal shoes with high heels. Walking towards the factory her hips swayed side to side slightly and he noticed the gentle bouncing of her blouse. I am not too old yet, Sándor mused, realising with some shock that the woman was actually Klára.

He had never seen her dressed like that before. Always in a two-piece outfit as befitting a secretary, smart but not attention-grabbing. Undoubtedly she had gone home first to change, she must be on her way to meet someone. Sándor picked up the phone and called a taxi for her.

Klára entered the office a few minutes later with a happy and smiling face, a picture of femininity.

'Klára, I hope I didn't spoil your plans for the evening.'

'No, no, you did not,' she replied cheerfully.

They talked about some office matters and then Klára said she would like to discuss a personal issue.

'What's bothering you?' Sándor had an anxious look on his face.

'Something concerning you.'

Sándor was taken aback. 'What could that be?'

'Do you remember our previous meeting in this office, six years ago?'

'Of course I do, why do you ask?'

'You had made a vow giving me your word that you would never make certain demands on me.'

'Yes I had, and I have kept my word!' Sándor replied indignantly.

'I know you have.' Klára said in a whisper, blushing. 'That is my problem, because I don't want you to.' And with a flip of her fingers she opened her blouse.

The V-shape of the open blouse revealed an unblemished cleavage. The effect of that on Sándor was instantaneous and intense. He had to muster all his willpower to keep himself in control. If only it was another woman he thought, I must not touch Klára.

With trembling fingers he attempted to button up her blouse. Touching her breasts would make him lose his restraint.

'Klára, I cannot accept your offer. You don't owe me anything.'

'This is not repayment,' she whispered throwing her arms around his neck and kissing him on the lips. Her firm breasts pressed to his chest and her moist, hungry lips pushed Sándor's resistance to its limits yet he untangled her arms gently, keeping hold of her hands, softening the effects of rejection. They stood there for several seconds gazing at each other, not knowing what to say or do next.

A car horn sounded twice, the taxi had arrived. Neither of them could say anything as they left the building and boarded the taxi. Sándor slid the pane of glass separating the cab from the passenger compartment to one side and gave the cabby some banknotes.

'Take me to "The Western" and then take this young lady where she wishes to go and keep the change.' He pushed the pane of glass to the closed position so that they would not be overheard.

'Klára, I could not take advantage of you. You are twenty-six and I am forty-three and I love my wife.'

'I would not interfere with your family life. If that were to happen I'd vanish.'

'I am deeply touched. You had offered me the greatest gift you can give any man. Why me?'

'That will remain my secret,' whispered Klára.

By the end of 1941 the German Army had marched into and occupied each and every country around Hungary and beyond. To avoid subjugation by the German Army, a reluctant Hungary was finally forced to enter the arena of war it was totally unprepared for. During dinner parties and other social events Tommy heard repeated mentions of phrases such as the Axis, the Allies, and the persecution of Jews. He overheard accounts that Jews in some countries had to display a yellow star on their coats and that they could no longer work in certain occupations.

To a seven-year-old boy it was quite intriguing, but insignificant.

1942

Early in the year Sándor had found the property he wanted. It was in an awful state but its location was perfect. Situated at a street corner on a south facing slope of Gellért Hill the house stood six feet above street level, in a garden contained by a sturdy wall. The buildings opposite being at a lower level, the property offered a magnificent 180-degree panoramic view. On the left one could see in the distance the island of Csepel on the Danube, ahead the hills of Buda in a semicircle and on the extreme right the Royal Palace. Within the periphery of the distant hills everything was at a lower level.

The war was raging elsewhere, and at home the rising popularity of the Arrowcross Party alarmed many people. Their symbol was a green cross within a white circle, tipped with arrowheads on each of its four points on an oblong red background.

The Arrow Cross Party followed the Nazi ideology of 'master races' and promoted the racist anti-Semitism of the Nazis. Their objectives were identical to Hitler's, they were Fascists to the core.

Julia and scores of other parents had been waiting at the school gates on the last day of the final term. What sort of final reports would their children come out with? When a child failed to reach a satisfactory standard in one or two subjects, they had to sit a subsidiary examination a week before the start of the next term. Failing to pass in either, or if they had failed in more than two subjects originally, they would have to repeat the same year with children younger than themselves. The shame of that made children try hard and incidents of 'repeating' were extremely uncommon. On the faces of the children emerging from the school building one could clearly see the proud and happy expressions and the subdued ones. Some even cried for not getting marks they had expected and were scared of a ticking-off from their parents.

Waving his school report frantically, Tommy ran into Julia's arms. Julia opened the little booklet and found each subject graded *Excellent*. This was certainly a great improvement on the previous year, the first year Tommy had attended school. It was not his fault catching whooping cough, measles and chickenpox one after the other and the usual bout of tonsillitis. But because he had missed more than the permitted number of days he had to sit the subsidiary examination in all but one subject. The one subject not re-examined was, of course, reading.

Learning about the good results in the evening, Sándor picked the boy up and gave him a loving cuddle. 'Tommy, you have done very well making us proud of you. From now on you will have to try hard to keep up to this standard. You deserve a prize for your achievement, what would you like?'

Tommy's reply was instant: 'A scooter please, Dad. A scooter.'

'All right, a scooter it will be but do remember the standards you will have to maintain from now on.'

Tommy, supported in mid-air by his father's powerful arm, was overjoyed. 'Thank you Dad, thank you very much. I'll do my best in school I promise!'

The scooter was in use virtually non-stop during the summer break. It was nice to see, Julia pointed out to her husband, how Tommy shared the scooter and all his toys with Judy. The two of them had seldom argued and never quarrelled. The early cuts and grazes healed quickly and, as they gained more experience, ceased to happen. Bobby was the only one who did not appreciate the presence of the scooter because he constantly had to change his places of slumber to avoid being run over.

'Mum, Mum!' Tommy was rushing in with Judy at his heels. 'Come and have a look in the chicken enclosure.'

Not knowing what to expect, Julia followed the children and found them peering through the chicken wire. She could hardly believe her eyes, a hen had managed to hide an egg somehow and it had hatched. There was a day-old chick running around in the enclosure stopping here and there and then setting off again, with its irresistible charm.

'Mum, can we play with it, please?'

'Tommy, a tiny chick is very delicate and you must not forget Bobby. It is not his fault that nature made dogs hunters. I am sure you remember what happened to the hen that escaped before.'

'Mum, Bobby is out somewhere and he may not be back for hours, can we play with the little chick please, pleeeease?'

To deny the request in the circumstances would not be reasonable Julia decided, so she caught the chick and placed it carefully on the grass. She fetched some chicken feed as well and sprinkled it over a small area in an effort to stop it wandering away. The chick calmed down after the initial shock and began to move about in an irregular pattern. The children realised that every time they reached out towards the little creature it ran in the opposite direction, so they just lay on their tummies, supporting themselves on their elbows and simply enjoyed the sight.

Absorbed in the antics of the chick, they had failed to notice Bobby strolling across the garden towards them. As he approached, the instinct of survival made the tiny chick flee for safety. It ran to a tiny gap in the fencing and was out in the street in an instant and out of sight. The dog took off at full speed to his permanent exit-hole Sándor had stopped filling up years ago. There was no point in doing that, this way he dug no more.

Tommy ran for help. 'Mum! Mum! Bobby's chasing the little chick!'

By the time Julia appeared the children were in tears. 'What happened?'

Tommy was crying hard, severely hurt by the evident desire of his trusted friend Bobby to kill the tiny creature. Just as he finished explaining, Bobby emerged, wriggling his way through his tunnel.

'Come here Bobby!' Julia commanded. '*What… have… you… done*?'

The dog strolled slowly up to his mistress and lowered his head to the ground as if ashamed of himself. He opened his jaws, coughed just once and from the depth of his mouth a soggy little bird rolled out protesting loudly about the method of transport back to the garden. Apart from being soaking wet it was unharmed. Tommy cuddled the dog and Julia turned away to hide her tears, having witnessed Bobby's display of devotion to his young master.

The dog demonstrated his selfless loyalty for a second time shortly afterwards. In the afternoon of a warm summer day Bobby began to howl. This was new. He barked occasionally but howl, never. Yet there he was sitting on his haunches, looking up to the sky like a wolf and howling.

'I'd better take him to the vet, he's getting old,' Julia said.

The statement shocked Tommy, he did not realise that his friend and confidant would not be at his side forever. The thought of life without Bobby scared him.

The weather being very warm, windows and internal doors had been left open at night to allow movement of air. Sometime in the middle of the night Tommy heard a dog barking vociferously in his dreams. The barking grew louder and louder and he awoke to find Bobby straddled over him on the bed as if protecting him from harm. The dog was barking and growling ferociously into the darkness, albeit there was no one in the room, only an unusual and distant droning sound was audible through the open window. Julia rushed in shouting,

'Don't be afraid my darling it's only a bombing raid!'

Both parents sat on the side of Tommy's bed. Sándor was stroking his son's head to allay his fears and Julia had her arm around the faithful, trembling dog when a muffled explosion was heard in the distance. A bomb had hit a house a mile away at Sashalom, killing the residents instantly. Another bomb had landed on an apartment block at Podmaniczky Street in central Budapest close to the Western Railway Station.

The strange circumstances of the bombing raid turned into a topic up and down the country: Why would numerous enemy planes fly so far and drop only two bombs? Why had they been dropped so randomly on unselected targets? How come there was no air-raid warning? How could they fly across the border unnoticed and as a result not intercepted? Were they really enemy planes or was it a callous propaganda exercise by the Luftwaffe to make people blame the enemy?

No one could be certain but the circumstantial evidence was overwhelmingly strong.

Buried in thoughts, Sándor walked away from the premises of his suppliers of chemicals, and the man in threadbare clothing walking in the opposite direction only registered vaguely. Sándor was jolted out of his ponderings. The face was familiar. He turned around, caught up with the man and called out, 'Ferie!'

The man in the rather worn outfit stopped and looked at Sándor, with a faint smile on his face. They had not seen each other for over twenty years, Ferenc Molnár used to be a fellow student at college and a friend.

'Ferie, have you got a job around here?'

'No, I haven't. I am looking for one.'

'Right. There's a cafeteria over the road let's go and have a cup and a good chat,' Sándor suggested. Ferenc Molnár was rather hesitant to accept but Sándor grabbed him by the elbow and took him across the road.

They sat at a corner table away from other patrons.

'What's wrong Ferie? I have the impression that you're down on your luck.'

'Sandy, you are an old pal. I don't intend to burden you with my problems. Let us talk about something else, how about old times?'

'Ferie, we can to talk about old times at some future date. Right now I intend to learn why a man with your ability and education is out of a job.'

'Sandy, I actually walked past you to avoid bothering you.'

'First of all you are not bothering me. Second, think of your family. I heard that you'd got married in the late twenties.'

Sándor realised he had hit a tender spot. Ferie sat back in his chair.

'Well, that's where it all went wrong. No, that is not true, it was some years later when Agie fell ill. In and out of hospitals, different specialists. By the time she had passed away, medical bills had gobbled up all we had. Fortunately, we did not have any children. Shortly after that I lost my job as general manager at a well-known clothing manufacturer. I've had nothing but odd jobs for the last two years.'

Sándor digested the information. Something was amiss. 'Why can't you find another post?'

'Because no company would consider employing a manager without making enquiries at his previous post.'

Sándor was aware of the danger of offending his old friend but not asking the next question would be just as bad. 'Ferie, what went wrong in your last appointment?'

'Well, you may remember that I am a great believer in socialist principles. I must clarify that I am not a communist. Communism is the other extreme to total capitalism. I want to see a society in between the two. Accordingly, I was badgering the board of directors to increase the wages of machinists because they worked long hours in cramped conditions for a pittance.'

Sándor was drinking his coffee in small gulps to give himself time to think.

Ferie continued, 'Don't worry about me I will manage, something will come along.'

'Not in your line, certainly not after two years without an appointment or reference. Not a chance and you know it. There is a way, but with a condition attached. Shall I carry on?'

'Please do, but take no offence if I don't find it acceptable,' replied Ferie.

'Fine, I will not be offended. Have you got a decent suit?'

'Not any more.'

'Right. I suggest that tomorrow morning you accompany me to my tailors and have a complete outfit made on my account. You can refund me one day in the future. The suit made, you are going to apply for positions in your field. Any interested or prospective employers you will refer to me for reference.'

Ferenc Molnár sat motionless like a statue. He didn't even blink for some time. Then he asked very quietly, 'What is the condition attached?'

'Ferie, I hope you would not find it too drastic. As a person with a conscience I do sympathise with some of your ideals. I am fully aware that certain employers are ruthlessly exploiting their workers. However, in the appointment you will secure, under no circumstances shall you profess or declare your beliefs. Would you give me your word on that?'

Ferenc Molnár did not hesitate, he proffered his right hand across the table. 'You have my word Sandy. I intend to repay you one day for your remarkable deed, hopefully with interest.'

The house on Gellért Hill had been rebuilt to a new design with a bay window at the front to enhance the panoramic view.

The Bay Window

**1943. Tommy on the terrace,
with a small section of the panoramic view behind him.**

Their new home delighted Julia and Sándor but not
Tommy. From a child's point of view the house was
nice and he found the new area and the streets with
steep gradients fascinating but he had a high price to
pay. Judy, who used to live just a few minutes' walk
from Tommy's home was now very far away. Even
when the two families went on their respective holidays,
the children found the short separation hard to endure.
They used to see each other almost every day until now,
currently there was no chance at all for that. For the first

time in his life Tommy experienced acute loneliness. At his age of only eight years he did not realise that he was actually in love. In the new neighbourhood and school Tommy found it hard to make friends.

Bobby was also unable to settle down. The change affected the dog badly. He could not find a favourite place for himself. Any place he lay down and curled up in he vacated after a while.

A few days after moving house Bobby disappeared. The three of them scoured the streets to no avail. Tommy cried himself to sleep that night. Julia, also missing the four-legged member of the family, expressed her fears to her husband. Sándor said that Bobby could have lost his way or, as it happens on rare occasions, the dog was trying to get back to their previous home, the only one he had ever known and had been used to.

Julia insisted on taking Tommy to school every morning because the difference in the flow of traffic made it necessary. Three cars a day going past the home they have just moved out of was more than usual. In this area cars, taxis and buses whizzed by, especially at the crossing of Sánc Street and Hegyalja Road, a busy main route.

Just beyond this crossing, Aladár Street branched off at an angle going downhill. This street came to view only after they had crossed the main road, revealing Bobby's lifeless body in the gutter some twenty yards away. Evidently a car or a lorry had hit the poor animal, vehicles he was unfamiliar with. Tommy attempted to run over to the dead animal but Julia gripped his hand and said, 'No, you must leave him in peace.' Tommy began to sob. Julia stroked his hair and turned around to take him home, shedding a few tears on the way.

To relieve the grief and distress of his son Sándor purchased a bicycle for Tommy and one for himself.

Tommy did not take long to master the art of balancing and soon afterwards father and son explored the surrounding area right up to the Citadella, the ancient fortress on the top of Gellért Hill. They also attended Mass every Sunday in the church at Döbrentei Place where Tommy was going to take his first Holy Communion. Julia would never join them. Asking his father about that, Sándor explained it was because she had a lot to do on Sundays, cooking dinner and baking cakes for visitors. The explanation baffled Tommy because they did not entertain guests every Sunday but he did not pursue the matter.

Ferenc Molnár telephoned one evening to say that his application for the position of general manager at a printing firm had been accepted and he would take up his post on the first day of the following month. Sándor invited him for a celebratory dinner and he became one of their regular if not frequent visitors. Julia liked Ferie Molnár with his subtle humour and his concern for others.

German being the second language in the country Julia hired a private tutor, Tante Helga, a lady of German origin to teach Tommy the German language in twice-weekly one-hour lessons.

Judy had been replaced but not forgotten. Tommy missed her more than his parents could imagine. He kept thinking of the many games they played, the things they used to do, how they used to sit side-by-side holding hands and chat and how they shared everything.

Tommy had a new friend, Tibor, a fair-haired boy with blue eyes of the same age, another only child who lived a few doors away. Tommy asked if Judy could come and visit. He was told that plans had already been made and if Judy would like to stay during school holidays she would be welcome.

The first snow was falling, turning everything brilliant white. The view from the bay window was exquisitely beautiful. The sparkling white snow outlined the edges of buildings, roofs, trees and even the unlit lampposts in the otherwise total darkness. Standing there with arms around each other's waist Julia said, 'How wonderful it would be with the streetlights on and the windows not blacked out.'

The war and uncertainty of the future worried them both. They turned on the radio every evening so they could hear the news that was also broadcast on Sundays from lunchtime onwards. France, Belgium, Holland and Norway had been under German occupation for some time and most of the news bulletins reported the events on the Eastern Front. The might of the 'victorious' German Army advanced as far as Stalingrad. In reality they had got snowed-in and suffered the effects of an unusually cold winter they had not been equipped for, so much so that men had frozen to death in their sleep. There was no mention or reference to that in the news.

Sándor brought cousin Robbie home from the orphanage at Christmas. He was fourteen by now but despite the age difference Robbie and Tommy got on well. He was very polite and courteous and more often than not he would just sit quietly by himself.

'Robbie is very mature for his years,' Sándor remarked.

1943

The tone of the news on the radio had changed in January. There were tactical withdrawals, difficulties with the terrain and supplies bogged down in the snow on their way to Stalingrad.

By the end of the month, Soviet troops and tanks had surrounded the demoralised and freezing German divisions commanded by General Paulus. At the beginning of February Paulus surrendered.

German prisoners of war after the surrender

The rest of the German Army began to retreat with Soviet forces at their heels. The Hungarian 2nd Army ordered to hold back the Russian advance was partly annihilated, partly captured. Better equipped for the harsh winter, the Soviet Army began moving westward re-capturing their country.

The families and loved ones of the 2nd Army and many other battalions had no way of knowing who had perished on the battlefield and who had survived and was in captivity. They were not to know that for many years to come and the consequences of that often turned out to be tragic.

The heavy losses of fighting men resulted in the re-activation of army reserves and, along with other men, Sándor received his call-up papers. It was not unexpected because he was in the age group for the reserves but even then Julia broke down. She wrapped her arms around Sándor, holding on to him for a long time. Tommy on the other hand was quite excited at the thought of his daddy becoming a soldier. Sándor had only two days before he had to report for duty and so he appointed Klára and Péter to run the company between them.

Tommy quickly discovered that being proud of his father in the army was no substitute for having him home every day. This was his third experience of personal loss after the distressing separation from Judy and the demise of Bobby, both with long lasting effect. Time and again he caught himself calling or looking for the dog.

Judy in 'Szentmihály also suffered a great deal from loneliness. Although she had been friendly with other children, the absence of Tommy, her life-long friend, created an emptiness no one else could fill. Night after night the young girl cried herself to sleep.

Julia was not the only one bursting into tears at the news of Sándor's call-up. Klára wept too, but only in private. She loved Sándor deeply, mostly as a man but also as a father figure. Despite her hopeless situation, knowing that she could never have him, she feared for him in the army and the realisation that from now on she would not have the pleasure of his company every week from Monday to Saturday she found very difficult to bear.

The news on the radio reported frequent withdrawals and unavoidable heavy losses as the front line kept moving westward across Russia. When family or friends visited, Tommy frequently heard about places like North Africa, Casablanca, also of the British, the Americans, the Jews, concentration camps and gas chambers. Asking Julia about things he had overheard she said it had nothing to do with him and listening to the conversation of other people amounted to bad manners.

Sándor came home on a forty-eight hour leave. Placing his army rifle in a corner he told Tommy not to touch it. Tommy was greatly tempted but he would not disobey his father. He stood a couple of feet from the weapon and observed the polished wooden butt, the black metal parts and that the weapon was slightly taller than he was. If only he could hold it and play with it! He was very proud of his dad looking really smart in uniform.

Tommy had stayed at Judy's place in August for three whole weeks. Judy was slightly taller but at their age such details had no importance. Seeing each other for the first time in many months the two of them embraced. In the following days they didn't leave each other's side apart from bedtime. Their happiness was contagious, but days and weeks passed very quickly and when it was time to part again Judy was in tears and Tommy realised that he would be much happier living in 'Szentmihály. They embraced once more. 'Please don't go,' Judy sobbed.

The news on the radio regularly reported further losses at the front, bombing raids at home, and some new regulations regarding Jews in certain occupations. Tommy heard so much of that lately and so often that it meant nothing to him any more. His friend Tibor came over to play or he visited Tibor. Life went on.

The telephone rang one day and following a short conversation Julia exclaimed, 'Your father is coming home!' She performed a pirouette demonstrating her delight at the good news to Tommy's astonishment.

Sándor duly arrived next day, wearing his civilian outfit.

'Why aren't you in uniform, Dad?' Tommy asked immediately.

'Because I have completed the training course for the Reserves and the Army does not want me just yet,' Sándor replied. 'I'll take it easy for a few days to make up for lost time with you and then I will go back to work.'

Early next morning Tommy decided to join his parents if they were awake. He stopped at the bedroom door and listened.

'…we'll leave the country when this is over… Two wars in one generation … In all probability we shall emigrate to Brazil, to Rio de Janeiro…'

That was his father talking! Tommy did not want to hear any more, the shock of what he had heard was too much. He tiptoed back to his room with his mind in turmoil. Leave the country? Why? When? What for? Hungary is our motherland, the home of our ancestors I was told many times. A country to be proud of. If we go away I'll never see Judy again! Tears cascaded down his face, being unaware of the reasons and because of the questions he could not ask. Listening to the conversation of his parents would amount to very bad manners.

The Soviet Army had re-occupied most of their country and advancing through the Ukraine approached Poland and Romania. Their aeroplanes flew further and further west on bombing raids. Towns and cities in the eastern region of Hungary became regular targets. Due to this development, the radios in every home had to be permanently switched on so that everyone could hear advance warnings interrupting the programme about enemy planes detected flying over the border: *'Air hazard! Air hazard!'* followed by the name of the town or towns in their flight path. This changed to: *'Air raid! Air raid'* and the name of the town they were approaching, later on followed by: *'Air hazard over'*, after they had passed on.

The news bulletins also reported the damage caused and the number of casualties of the raids on previous days.

1944

In early 1944, Adolf Hitler lost patience with the reluctance of Regent Horthy to fully tow the Nazi line. He invited Horthy to Germany for a three-day consultation. It was a trick.

At the second morning of the talks, 19th March 1944, the people of Hungary awoke to find German troops, motorcyclists, troop carriers and armoured cars everywhere. Coming from all directions and eliminating border guards the German Army occupied Hungary overnight and set about arresting people, the outspoken opponents of the politics and methods of the Third Reich, from all walks of life.

Tommy's German tutor born and bred in Hamburg, turned up in tears, really upset.

'Two SS officers turned up early this morning and arrested my husband,' she said weeping. 'Despite reasoning and pleading with my fellow countrymen, he was taken away in handcuffs to an unknown destination. One of the two arresting officers said, "You should be ashamed of yourself for marrying a racially impure non-Aryan man".'

She dried her eyes with a hanky. 'And he called me a whore.' She broke down after that.

Julia hugged and consoled the weeping woman who stayed with them all evening and when she decided to leave Julia ordered a taxi for her.

The lesson did not take place and that was all right by Tommy but he felt sorry for his teacher because she was a nice person.

Sándor said that owing to the situation he would stay at home as much as possible, Klára and Péter could run the business with him available on the telephone.

'Dad, there are German officers in the middle of the road looking at our house,' Tommy said a few days later. Sándor, refraining from looking out directly, walked past the window. He observed a group of three officers and an evidently very co-operative civilian pointing at his house, apparently providing some information. He wondered what could have made these German officers interested in his home.

'The subservient pig,' he muttered.

'What does that mean, Dad?'

'Tommy, I ought to explain certain facts to you,' Sándor said and squatted down to face Tommy. 'As a country we are fighting a war that has nothing to do with us. We did not start it, we did not want to be in it. We entered this war in an attempt to avoid occupation by the German Army in the manner they had subjugated all other countries around us. A large number of men, some young, some with families, have already perished at the front. The war is getting nearer every day and people of all ages, including children, die in bombing raids. Germany started the war by invading other countries and now they are here in ours because they do not trust us. They are not here as our friends. Does this make sense to you?'

'Dad, if the Russians are the enemy and the Germans are not our friends what are they?'

'The Russians see us as an enemy because we are fighting them. The Germans with whom we are supposed to be allies can only be described as a different sort of adversary. They are not here to protect us. Tommy, you must not tell anyone ever what I have just told you and you must promise me that.'

'I promise.'

His father's explanation helped Tommy to comprehend the situation and events of the past year or two, although there were things about it he could not see clearly.

Clarification was not long forthcoming. The doorbell rang two days later and Julia found two German officers there who pushed past her into the hall and entered the lounge.

'Was wünschen Sie?' asked Sándor in fluent German. (What do you want?)

'We are inspecting the premises. The position and location of the building are perfect for the German High Command,' replied one of them, walking over to the bay window and gazing at the panoramic view. The other one had attempted to go into the reading room with the wall-to-wall bookcase reaching almost to the ceiling but Sándor stepped in his way.

'Excuse me, this is my home. You have no right to walk in without asking me first!'

The officer glared at him with an expression of dismissal.

'Your ownership of the property is insignificant. Should we find this place suitable for our purpose you will be given two hours to pack and remove what you want to take with you. Understand?' Abruptly he pushed Sándor aside and entered the room. They inspected every nook and cranny except the attic and returning to the lounge declared that it was the best situated property they had seen so far for the High Command but a larger one would be preferable. They departed without saying 'thank you' or 'goodbye', leaving the front door open on their way out, unbuttoned long coats billowing behind them in the wind.

Tommy observed his parents facing each other motionless with unsmiling, grim expressions. Something was wrong.

On their way home from school a couple of days later a weird, khaki coloured open-top German Army car pulled up beside two men walking on the other side of the road, its doors opening before the car came to a halt.

The driver and another German soldier leapt out of the vehicle and grabbed hold of one of the men, twisting his arms behind him and forcing him into the rear seat of the car. The other man protested and tried to intervene. The driver of the car hit him in the face so hard that the man stumbled a couple of steps backwards. Recovering his balance, he continued to protest but a rifle butt hit him in the abdomen making him crumple up in agony. He fell down. In the meantime the other soldier clamped handcuffs on his captive at the back seat of the car. The driver then leapt into the vehicle and drove off.

The whole incident happened so fast that by the time Julia grabbed Tommy and buried his face in her skirt he had seen most of it.

In the following weeks they saw several of the weird-looking vehicles being driven around. Tommy soon learned that they were called 'Kübelwagen', 'Bucket car'.

The front moved steadily westward and the Soviet Armies advanced to the Carpathian Mountains. Their bombers flew closer and closer to the capital. Sándor and Julia awoke one night hearing the air raid sirens for the first time. Julia collected Tommy from his bed.

'We could go to the cellar of Paul Széchy's house as arranged but it would offer no protection against a direct hit, it is only a basement,' Sándor said.

They went to the bay window. There was nothing to see in the total darkness but the faint droning sound of many planes was audible.

'What's going on?' Tommy asked with a yawn.

'Nothing much Tommy, but any moment now you may hear a big bang. Stay between us and don't be afraid.'

The droning sound was still very distant when a small but very bright light appeared out of nowhere, high up in the sky far away on the left. Descending slowly it became brighter, illuminating the area beneath it. Another one followed it further ahead. They were flares attached to parachutes, eventually nicknamed as 'Stalin's candles', helping the bombers identify the target area. As the flares descended to the ground, large orange and red flashes shot up close to each other, covering the area. There was no sound for several seconds and then the rumbling of explosions could be heard in the distance.

'They're bombing the industrial area of Csepel Island,' observed Sándor.

The bombing continued in several waves, the bombers chased by searchlights. Huge fires started in the wake of the raid turning the colour of the clouds above glowing pink, illuminating the night.

Gradually the droning sound got louder and suddenly a flare lit up far ahead, high up in the sky, its brightness too much for the human eye. Descending steadily the blindingly bright light reflected downwards by the white parachute made the buildings below it clearly visible. It was a purely residential area. The droning had become very loud, the bombers following the plane dropping the flares.

'God help the people in those houses,' Julia said. She was shaking. Sándor embraced both Julia and Tommy. 'We are all in God's hands.'

The darkness made the planes invisible but searchlights criss-crossing the sky occasionally picked up one of the bombers, making the ack-ack guns start up with their rapid clatter. The planes passed on unharmed, dropping no more bombs. Soon the sirens sounded the "All-clear". They went to bed with Tommy between his parents. He fell asleep quickly, unlike them.

The doorbell rang the next day. Julia opened the front door and found a German officer there with the "II" insignia of the Wehrmacht on his lapels. He introduced himself as Major Weissler and requested to speak with Mr Tottis. Julia asked him if he would wait a moment and went indoors to tell her husband. Sándor said that this was a different, more civilised approach and to show the man in. He stood up to receive the visitor.

The Major entered the room and observed that father and son had been playing chess. He introduced himself, apologised for the intrusion and said that he was in need of information. Out of a square leather case attached to a diagonal leather strap over his shoulder he produced a map.

'Move the chessboard Tommy.'

The boy carried out his father's request and returned, standing on his left.

The major asked various questions, pointing at certain areas on the map. Sándor, nerves taut, fearing the consequences of his refusal to cooperate, kept replying, 'Ich weiss nicht… Ich kann nicht… Ich weiss nicht…'

With his basic knowledge of the German language, Tommy understood most of the questions about places and people, some of them known to him and his father. He was brought up to tell the truth at all times, why did his father tell lies saying he did not know? He could not have forgotten so many things! When Sándor issued yet another denial he could not let it pass.

'Daddy, we *do* know that place, why do you say you don't?'

The back of Sándor's hand hit him hard in the face, the heavy gold signet ring bearing his initials made the boy's nose explode. The act of being hit like this was so uncharacteristic and unexpected that Tommy did not feel any pain and the events of the next few minutes etched themselves on his memory.

Major Weissler folded his map and replaced it into the leather case. Then he straightened up and fixed his eyes on Sándor.

'I understand, Sir,' he said and saluted Sándor in the traditional manner with the fingertips of his right hand touching the shield of his cap. Not the Fascist salute.

He walked to the door, stopped at Julia standing there, petrified by what she had witnessed and said, 'The little boy needs his face washed.' He nodded, clicked his heels and walked out of the house closing the front door behind him.

Tommy's nose hurt. His father sat him on his lap facing him, legs astride. Sándor was visibly upset.

'Tommy, I am indeed sorry for hitting you. You did not deserve it, you did not do anything wrong. We had told you that the truth must be told at all times, never tell lies, and you have heard me telling some. Then again, the circumstances we are living in are different. Telling this officer what he wanted to know would have put at risk some friends and other people. Had he been the arrogant type, like the ones we have had here before,

I would be in trouble for refusing to give him the information he had expected. Major Weissler behaved like a gentleman when he realised that he would learn nothing from me. I don't think we need to worry about repercussions. Let that be a lesson to you, not all German soldiers are the same, there are good and bad people everywhere. Please forgive me, I had not intended to hurt you.' His arms enfolded the son he loved so much and struck so hard, however unintentionally.

Tommy hugged his father and cried although he was not quite sure why.

He cheered up before long and Sándor suggested they go for a stroll in the spring sunshine.

Walking along hand-in-hand in Mihály Street they saw a well-dressed man coming out of a house and get into a car with 'CD' plates. He drove off.

'Dad, what are "CD" plates for, what do they mean?'

'The letters "CD" form an abbreviation of two French words: *Corporation Diplomatique*. A car with a plate like that is used by a foreign embassy. The man we saw was Raoul Wallenberg from the Swedish embassy. I have heard that he is trying to save people from being deported.'

Sándor was right about Major Weissler, there were no consequences to his visit, but a week later two other German officers presented themselves. The older one with a black eye-patch introduced himself to Julia as Colonel Eisner, the younger one was his adjutant. The colonel asked to speak with Mr Tottis in private. Julia took him to the lounge. The adjutant remained in the hall.

The colonel introduced himself, 'Herr Tottis, I am Colonel Eisner attached to the German High Command. Although the house is too small for all our staff we have decided to commandeer it because of its unique location. On behalf of the High Command I am taking possession of the house *as of now*. To comply with the regulations, you and your family are allowed two hours to pack whatever you wish to take with you and move out. Once you have left the premises there will be no grounds at all for returning.'

In a softer tone he added, 'That is the standard directive. All I ask you is that you carry it out as fast as you can. Do you have somewhere to go?'

'Yes, we have. I have expected this as the probable outcome of the other officers inspecting our home.'

Sándor and Julia began packing clothing, towels, toiletries, and a few of Tommy's toys into suitcases. The portable typewriter, cooking utensils, and other items they considered essential went into boxes. When everything they intended to take with them was in a pile in the living room, Sándor called for three taxis. They loaded the baggage into the three vehicles, Sándor boarded the first one, Julia and Tommy the second, the third one just followed them.

The flat in Báthori Street they moved into was on the Pest side of the river near the Houses of Parliament. It was fully furnished and on the second floor of an apartment block. The last occupant must have passed away some time ago because dust covered every piece of furniture, the floorboards and windowsills. Located at the back of the block their new home was dark. The sun shone in for a very short time and the furniture, albeit in good condition, was old-fashioned. Carrying their belongings over from the lovely home the German High Command took over, Julia broke down. Sándor tried to console her saying that the situation could not last forever, the important factor was that they were together. Tommy, also upset by the events and seeing his mother in tears wondered, why wouldn't they stay together?

A U-shaped gangway encircling the paved inner court served five flats, the same on each floor. At the top right of the U-shape was the main staircase and lift, their new abode at the other extreme. Between their home and the next one occupied by a family with a thirteen-year-old daughter, loomed the dark and narrow emergency rear staircase. The flat at the centre of the 'U' housed an elderly couple keeping themselves to themselves; beyond that, a family resided with three noisy children. Dr Herzog with his invalid mother in a wheelchair occupied the flat adjacent to the main staircase and he had converted a large room into his surgery.

The basement had been transformed into a large makeshift air-raid shelter by the removal of the individual coal cellars, originally one for each dwelling. Steel connecting doors had been fitted at either side, providing an escape route between adjacent buildings in case one received a direct hit. The bleak enclosure contained only wooden benches. As the number of air raids increased, the sixty or seventy inhabitants of the building had become acquainted with each other if only vaguely. Their reaction to danger took various forms; some sat in silence while most of them kept a conversation going. One or two shook with fear or cried, and a hysterical woman proclaimed every few minutes that they would all perish, there was no hope, despite her husband trying to calm her down.

The radio switched on all through the day made more and more references to Jews and regulations concerning them. Tommy wondered about the reason for the large number of regulations issued, penalising Jews and curbing their freedom. The only Jews he could think of were the ones in the Bible and they had lived and died long ago.

Seated in an armchair, Sándor called Tommy over to him. The boy sensed something was wrong because his mother kept bursting into tears in the last couple of days and when he asked her about it she stroked his hair, tried to smile and told Tommy not to worry about her.

Sándor stood Tommy between his knees and placing his hands on his shoulders looked at him with concern.

'Tommy, I have something to tell you. We must adhere to a new regulation, regardless how unjust or disagreeable. As from tomorrow morning we shall have to display a yellow star every time we leave home, even if only going to the air-raid shelter. Under no circumstances can we go without it. Your mother has already stitched one to your coat.'

He saw the shock registering on his son's face. 'Why is that? We are not Jewish!'

'No, we are not. Nevertheless, according to new regulations we are classified as Jews because we have Jewish ancestors within the last two generations. One of my grandparents was Jewish and your mother was born to Jewish parents. The fact that they were non-practising Jews makes no difference. Mum changed her faith to marry me. I am sure you can now understand why you must be wary of German soldiers and their Hungarian followers, members of the Arrowcross Party.'

The feeling of injustice made Tommy cry. He wrapped his arms around his father's neck, laid his head on Sándor's shoulder and sobbed. 'Dad, I don't want to have that star on my coat, do I really have to wear it?'

Tommy did not know that to Jewish people the Star of David was a symbol to be proud of even in this form. To him the vision of being labelled with a sign of any sort amounted to undeserved punishment. The more he thought about the situation the more convinced he had become that he was penalised, just like Jewish people, for no other reason than being Jewish. The magnitude of the event hurt him in a way he had not experienced before and his sobbing got heavier. Sándor embraced his son and held him close until he had stopped crying.

Going to school, Tommy had seen other people with yellow stars but not many. Most people walked by without a glance but some made faces at Julia and Tommy or made nasty remarks and a few even spat at them. Tommy dreaded the prospect of having to wear the star at school all day, every day. Noticing other children displaying their Jewish origin helped a little, but in his class he was the only one. Fortunately, his classmates took no notice and none of them seemed bothered by it. The only adverse reaction came from a middle-aged teacher who avoided looking at him or asking him questions.

Sándor and Julia noticed the change of atmosphere in the shelter when people entering the gloomy place realised that some of their neighbours were Jewish. Two families distanced themselves as much as they could, the rest ignored the ones with yellow stars, some because befriending Jews was discouraged, the rest because they were too embarrassed by this form of persecution and did not know what to say.

The few Jewish families in the apartment block gathered in a small group, partly due to religious cohesion, mostly because the isolation that had arisen.

Jewish males in the age group of eighteen to fifty had to report at appointed regional forced-labour camps. Most of them should have been in the army but one of the first anti-Semitic edicts in 1943 was the exclusion of Jews from the armed services. That was the reason for Sándor's demob.

Sándor had to report to a camp far beyond the outskirts of the capital and surrounded by high walls with sentries at the gate checking the identity of everyone passing through.

Registration of each individual, the issue of the uniforms, a pale version of the standard khaki and the allocation of bunks took up the first half of the day.

In the afternoon they assembled in a group on the parade ground and the camp commandant informed them of the order of the next few days: training along army lines and physical exercise. The commandant, unfit for active duty owing to injuries sustained at the Russian Front, had the rank of Captain.

In the following three days Sándor had his share of marching, running, press-ups and climbing obstacles. As he and men in his age group had lived by the same routine in the previous year while in the Army, it was tolerable. A number of older men did not fare well. Some collapsed from exertion and had to be either helped or actually carried back to their bunks. A few of them had suffered heart attacks and finished up in hospital. No one knew whether they had survived or not.

On the fourth day at the morning parade, the sergeant in charge called out five names and Sándor's was one of them. Two soldiers escorted the five men to the commandant's office and lined them up in front of his desk. The two-man escort left the room.

'At ease!' said the commandant. 'I am Captain Kövessy. You are going to undertake the administration of this camp in the adjacent office. I have picked you for your long experience in purchasing, commerce, organisation, and because all five of you have unblemished army records. I expect you will have questions to ask. Do not hesitate to approach me. I will now allocate each of you the tasks you will be responsible for.'

Following the training exercises, the inmates of this and other camps, the 'Labour Service' as it was officially called, went out under armed guards to clear and shore up bomb-damaged buildings, bridges, and roads damaged by bombs. They returned to camp in the evening, worn out by the unaccustomed effort. However, it was a lot better than deportation to concentration camps.

The commandant called his administrators into his office a week after they had started as such. 'Well done! I am confident I can rely on you. You have my permission to telephone your families once or twice a week but they can only phone you in cases of *extreme* emergency. Apart from you and me, no one must know of this arrangement. Do you wish to comment?'

'Sir! We appreciate the gesture,' one man replied. 'We shall not abuse the privilege.'

Another one cleared his throat and said haltingly that his wife was due to undergo an abdominal operation the day after he had to join the Labour Service and asked if he could call immediately. Also, would it be possible for him to visit her in hospital?

The commandant consulted a booklet of directives and seemed engrossed with the subject.

'Yes,' he said finally. 'It would be possible under certain conditions. According to regulations, an armed guard with orders to shoot in case you try to escape must accompany you. Handcuffs attached before leaving camp cannot be removed until your return. However, the regulations make no reference to clothing, so it is up to you whether you go in uniform or wear your own attire.' He waited for comments and then continued, 'I am afraid I cannot grant permission for more than one visit per week except in emergencies, meaning that you can leave camp only once in every five weeks on a rota system. However, you are free to swap places. That is your prerogative.'

Making herself a cup of coffee, Julia poured the milk into the hot liquid and it curdled.

'Tommy,' she called out, 'I have a lot of washing to do, would you run down to the shop and get some milk please? Don't forget to put your coat on, you almost went without it last time!'

'Yes Mum. May I have some money please?'

Going to the shop provided a welcome break from homework so Tommy put his coat on, the money in his pocket, and hurried off.

There was a small queue of two women behind an elderly man being served by the lady shopkeeper when he arrived and by the time the woman in front of him was about to depart two other women stood in line behind him. He turned to look around and the woman behind him noticed the yellow star on his coat.

'You repulsive little Jew!' she bellowed. 'I am not going to wait behind you! Go to the end of the line this instant!'

'I am not really Jewish, I am Roman Catholic,' Tommy replied with determination.

'You despicable, lying Jewish brat!' screamed the woman. 'Do you think I am stupid? Wearing the yellow star proves that you are Jewish! Now *get* to the back!' She lashed out with her handbag.

Tommy had managed to dodge the bag, gritted his teeth in anger at being unable to retaliate and stood behind the other woman in the queue. In due course it was his turn at the counter.

The shopkeeper placed the bottle of milk in front of him and Tommy gave her the money. Giving him the change she slipped a small bar of chocolate into his hand.

'I didn't ask for that,' Tommy said wide-eyed.

'I know you didn't but I would like you to have it. Please.'

'Thank you very much, very nice of you. I'll tell my mum.'

He did tell his mum and the episode made Julia angry and distressed. 'I cannot believe that anyone, particularly a woman, would treat a child like that. Had I known that I would not have allowed you to go on your own.' She fell silent for a short while and then she said in a whisper, 'I must thank the shopkeeper for her compassion.'

School broke up and Tommy was home all day to Julia's great relief. Most air raids took place at night but when a daytime raid passed over the city, not knowing if the school had been hit or damaged, was awful.

Deportation of people, mostly Jews, to unknown destinations gathered momentum. A large number of families obtained temporary citizenship documents from the Swedish and the Swiss embassies who had tried to help in this way. In most cases it proved to be a futile effort according to accounts of non-Jewish friends because German soldiers and Arrowcross men carrying out the round-ups tore the documents to pieces.

Some of the persecuted looked for non-Jewish people who would be prepared to give them refuge in their homes. Anyone daring to hide Jews and many had, imperilled the lives of their families and their own. Klára Szabó, a frequent visitor, repeatedly offered to hide Julia and Tommy in the comfortable apartment she had moved into from the rented room she had previously occupied. Julia could not accept the courageous offer but was grateful for it.

Mr and Mrs Roth, the elderly Jewish couple who lived two doors away had stopped Klára after one of her visits to Julia and Tommy and invited her into their home. They told her that they had a handful of jewellery but no family. They asked Klára to take charge of it until the war was over. In the event of neither of them surviving the persecution she could keep the lot. Klára insisted on giving them a receipt, she was glad to help.

At last the day had arrived when Sándor could visit his family. He wore his civilian clothing and even though the sleeves of his jacket slid over the handcuffs on his wrists the position of his arms and hands gave them away. His escort, a tough looking corporal not much younger than himself with a rifle on his shoulder, followed two steps behind.

The prospect of seeing his family allayed Sándor's feelings of anger, injustice and shame at being treated like a criminal. Passing some derelict buildings on their way to the railway station the corporal issued an unexpected command: 'Halt! Left turn!'

Startled by the command and not knowing what was going to happen next, Sándor turned into the narrow alleyway when, without warning, the corporal manually turned him around. With the key already in his hand the corporal removed the handcuffs.

'Should you try to escape I *will* stop you,' he said.

'Corporal, you are taking a huge risk.'

'I have asked permission to do this. We can now walk side by side like friends. In case of trouble I can look after both of us. I've been in the army all my life.'

'Even with permission this is a brave and noble act from you and the Commandant.'

'Oh, you mean the Captain. He is that all right, brave and noble. I know that because I was his batman, his personal aide, at the Russian Front.'

Arriving at the Báthori Street apartment the corporal was genuinely embarrassed.

'Madam,' he said to Julia. 'You cannot imagine how awful I feel having to escort a fellow Hungarian who is not guilty of anything.'

On the return journey to camp they slipped into the same alleyway once more to fit the handcuffs back on.

Klára Szabó bought a larger handbag. She had stored the jewellery of Mr and Mrs Roth in a drawer of her wardrobe but then she realised that while she was at the office her home could suffer bomb damage or even a direct hit. She decided to keep the jewels with her; if she were to become a casualty of this war their place of concealment would not matter at all. She received a telephone call one day from Sándor.

'Mr Tottis, how nice to hear from you, how are you and what can I do for you?'

She always addressed him by his surname. Sándor had asked her more than once why she refused to call him by his Christian name and she replied that she could not allow Julia or anyone else think that there might be more than an employer and an employee relationship between them.

'Klára, I only want to thank you for your help and concern for my family.'

'No need! What did you expect me to do, ignore them?'

'Klára, I can't spend any more time on the phone. Look after yourself.'

'If you need me for any reason or purpose *call me!*' She shouted the last two words down the line. Replacing the receiver she burst into tears, terrified of never seeing Sándor again.

Sándor had noticed that a variety of soldiers escorted the other four men on their day off. He had no idea whether this was by design or had any significance. Shortly before his turn he asked the commandant if Corporal Sulyok could escort him again.

The commandant was amused. 'I have no objection but the corporal might have. He is a soldier with a conscience, a rare specimen. Most soldiers obey orders unquestioningly as they were trained to do. Corporal Sulyok is outraged by mindless prejudice. You will have to ask him yourself.'

Sándor grabbed the opportunity when he spotted the corporal walking by the office. After a moment's hesitation the corporal agreed.

Sándor's next visit home went without a hitch. Julia informed him that some monasteries and convents provided refuge to children whose families had fled the Eastern regions from the Soviet onslaught. According to the 'network of whispered information', only a few children in their care had been left by genuine refugees, the nuns and friars give shelter to all children without asking questions about their origin.

Julia had asked Corporal Sulyok at his previous visit what his favourite meal was, not provided by army catering. The corporal revealed his craving for stuffed green peppers in tomato sauce with new potatoes, a dish his mother used to cook for him every time he was on home leave. Sadly, his mother had passed away and he had not enjoyed such a meal since. Served with his favourite food at the dining table, except that new potatoes were out of season, the corporal was astounded. Julia was pleased that he had asked for a second helping.

Reminded that soon the weather would turn cold, Sándor left wearing an overcoat and hat.

At two o'clock on 15th October the Regent of the country, Miklós Horthy, interrupted all radio programmes for a broadcast. He declared that following secret negotiations with representatives of the British, American and Soviet governments he was extricating Hungary from the war by surrendering, thus preventing further bloodshed. The majority of the population, the persecuted category in particular, was jubilant but their joy was not to last. Shortly after his broadcast the Gestapo arrested Horthy and placed him into 'protective custody' in Germany. With Nazi approval, the Arrow Cross Party seized power and declared Ferenc Szálasi,

'The Leader' (The Fuehrer) of the party, a fervent follower and admirer of Hitler, prime minister.

Almost immediately members of the Arrowcross Party appeared on the streets armed to the teeth, most of them young thugs without uniform or even a decent set of clothing, wearing armbands with the Party's emblem. How they had managed to be exempt from army service no one knew. They acted like militia, had no discipline and made up rules as they went, ignoring and overruling the regular police force.

The rounding up and deporting of Jews gained momentum in cattle trucks distinctly marked:

5 horses or 40 Jews

Boarding off a sector of a central district in Budapest the building of a ghetto got under way.

The Soviet Army had passed through the Carpathian Mountain range advancing west all the time. The bombing intensified by the increased number of air raids.

'Tommy, Dr Herzog promised me a splint for the finger I strained, would you go over and pick it up please?' Julia said.

'Yes, Mum, in a minute…'

The doctor answered the knocking on his door. 'Hello Tommy, do come in.'

The door to his surgery across the end of the hall was open. The doctor entered and picked up his medical bag from the floor beside his desk.

'I borrowed a splint from the hospital. Ask your mother to return it when her finger is better.'

Tommy noticed a long and fairly thin sausage-shaped glass container on the doctor's desk. It was fitted with a device one would expect to find on a soda siphon but more delicate. Tommy asked what it was for.

'That is an aid to carry out minor operations like stitching up large cuts or wounds. The bottle contains ether. Ether freezes the area it is sprayed on, deadening sensation, but the effect does not last long. If it did, the patient would get frostbite. Let me show you, I promise it won't hurt. Give me your middle finger.'

He sprayed a short burst onto the ball of Tommy's fingertip. For a split second Tommy experienced something similar to a burning sensation and then his fingertip went cold and lost all feeling. He could move it and touch with it but it gave the impression that it did not belong to him.

'That is amazing! Thank you Dr Herzog.'

Sándor's turn to leave camp again occurred in late October. He was glad to have his warm overcoat and hat on – the weather was already wintry and the journey took about an hour and a half. Escorted once more by Corporal Sulyok, they had passed through the gates at nine o'clock precisely.

Just after ten o'clock, a harsh voice amplified by a loud horn jolted Julia and all the other inhabitants of the apartment block.

'Attention! Attention! Jews living here must assemble in the courtyard with a small bag or case they can carry. We are going to check the papers of all residents. Open your front doors and leave them open. Locked doors with no keys left with the caretaker will be broken down. Jews must be ready to march in one hour.'

Apart from a feeling of terror, Julia was angry with herself. She had found a place for her son in a convent but delayed the day of parting. Now it was too late. Her mind was racing. What have I done?... I have put Tommy in danger by keeping him with me... My selfishly hanging on to him could cost him his life... What sort of a mother am I to let that happen?... Sandy is on his way here and he will find an empty home... I must write a note!

Dr Herzog tidied up his desk and the files of his patients, making it easy for another doctor to take over his practice, built up over many years. He placed a wedge under the open front door and attended to his mother in the wheelchair.

Sándor and Corporal Sulyok boarded the tramway at the Eastern Railway Station, changed to another at the 'Small Boulevard' as it was called by Budapestians and alighted at the stop at Báthori Street. This part of Báthori Street was rather narrow. Halfway down its length there was a small square and road junction. From there the rest of the street running down to Parliament Square was much wider.

The entrance of the apartment block coming into view as they entered the square made the two men stop. Armed with a submachine gun and with his back to the street, an Arrowcross man stood under the arch of the main entrance preventing escape from within. The significance was clear to both of them together with the consequences for the inhabitants.

'I must get my family out of there,' said Sándor.

'You can't,' responded the corporal.

'Yes, I can! I speak fluent German. I can bluff it out.'

'What if you fail?'

'At least I'll have tried.'

'And I'd get court-martialled for aiding and abetting a prisoner to escape. Do you realise the sentence for that is the same as for treason?'

Sándor looked at the soldier. 'I am sorry that thinking of a way to save my family I did not consider that, but you cannot expect me to stand here and do nothing, can you?'

'In the circumstances I can and I will!' the corporal said sternly. 'And I expect you to keep walking up and down here as if you were waiting for someone until my return, and *That's An Order!*'

The command issued, the corporal turned on his heels and walked off in the direction of the apartment block. He walked through the main entrance unhindered and instead of using the main staircase he crossed the courtyard to the back staircase, observing covertly. Some people carrying small bundles had already gathered and a young Arrowcross man was checking papers on the first floor.

I'm in luck thought the corporal, they've only checked the ground floor and a couple of dwellings on the first floor so far. Ascending the stairs two at a time to the second floor he turned towards the flat at the end of the gangway. The door was open and he walked in without knocking. He listened in the hall and hearing Julia talking to Tommy, entered the room.

'Have no fear, I can fool them! Pack quickly and come with me.'

Julia visualising what the corporal was attempting to do was speechless but only for a moment.

'You won't get away with it, but I will forever be in your debt if you take Tommy with you.'

'I can take both of you but we must hurry.'

'They'll ask for my papers, everyone must produce them but they may not bother about a little boy hand-in-hand with an armed soldier. I cannot go with you!' She was almost shouting.

'Can you take some clean underwear and a shirt for him and his toothbrush?'

'Of course I can. I'll stuff some under my tunic and some in my pockets.'

'Please, can I take my Shuco car?' Tommy asked, holding his favourite little two-seater sports car with functioning gear lever and steering in his hand.

'Well now,' said the corporal, 'we certainly cannot leave that behind,' and slipped the toy car in his pocket.

'Wait a minute,' Julia said to the corporal. 'We have a sum of money here for emergencies. I am going to keep half of it, would you give my husband the rest? And you must tell him that the Sisters of Mercy at their convent on Somlói Road, Gellért Hill, assured me of a place for Tommy. Don't forget!'

She embraced her son, told him to be brave and then turned abruptly to hide her face. The corporal noticing the heaving of her back and shoulders grabbed hold of Tommy's hand and they swiftly left the room. In the hall he ripped the yellow star off Tommy's coat – it had almost been overlooked.

They stepped out onto the gangway and caught sight of the young Arrowcross man with a rifle slung across his back and a pistol in his waistband entering the home of Dr Herzog at the other end of the 'U'-shaped gangway. The corporal stopped to watch.

The young brute opened all side doors in the hall and, finding no one, entered the surgery. The corporal and Tommy had a clear view of the large desk with the old doctor slumped over it, his head sideways and his arms in semicircles. Near his right hand was an empty syringe. Behind him at the window facing the street his invalid mother sat in her wheelchair with her head dropped forward and down. Both of them were unmistakably dead. The Arrowcross thug stood there, his feet rooted to the floor. He had never seen a corpse before and now he was in the company of two. Then he spat on the floor. They are nothing but stinking Jews, the scourge of Aryan folk, he told himself and left.

The corporal hurried Tommy to the back staircase. They descended to the ground floor and crossed the courtyard. Swinging Tommy's hand forwards and backwards, playfully, the corporal walked through the vestibule. The ruse worked, the man with the submachine gun ignored them and in a moment they were out in the street.

Sándor's throat tightened at the sight of the corporal and his son walking out of the building. He half-expected, half-hoped to see his wife coming out behind them but she did not. To avoid suspicion he had to keep his emotions under control and waited for them to approach. Tommy did not notice him until they drew near. Then the corporal let Tommy go and the boy almost flew into his father's arms.

Listening to the corporal's account of the situation Sándor understood Julia's dilemma. The money and the message passed over, he suggested to the corporal that as they had about three hours before starting their journey back to camp they should watch how events developed.

Time passed slowly. Eventually the young Arrowcross man appeared leading a small column of women, children and elderly men with their meagre belongings out of the building. At the rear of the group the other man with the submachine gun made sure that there would be no chance of escape. The Arrowcross men drove the column towards the Danube's embankment. The two men and the boy followed from a safe distance.

Other small groups joined the one Julia was in and they kept going towards the Chain Bridge, built in 1848, the first one to span the mighty Danube connecting Buda to Pest.

They trailed the group escorted on one sidewalk of the bridge on the other sidewalk. At the Buda side, on the lower level of the two-tier embankment, a large number of people stood waiting assembled in columns

**The lower embankment at the Chain Bridge
the march started from. Photo taken in 2002.**

of six abreast. The new group arriving was quickly absorbed.

By the time the two men and the boy got to the railings of the upper embankment and looked down, Julia could not be seen. They decided to walk ahead and try to see her as the column went by. Watching from above as the marchers began to move northward in the direction of Margit Bridge and going past them down below, Sándor calculated the number of people being over six hundred.

The tail end was in sight when Tommy spotted his mother looking up at him and raised his hand to wave to her. Sándor swiftly grabbed hold of his wrist and stopped him. 'Sorry Tommy, right now you must not do that.'

They followed the column past Margit Bridge and further up to the Freight Terminal where transfer of cargo took place between ships and railway wagons but there they had to give up. The column of unfortunates kept going further north towards the Ujlaki Brickworks, quite some distance from here with its gigantic expanse of storage areas and its own rail terminal. Time had to be spared to take care of Tommy. Back at Margit Bridge they boarded a taxi.

'Number six Alkotmány Street,' Sándor instructed the cabby.

On arrival he asked the cabby to wait and they entered the office. Klára's face lit up at the sight of them. Julia had told her about the corporal so she knew that he was a friend not a foe but the boy's presence without Julia alarmed her. Sándor hurriedly explained what took place and asked Klára to take Tommy to the convent. The two men would go by taxi to the railway station to catch the train back to the camp.

Klára turned to the corporal. 'Please look after him he means a lot to me… and many other people…' she hastily added. Grabbing hold of the lapels of the corporal's uniform she pulled him down and kissed him on the cheek. The face of the seasoned soldier turned crimson.

'Tommy,' Sándor said in a tone that conveyed the gravity of the situation. 'You will be on your own from now on. Have courage and use your own judgement. I will try to visit you at the convent and I am sure Klára will in place of your mother and me. I must go now.' He kissed his son, gave a warm hug to Klára and the two men departed.

Klára sat down by her desk, embraced Tommy and wept silently for a long time before they set off on the journey to Somlói Road.

Tommy recognised the convent, he and his father had cycled past it many times. The Mother Superior took his hand and led him around showing him the washroom, toilets, and the dormitory. She told him to call her Sister Zoé and asked no questions. Finally, he joined other children in the Common Room.

'That's my place!' a boy shouted at Tommy at the evening meal when he sat down on a bench at one of the long tables and pushed Tommy away. Even though he found a place to sit, nobody asked him anything or engaged him in conversations flowing all around him.

Snuggled up in bed on his first night, sleep avoided him. The darkness, the result of blacked-out windows, troubled him, although once his eyes adjusted to it he could make out beds nearest to his. Despite the large number of children in the dormitory Tommy experienced devastating loneliness. The memory of his mother taken away and the manner of it made him feel panicky that he might never see her again. He did not realise at the time that he might not see his father either but the snippets of conversations he had overheard in recent years surfaced, creating abstracted and fearful images in his mind ... deportation ... concentration camps ... torture ... gas chambers ... crematoria. Tommy had no idea of the functions of gas chambers and crematoria but they implied some device of very scary nature. He curled up in a ball, pulled the blanket over his head and cried for a very long time until sleep relieved him from his torment.

The light was fading by the time the column Julia was in reached the holding area at the Brickworks where they joined thousands already there, some for many days.

Transportation could not cope with the increasing number of deportees marshalled there by the joint effort of German troops and Arrowcross thugs. Confined in that barren place they had nothing to eat, toilet facilities were non-existent and queues at the very few water taps were endless. People with no cups could only cup their hands to quench their thirst. Washing themselves was not possible.

The Újlaki Brickworks

Sitting on the hard ground with other late arrivals, Julia kept thinking that she was having a nightmare.

The situation she was in could not be real she pondered. Then she noticed a small group forming around a screaming woman on the ground. Are they beating her she wondered, and for what reason, and then she realised with shock and horror that the woman was giving birth. Oh God, she reflected, my nightmare is negligible compared to hers.

Darkness shrouded the surroundings quickly and totally. Julia could only make out people in her immediate vicinity. With darkness came the cold that would not let her sleep. The general din abated and individual sounds became more audible. There were hysterical screams and voices trying to calm the sufferers. Incredibly, now and then people argued over a small piece of ground or blanket. She dozed off and woke almost immediately, dozed off again and woke up countless times until dawn.

They suffered the next day in utter discomfort unable to empty their systems with any form of dignity, feeling unwashed, dirty and very hungry. The round-ups had been suspended. No more people arrived.

The aerial attacks continued with the inclusion of new and fiendish devices causing death, devastation, and horrible injuries. One barbarous contraption was the incendiary bomb which spewed burning liquid all round. This liquid 'flowing fire' sometimes ran into the bomb shelter of the building that was hit, burning alive the surviving occupants.

Another deadly device was the bomb with a timer, consisting of a short length of wire holding back the spring-loaded firing pin. Enclosed in the small chamber through which the wire ran was a glass vial filled with corrosive fluid. Upon impact the glass shattered, releasing the fluid to corrode the wire. The thicker the wire the longer the time before it corroded to such extent that the pressure of the spring behind the firing pin would snap it, releasing the firing pin to detonate the bomb. These bombs were made to explode long after the air raid had passed and the civilian population were out and about unaware of danger.

As darkness enveloped the Brickworks once more, Julia fell asleep at last. She had no idea how long she had slept when she felt someone shaking her. Opening her eyes in the gloom she seemed to detect three policemen a few yards behind each other, stepping carefully between people on the ground, going further in. Then three more appeared and came to a stop. For a minute or so nothing had happened and then the policemen changed course and came across in her direction saying in low voices, 'Stand up please, stand up please,' as they walked past her. She could hear other voices saying the same. They stood up and heard the command to march.

March they did, wondering why they were going back towards the capital, about two hundred of them escorted by six uniformed policemen. When anyone had tried to ask questions the policemen raised their forefingers to their lips signalling silence. Long before dawn they stopped within a stone's throw of Margit Bridge, tired, hungry, and uncertain of the situation.

The policemen ran up and down the column saying softly, 'Scatter, scatter, scatter…'

Somebody held onto one, asking, 'Who are you?'

'We are policemen of the Fifth Precinct and we don't like what is going on,' he replied and they melted away into the night.

Julia was walking aimlessly. Two people had offered to shelter her and Tommy: one was Klára and the other Irma, a long-standing friend and a widow. Instinct of self-preservation urged Julia to get in touch with one of them but her conscience prevented her. Sheltering Jews was punishable by death, how could she ask anyone to risk so much?

The city was awakening, people wearily walking to their place of work, trams rattling their way along the road. I must get off the main road, thought Julia so she turned into the maze of side streets. Her eyelids felt heavier and heavier and the effects of hunger and tiredness rendered each step more and more strenuous. She needed to rest. Leaning her back against the façade of a building, with her feet further out to stop her knees buckling, she closed her eyes. Apart from the faint hum of a tramway moving along at the distant main road, the narrow side street was eerily silent. She instantly dozed off.

In spite of being exhausted she was vaguely aware in her semi-conscious state of the occasional footsteps of people walking by. Then someone went past her and the clip-clop of heels ceased and started to come back, stopping right in front of her. The feeling of terror made her eyes open wide. A middle-aged woman was scrutinising her with blatant curiosity. 'You wouldn't be Julia Láng, would you?'

The face was vaguely familiar but she could not place it.

'Miss Jutzie, it is me, Therese, remember me?'

Of course! Therese, the sixteen-year-old maid employed by her parents when she was aged twelve, Latzie nine, and Imre only six. Therese, who had slept in the tiny room next to the kitchen and with whom she had shared the secrets of teenage girls as the years passed by. Julia went into an uncontrollable fit of crying.

'Come now, you are safe with me, but let me remove the yellow star,' said Therese. 'I can't take you home with that on.'

'Therese,' Julia said haltingly, 'I… need a bath and some sleep… I will not burden you with… my presence.'

'You won't be a burden. Come along now.'

After a long and refreshing bath, Therese put Julia to bed. She awoke late afternoon and found her clothes washed, ironed, and placed on a chair. Therese cooked a meal and they recounted the events of their lives. Julia was desperate to make phone calls but Therese and her husband Béla were not on the phone. Using a neighbour's phone was unthinkable. The only possibility was a phone booth on the nearby main road.

However, this seemingly simple activity had a dangerous aspect. Stitching back the yellow star would imperil Therese and her husband. Going without it Julia could be caught in a random identity check and not displaying the yellow star incurred the penalty of death. Therese could not make the calls, her unfamiliar voice could be mistaken for an *agent provocateur*. Julia went on her own risking all – there was no other way. She flatly refused to allow Therese to accompany her.

Walking along and trying to find a phone booth she felt refreshed and fit again but scared. Isn't it strange that I'm scared to walk in the streets of my hometown, in the country where I was born, where all my ancestors were born, she reflected. What sort of madness is this? My father lost an arm in the last war and was decorated three times for bravery. We were Hungarians *then*. Now he would not be accepted as one, he would be a *Jew*.

The phone rang in the Office of Administration and Samuel answered it.

'Hello? Who? Yes, of course you can.' He turned around, 'Sándor! Call for you, a woman.'

Sándor hurried across, convinced it could only be Klára, something must be wrong with Tommy. She wouldn't call unless it was an emergency.

'Klára? Hello Klára. What's wrong?'

The voice was not Klára's. His wife was talking to him but he could not believe it. People taken away to be deported did not return! As he listened to her story and finding relief by it he began to sob. Samuel put his arm around his shoulder in a gesture of support and in an attempt to comfort a friend. The other three men in the room presumed that Sándor had received bad news and looked at him with great sympathy. They were familiar with personal tragedies.

After talking to Sándor, Julia could hardly wait to tell her little boy the good news that she had escaped from her captors. She dialled the telephone number of the convent. The phone rang only twice before a stern voice said, 'Convent of the Sisters of Mercy. Can I help you?'

'Hello Sister. I would like to talk to my son, Tommy Tottis.'

'I am sorry, I don't know anyone of that name.'

'But I know he is there, a friend of ours left him in your care three days ago!'

'You are mistaken, we do not have him here. I must go now. Goodbye.' The line went dead.

The nun answering the telephone had lied and denied the existence of her son – the right thing to do in the circumstances Julia admitted, because she could have been an agent provocateur.

The next call Julia made was to Irma at Óbuda, on the northern outskirts of Buda. She had decided to ask her for shelter because asking Klára was a bit awkward for her. She did like Klára very much indeed but she was, after all, her husband's employee. It did not feel right to ask her. The phone kept ringing and no one answered. The same thing had happened the following two days. Irma was not at home.

Therese introduced Julia to her neighbours as a cousin when they had to go to the shelter, a war widow. That was a good yarn and everybody accepted it. Béla, a factory worker in his fifties, left early in the morning and got home after six in the evening. One evening he fidgeted a lot.

'Madam, I mean no offence. I have nothing against you but you must consider our situation. Going to work yesterday morning a man called Rácz who lives on the second floor with his family, caught up with me. We often go to the bus stop together but I hardly know him. Yesterday he had an Arrowcross armband on his sleeve. My wife and I talked about it through most of the night. She is very upset but I explained to her that we couldn't risk sheltering you much longer. I am not asking you to leave until you find somewhere to go but please do try.'

Two more days passed before Irma answered the phone. She had been in hospital having her appendix removed and Julia was more than welcome. Julia rang Klára immediately, explained the situation and asked her to inform Tommy about it on her next visit.

Tommy in the meantime had settled down and accepted his new surroundings. Children adapt easier to changed circumstances than most adults, they are more resilient.

Tommy had explored not only the corridors and some of the rooms in the building but also a corner section of the garden bordered by overgrown rhododendrons. A small boy like him could actually climb inside the dense bush and create a hiding place there.

The plain, whitewashed building situated on Somlói Road had a sloping rear garden that extended down to the principal Convent of the Sisters of Mercy. This imposing redbrick structure with a steeple at its centre had its façade looking over Ménesi Road, parallel with Somlói Road.

THE CONVENT OF THE SISTERS OF MERCY WITH THE WHITEWASHED BUILDING BEHIND IT

The Army had procured this large building. A large, makeshift sign hanging over the main entrance read:

No. 505 Field Hospital

Most of the Sisters worked day and night as nursing staff, treating the injured and the dying ferried back from the front as it was getting nearer and nearer, day by day. A small group of nuns looking after fifty-three children, most of them under the age of ten in the other much smaller building, had to cope with the cooking, the washing of clothing, the bathing of the little ones and the cleaning of the premises. Twice a week a friar, a different one each time, visited from a neighbouring Cistercian Order and took up his post in the confessional of the tiny chapel to provide the necessary cleansing of souls for the sisters and some older children.

Klára rang the bell at the convent. The door opened and two nuns greeted her, the same two she had passed Tommy over to recently. The same pair of nuns attending the door at all times performed a very basic form of recognition system. Nobody they had not seen bringing a child in would have got past them.

Tommy hugged Klára, they kissed each other and she gave him some biscuits she had baked.

'Tommy, I have very good news for you. Your mother has managed to escape her captors and she is in hiding at her friend Irma's place in Óbuda.'

'Oh, Klára, thank you, thank you, I know where that is, I have been there many times!'

'Shhh, Tommy. Nobody must know about this. If it leaks out it could cost both their lives.'

Tommy was jubilant, his mother was safe. His anxiety had ended.

Arrowcross men marshalled the Labour Service unit László served in to the local railway station on a November morning. The thugs herded them into a long line of cattle trucks much more forcibly than cattle would have been and sent them to a concentration camp. The frontline was getting nearer every day and economies had to be made so the Nazis disposed of the Labour Service. Unbeknown to László, his wife and their two-year-old daughter had been travelling for the second day running in another cattle truck, the train approaching its destination: Auschwitz-Birkenau.

Magda should not have been on the train but she had refused to part with her daughter.

Some days later, the unit Sándor served in assembled for the morning parade as usual. The writing was on the wall, German troops and Arrowcross men had replaced the familiar guards. There was no parade. Ordered to march to the railway station they had to board a long line of cattle trucks clearly marked: **5 horses or 40 Jews**.

Incarcerated in the wagons with no food or water and no toilet facilities was very hard to endure. Since only their body-heat kept them warm, the men pushed against the walls of the truck suffered the cold most. Men in the middle, surrounded by other men, repeatedly swapped places with those against the walls to give them a chance to warm up. However, when the first man collapsed they just left him lying there as they had allowed two more to die on the three-day journey. All of them had the same impression that the men who passed away prematurely could have been the lucky ones. Along with his fellow internees' reflections, Sándor's thoughts had never been far from the awful realisation that Julia and Tommy and the rest of his family could also be on a journey in cattle trucks like the one he was travelling in.

The only consolation he kept clinging to was that his wife and his son had a chance to escape the brutal and senseless carnage, the Soviet Army closing in on Budapest might get there in time to save them from harm.

Tommy complained to Klára early in December about the delayed visit by his father. Klára tried her best to allay his anxiety, explaining that the increased bombing and shelling made public transport very erratic and at times non-existent. Long journeys were not possible in the time allowed for him to leave camp. Privately she had her own fears and doubts. They hugged and kissed each other and the boy thanked her for coming to visit him.

Walking away from the convent, Klára compared her own experiences of growing up without parents to children like Tommy, forcefully separated from theirs. On the day she had to leave Tommy at the convent she had decided that, in the event of his parents not returning she would adopt him. Tommy was Sándor's son, the man she loved so much.

Waiting for a bus to come along she observed the ruins of the building on the opposite side. A bomb had hit the six-storey block some time ago, demolishing the middle section of the top three floors. The 'V'-shape breach on the façade made rooms visible in cross-section – a little bit of flooring with a chest of drawers in a corner, pictures on a wall. Somebody's home once. In another half-room a piano dangled precariously over the edge in an odd angle, the result of the floor falling away from under one of its legs. The weight of the fallen masonry made the lower floors collapse and the building had been abandoned.

Unseen and unknown, the rubble of masonry inside the façade concealed a time bomb dropped during a recent air raid. As timer-controlled bombs do not explode on impact, the sound of its landing had been lost in the general din. Deep in the rubble it lay motionless, the acid eating away the wire holding back the firing pin. At that moment the wire snapped and the explosion threw huge lumps of masonry, bricks, tiles, shards of glass, timber, upwards and sideways. The shockwave slammed Klára against the building behind her and her head smashed against the stonework. Unconscious, she slid down to a sitting position on the pavement, but sustained no other injury while around her and across the road lay the injured, the dying, and the dead.

The fighting advanced towards the capital and more and more artillery shells hit buildings at the eastern approaches. Shops displayed ever more empty shelves. People kept building up stocks in apprehension of having to live in shelters while supplies had dried to a trickle.

In the concentration camps the elimination of Jews had accelerated to make room for those en route and the ones yet to be rounded up. Some Arrowcross men took the enthusiasm for elimination to its extreme. Marching their captives to the holding area they had simplified the process by lining them up at the edge of the Danube's embankment and shooting them one-by-one or machine-gunning them, making them fall into the river.

The few who had survived the bullets drowned in the freezing water – women, children, and elderly men.

Worse was to come. The rapidly advancing Soviet army made the murderous Arrowcross thugs even more sadistic and brutal. They executed the most helpless, patients in beds, their doctors and nurses of the city's two Jewish hospitals on Maros Street and Bethlen Square and residents in the Jewish poorhouse on Alma Road.

MEMORIAL TO VICTIMS SHOT DEAD AT THE DANUBE'S EMBANKMENT

Budapest Hungary

THE SHOES, MADE OF METAL, WERE CREATED ACCORDING TO THE FASHION OF THE TIME

Photo from an Internet Holocaust site

Nine days after the explosion of the time bomb, Klára regained consciousness and slowly became aware of her surroundings. She was in hospital but had no idea why or what had happened to her. Her recollections were dislocated, hazy and did not fit together. As she slowly emerged from her coma, a nurse told her not to talk just yet. Her life was not in danger and she would leave hospital soon. Nurses had to make diagnostic comments because doctors were few and far between. Patients had to vacate beds as soon as they were capable of looking after themselves.

By the next morning, Klára's memory had improved greatly. She clearly remembered the events of the past, right up to visiting Tommy at the convent but had no recollection of leaving the place or what had happened afterwards. She inquired about this memory void and realised that her speech was slurred. The nurse explained that she had sustained two nasty cracks at the back of her cranium which luckily had not caved in, but the resulting concussion had caused the loss of memory – a common occurrence.

Klára asked about the clearly audible artillery and gunfire and the nurse told her that the Soviet forces were fighting their way across the city street by street. A sudden memory flashed up in Klára's mind.

'Where is my handbag?'

The nurse bent down and picked up the handbag from the floor, the bedside cabinets having all gone, used for firewood. Opening the bag Klára found all her personal belongings there but not the jewellery of Mr and Mrs Roth.

The unstoppable advance of the Soviet Army had forced the German defenders to retreat to the west bank of the Danube, the Buda half of Budapest. To stop the Soviet advance, German sappers attached explosive charges to all bridges across the river and exploded them. When the explosive charges detonated nothing seemed to happen for a couple of seconds and then, one after the other the bridges, including the historic Chain Bridge and the graceful Elisabeth Bridge, the longest suspension bridge at the time in Europe, gently collapsed into the fast-flowing river below. There was no way the Soviets could cross or build a temporary bridge without being shot to pieces from the hills of Buda so they had brought in more artillery and launched frequent raids by groups of four or five fighter-bomber planes attacking the German positions.

Quite some distance north of the capital and beyond the rectangular bend in the river, Soviet divisions eventually succeeded in crossing the Danube enabling them to advance toward the German encampment in and around Buda.

The Mother Superior forbade any form of Christmas celebrations in the whitewashed building sheltering the children on Somlói Road. The nuns had more than enough tasks to fulfil, and Sister Zoé was aware that most of the children in their care would not appreciate such a festivity.

Holy Mass was said several times on Christmas Day in the chapel, enabling all the Sisters to attend in turn. Although the rattle and noise of war raging in the area was clearly audible, the convent being on the western slope of Gellért Hill seemed to be relatively safe because no encampments existed on that side, therefore no targets either.

Christmas passed without Klára visiting and Tommy realised something must have happened to her. Klára, a loving and kind-hearted person was his last link to his parents. Her total absence left him with nothing to look forward to, making him feel very lonely and cut off from everyone he knew. He was still hoping for a visit from his dad, but two months had passed since their last meeting and Tommy had an intuition that something bad must have happened, preventing his father from coming to see him.

Two nuns and three older children prayed silently in the pews of the tiny chapel on the top floor in preparation for their confession. A friar, Father Udo arrived, genuflected at the bottom of the central aisle and entered the confessional stall. He was saying a short prayer when a stray artillery shell smashed through the roof and, hitting the tiled floor, exploded.

The people in the pews died instantly. A large chunk of the shell's cast iron casing shot through the confessional and struck the friar in the face. The woodwork of the stall took most of the impact but the flying chunk of metal had enough momentum to fracture his left cheek and pierce his eye.

The explosion shook the building and terrified everybody within. The nuns shepherded the screaming and panicky children into the Common Room and told them to stay put while they rushed to the chapel. Surveying the scene – one that they had never imagined let alone witnessed – two of them fainted, one threw up. Nevertheless, they set about removing corpses and parts of bodies.

Those who could not cope with the sight embarked in digging graves in the garden. Only after burying the remains did a nun open the door of the confessional and found the unconscious Father Udo. They carried him on a stretcher down the sloping garden to the Field Hospital.

1945

The explosion was a decisive factor in Tommy's plan to find his mother. He had been thinking about it for days and had figured out how he could escape from the convent despite the securely locked front door and the metal grilles on all ground-floor windows. However, finding the three-storey building at the corner of Zápor Street and Timár Street where his mother was in hiding presented a bit of a problem. The place was almost three miles from the convent. He had travelled there with his parents by public transport but that was no longer possible. Trying to follow the route was out of the question because it was very long and full of twists and turns. One thing he was certain of: Timár Street ran perpendicular to the Danube right down to the edge of it. He was familiar with the Danube's embankment from this southern section all the way up to the Freight Station he had been to recently, and assumed that following the river beyond that point he was bound to come across Timár Street on his left. The dangers to life and limb did not occur to him, children being unable to comprehend the hazardous nature of their planned escapades.

At the crack of dawn on the first day of 1945, Tommy slipped through the back door, hurried down the sloping garden and entered the Field Hospital. The main corridor deserted and silent so early in the morning prompted him to walk on tiptoes to the front entrance and out to the road. No one saw him.

Familiar with the road from his cycling days he turned left and ten minutes later he was at the main road leading to the river and to the bridge named after the

Austrian Emperor, Franz Joseph. So far he did not see another soul and that had scared him but also made him realise that there were no Arrowcross men around either. The noise of explosions did not worry him. He had got used to hearing them.

Photo from the Internet

When he turned into Gellért Place, the road junction at Franz Joseph Bridge, he was confronted with a front-line scene: a huge field gun in an upward angle pointing to the other side of the river and surrounded by both Hungarian and German soldiers.

Ahead of the gun and all along the embankment, stalks of sweetcorn hung side-by-side and upside down, suspended on lengths of stout wire running between posts. The resultant screen concealed the equipment and personnel from the other side.

A soldier spotted him and ran over. 'What are you doing here all on your own?'

Tommy had not foreseen that questions would be asked during his journey and he immediately realised that, despite his upbringing, he could not tell the truth.

'My father is with the artillery at the Southern Rail Bridge. I had visited him at Christmas and got stuck there when the shooting started to get heavy. This morning he suggested I find my way home because the situation here is getting bad.'

'He was right. But you must take care on your way.' The soldier patted Tommy on his back and allowed him to pass on.

Tommy continued his journey walking along the narrow pavement skirting the foot of the almost vertical rock face of Gellért Hill. He observed patches of rust appearing on the rails of the tramlines set in the road surface beside him, due to lack of use. Further ahead soldiers kept moving about, making him wonder if they were the crew of another artillery post. The sound of aeroplanes could be heard in the distance, getting closer, but looking up he could not see any because of the sheer rock face on his left, but he heard someone shouting.

'Come here! Run! Run!'

A soldier waving his arm ran towards him and Tommy started running to the soldier unaware of the reason for the urgency. The sound of the planes changed to a higher pitch and got much louder. All of a sudden a burst of bullets swept by and clattered along, hitting the road surface beside him.

The soldiers ahead disappeared out of sight except the one rushing towards Tommy. Grabbing hold of the boy's hand he dragged Tommy toward a protruding boulder.

Just beyond this huge rock, out of sight, a small entrance led to a cavern beneath the cliffs normally guarded by a wrought iron gate, now wide open. This was the place the soldiers had vanished into and where Tommy was pushed in by one of them who probably had saved his life.

The pavement at Gellért Hill.
The cavern is beyond the bend on the road.
Photo taken in 2002.

'What on earth are you doing wandering in a war zone on your own?' the soldier asked Tommy in the safety of the cavern.

Tommy repeated the story he had told before. The soldier with a concerned look mused, *if that is true I'll eat my hat*, and asked no more questions. The rest of the soldiers looked at Tommy with tired eyes and none of them uttered a word.

The cavern.
**The elliptic wrought iron gate had been replaced by a plain
steel door. Photo taken in 2002.**

A boy Tommy was friendly with in the convent alerted
the others to his absence and then told one of the sisters.
The Mother Superior, Sister Zoé ordered an immediate
search of the building and grounds. The search
unfruitful, Sister Zoé could not conceal the fear and
worry in her heart. Despite the many precautions they
had taken to protect the children in their care, evidently
they had not considered the possibility that a child
might try to escape from the refuge. What would happen
to Tommy in the war-torn streets? What could she say,
how could she defend herself when the parents or a
guardian turned up to collect him? She went to the
ruined chapel, the altar wrecked and a large part of the

roof missing, knelt down, raised her eyes to the grey, wintry sky and prayed for the boy. She also wept for him with slow and deep sobs.

The air attack over, Tommy continued his journey past Elisabeth Bridge to Döbrentei Place and the church he used to go to with his father. He kept his ears tuned to the sound of aircraft and his eyes on the road ahead so that should the planes return he could take cover quickly. The artillery was firing on and off and shells exploded here and there but not in his close vicinity. He walked past the steps and locked entrance gates leading to the Royal Palace on top of Castle Hill. There the changing of the guards used to take place his father told him not very long ago. The thought of him made Tommy's mind concentrate on matters he could not fathom. His father had always kept his promises yet he did not visit the convent, something must have stopped him. Where was he now? Why was this going on? What was the purpose of persecuting Jews and other people when they had done nothing wrong? Why? Why? Why? His young mind could not find an answer or an explanation to the question.

A man wearing a tattered overcoat and a soft beret stepped out of a doorway. He had a haversack on his back that sagged, revealing lack of content. Waiting for Tommy to walk past, he fell in beside him saying nothing and sucking a sweet. He retrieved the brownish substance from his mouth and offered it. 'This is my last one, do you fancy it?'

'No thank you,' Tommy replied, unable to figure out the motives of the stranger.

The man popped the sweet back into his mouth and said no more. At the next intersection, the remnants of Chain Bridge on the right, Fő Street ahead, the man turned left going into the road tunnel running below

Castle Hill. Tommy felt relieved, not knowing who the stranger was or what his intentions were.

The man had different thoughts: poor kid, almost certainly Jewish like I am but I cannot take the responsibility of looking after him.

Fő Street ran parallel with the river. Thankfully, there was not a soul in sight. Tommy acknowledged that everyone must be sheltering in basements and cellars. He heard the familiar whistle of an artillery shell, the shrill tone deepening to a shushing sound indicated a descending trajectory. It was a lot louder than previous shells. The shushing sound suddenly ceased and a split second later a deafening explosion followed from somewhere above. Huge chunks of masonry, rafters, roof tiles, floorboards, furniture pieces and a bathtub cascaded down from the top of the four-storey building immediately ahead of him, some of the smaller debris landing at his feet. Tommy instantly realised he could have been buried under the huge pile of debris on the pavement extending to the middle of the road. No one would look for him because no one would know he was there. He sat down on the steps in the recess of an entrance. The question of turning back presented itself in his mind.

Where would I go if Mum wasn't there any more? Or if I were to find only a heap of rubble? On the other hand, I could find the convent in ruins on my return so I might as well carry on.

Moments after making his decision to continue his journey, he heard fighter planes and the rat-at-at-at of their machine guns somewhere further ahead. Snowflakes began to fall. Little delicate ones. There had been hardly any snow so far this winter but it was quite cold.

Fő Street ran into Bem Square and entering it the objective of the fighter planes came into view, another field gun and its crew, dug into trenches. Walking fast in a diagonal line towards the embankment and Margit Bridge he was halfway across the square when the planes returned. This time there was only one choice. He sprinted to the nearest point of the irregular trench, jumped in and landed on top of a soldier who, seeing the boy running to the dugout had tried to catch him and stop him getting hurt. Other soldiers gathered either side of him in the narrow ditch asking questions all at once but an arrogant male voice, 'I will handle this!' silenced them.

A tall man pushed his way past the soldiers in the confined space. He had a German army long coat on and a German helmet covered his head. A diagonal shoulder strap supported a large pistol in a holster attached to his leather belt on the right. Tucked under his belt on the left he had two black-and-red striped Vécsey-type hand grenades with wooden handles. Apart from the coat and helmet the man wore normal civilian shirt and tie, trousers and shoes. The authority he exercised over the soldiers he had accomplished by the Arrowcross armband above his elbow. His voice was harsh, 'What's your name and where did you come from?'

Tommy told him his name and gave the same explanation as before. He varied it though, saying that his father served with the unit stationed at Franz Joseph Bridge because that unit really existed.

The suspicious and sceptical Arrowcross man tried another trick by asking what type of gun was there. Tommy could only recall one type he had heard in conversations at home. 'Bofors. And those are Vécsey grenades.' He pointed at them to impress the man.

'Why did you go alone, why didn't your mother go with you?'

'She was unwell and I went by tramway before Christmas.' Tommy could not believe his own ears hearing himself telling fluent lies, but they were effective so far.

The man bent forward, bringing his face level with Tommy's. 'I am sure you are a Jew. Admit it!'

'No, I am not. I am Roman Catholic,' Tommy said irritably.

The man demanding absolute proof that he was not Jewish stunned Tommy.

'Come on,' the man said. 'Prove it!'

Tommy found his request shocking, but he had to do what the man insisted upon. To his amazement the man smiled at him. 'All right, so you aren't a bloody Jew.'

Tommy was both astonished and incredulous. He could not comprehend how the Arrowcross man had figured out that he was not Jewish. (At that time in his life Tommy was unaware that boys of Jewish faith are circumcised shortly after birth.)

'So now you are trying to get back home. Where is your home?'

Tommy had no real home address anymore so he blurted out his destination. 'Number 10, Zápor Street, Óbuda.'

'Right, I will escort you there. I'm going to teach that mother of yours a lesson in how to take care of her son!'

The statement was unexpected and shocking, making Tommy realise the dangerous situation his mother would be in when confronted by this man. The feeling of guilt and fear of the consequences was difficult to bear.

'Come on!' the man said, climbing out of the trench. 'Help him!' he instructed the soldiers and one of them hoisted Tommy up and out of the trench.

'I have no idea where Zápor Street is – you must show me the way,' said the man.

This is awful, he is forcing me to take him there, Tommy reflected feeling like Judas Iscariot but he had no other choice. They walked through the underpass at the foot of what was left of Margit Bridge and further on came across an army field-kitchen set up in the once immaculately maintained grounds at the rear of Lukács Thermal Baths.

'We might as well eat something while we have a chance,' the man said.

The meal consisted of sliced cabbage cooked in thin, watery tomato juice. Tommy was very hungry, it was about lunchtime and he had not eaten anything since the previous evening. Consuming the unrefined, insipid food, he reflected on the episode in 'Szentmihály when having eaten the meat and potatoes he refused to eat the cabbage. How much tastier the cabbage cooked by his mother was! He would never again refuse his mother's cooking, not ever, he vowed, realising suddenly that he might never have another opportunity to do so.

They walked away from the field kitchen and following the river became aware of machine gun and small arms firing audible somewhere ahead of them, different to the sounds of artillery across the Danube. Shells frequently exploded here and there, mostly away from the embankment and they had to dive into doorways to shelter from air attacks. Tommy kept thinking of ways to flee from the clutches of the Arrowcross man but no worthwhile idea emerged, there was nowhere to run or hide.

There was smoke rising in the distance where Tommy remembered the Freight Station should be. Gradually, as they got nearer it turned black and dense over the area. Some wagons had been set alight by incendiary shells, flames spreading from one truck to another. Gathered under an archway, a small group of German and Hungarian soldiers watched the scene with total resignation, there was nothing they could do about it.

The Arrowcross man stopped and surveyed the scene. Tommy watched the fire in awe. A figure emerged from one of the burning and smoking wagons, walking in their direction. It turned out to be an elderly man carrying two pairs of knee-length boots in each hand hanging from his fingers by the 'pull-on' loops stitched to them. The boots were the quilted felt variety, a type of footwear issued to soldiers in winter to keep their legs and feet warm.

The Arrowcross man stepped in front of the old man, blocking his way and roared at him.

'You filthy thief! The Leader ordered all looters to be executed!'

The old man looked offended. 'I am no thief! The wagons are on fire! I'm salvaging what I can.'

'You are stealing army property!' retorted the Arrowcross man, removing his long-barrelled pistol from its holster and pointing it to the old man's head. The old man ducked the very instant the gun was fired. His hat flew off revealing grey hair but no visible injury. Bent sideways and peering up at the Arrowcross man, he had an expression of total disbelief on his face. In a simultaneous movement the Arrowcross man pressed the muzzle of the gun against the old man's ear and pulled the trigger.

The force of the shot knocked the old man to the ground, his body lying on the cobbled road surface and his head sideways on the pavement. Nothing happened at first then blood began to ooze from his nostrils, mouth and ear, flowing faster and faster, forming a pool around his head.

'This is the fate of all looters!' proclaimed the Arrowcross man with an air of accomplishment, looking at the group of soldiers as he replaced his gun in its holster.

Even though hardened by years of frontline fighting, the soldiers' facial expressions reflected incredibility and shock. None of them moved or uttered a word. They just stood there motionless, staring silently at the Arrowcross man.

Tommy could not take his eyes off the old man who was a living person just a few seconds before. He really wished that the old chap would stand up and dust himself down.

The fact that a life can be extinguished in a fraction of a second he found very difficult to accept. He also had a vision of what would happen to his mother and him once his lies were uncovered. The realisation terrified him. He tried hard not to cry. He knew he must not.

They resumed their journey and Tommy was contemplating the inevitable. The further north they ventured the more audible the din of incessant gunfire had become. By the time they turned left into Timár Street it was very loud, coming from the right, mostly rifle and machine-gun fire. At the first crossing in their path, the Arrowcross man peered around the corner but it was just a short cul-de-sac. They crossed over and approaching the slight bend on the road met a soldier with a tourniquet on his upper arm, panting from exertion.

'What's going on around here?' asked the Arrowcross man.

'The Russkies attacked from the north. They are pushing their way south bit-by-bit. I must get to the medics. Watch the crossroads or you'll be shot to pieces!' he shouted running off.

Beyond the slight bend in Timár Street the roads were mostly of the grid system, straight parallel roads intersected by other straight parallel roads at right angles. They walked up to the next crossing amidst the noise of non-stop gun battle coming from the right and sheltered behind the corner of the building. When the gunfire abated the Arrowcross man said, 'Come on, we'll run across.' Machine-gun fire and whizzing bullets greeted them sprinting across the road.

At the next crossing the Arrowcross man tried to look around the corner. Wearing the German helmet he was instantly shot at, almost as if the snipers expected him to be there. The man's face drained of colour and he looked scared. The firing of guns continued for several minutes and then ceased.

'Run!' the man yelled and they did. This time a rapid firing commenced as soon as they stepped out into the open. Fortunately, due to the lack of time to take aim and the distance involved, the bullets went far and wide. Once behind the corner the man did not keep walking to the next intersection. He just stood there, noticeably rattled.

'How many crossings to Zápor Street?'

'I'm not sure, three or four. I've never used this route before.'

The man looked at his wristwatch. 'Twenty minutes past three. It'll be dark by four. I'd better start getting back to my unit. Take care of yourself!' He shouted and dashed back across the road towards the river.

Bullets whizzed again missing their target. Tommy watched the Arrowcross man darting across the intersections and disappearing beyond the bend in the road. Not until then did he feel assured that the evil man had gone for good and would not return. He was trembling at the realisation that the threat of execution had been lifted and at the thought of being so close to his destination.

Just before he got to the next crossing volleys of firing had started up again, bullets bouncing off the road surface and walls. It went on and on audibly at other crossings as well. He stayed behind the corner of the building and when the guns fell silent dashed across. Whether he had gone unnoticed or identified as a child, not one shot was fired. Encouraged by that he ran up to the next crossroads and instantly recognised the three-storey block at the diagonally opposite corner. He arrived at his destination but still had some perilous obstacles to overcome.

Gunfire made Zápor Street even more risky than the previous streets Tommy had to run across, because the entrance of the building opened into Zápor Street. Luckily the doorway provided a recess, albeit a shallow one. The gates would be closed, of that he was certain, and that created another problem. Owing to the occupants almost certainly sheltering out of earshot in the cellar or basement, how could he gain entrance? Yet the biggest worry for him was the question of his mother being there. Fear of not finding her sent Tommy's heart pounding, he could almost hear it. He waited for the shooting to cease and then he darted with great determination diagonally across the junction and ran along the façade of the building to the entrance. By the time a short burst of bullets clattered behind him he was in the comparative safety of the recess.

Tommy pressed the bell button hoping someone would hear it. Getting no response he tried again. Once more there was no reaction and that scared him. Grabbing the ironwork with both hands and using all the strength he could muster, he rattled the gates.

The basement down below gave shelter to families, elderly couples, Irma and Julia. The men were elderly, children few. Each family huddled in their tiny allocated space. Light was provided by home-made oil-lamps consisting of a cup or a tin containing cooking oil with a slice of wine-bottle cork floating on the surface and a length of string through its centre acting as wick. A bit of foil placed over the improvised wick prevented the cork getting singed by the flame. The small flickering flames produced only a little light yet a potent odour the inhabitants had to put up with.

Most of them ate sparingly, no one knew how long the siege was going to go on for. They warmed tinned food and cooked dried vegetables on a solid-fuel range in a ground floor apartment and used in turn by each family. The din of war was clearly audible, if slightly muffled with the exception of artillery shells exploding nearby, shaking the building. People tend to accept the harshest, most awful situations and circumstances if and when there is no escape from them, thus the people in the basement had got used to the bangs but they sighed with relief after each one that the apartments above them had been spared once more. Infrequently, but never for long, the noise abated and the silence was enjoyed by all.

During such a lull, an unusual sound caught the ear of an elderly woman who occupied a small area with her husband by the entrance to the basement. Having detected it again, at another break in the noise of gunfire, she suddenly exclaimed, 'Would everybody please keep quiet! I think someone is at the gate trying to find shelter or draw our attention.'

In the few seconds of total silence before the shooting resumed, most of the other occupants also detected the rattling of the gates.

'Maybe an injured person needs help,' said someone.

'How do you know it isn't the army trying to make use of our homes as firing posts?' asked an elderly man. 'We did that in the last war.'

'It could be someone in need,' said the woman who had first heard the noise. 'If they are soldiers I won't let them in.' Collecting the keys hanging from the hook by the exit she went off to investigate.

Nobody said a word. The apprehension was discernible. All eyes turned to the doorway when the woman returned but in the gloom of the shelter not much could be seen.

'I have a young boy here,' announced the woman, 'trying to find his mother. His name is Tottis, Tommy Tottis.'

Julia shot forward, her mind in absolute turmoil. It's not possible! It can't be my son! How would he find his way over here with the war raging outside! She ran across the shelter and, realising that the boy was indeed Tommy, sank to her knees. Mother and son embraced each other, tears pouring from Julia's eyes making Tommy's face wet.

Deeply moved by what she had witnessed, the elderly woman let Tommy's hand go and returned to her place. Some women also shed a few tears. Others had raised an eyebrow. Only one person was annoyed about Tommy's arrival – Irma. After she had recovered from the effects of her operation, Julia's presence in her home had begun to irritate her – and sharing food and a tiny area in the shelter did not help. Now the boy as well, another burden, she thought.

Julia noticed Tommy wincing in her embrace. 'Tommy, what is wrong? Are you hurt?'

'I don't know Mum, I didn't notice it before but I have a stinging sensation above my left knee.'

Julia bent down to look but the nearest little oil lamp being yards away she took a few seconds to notice trickles of blood running down Tommy's leg into his left sock. She picked the boy up in one swift movement and carried him to the tiny area she shared with Irma. Depositing Tommy on her makeshift bed and holding the little oil-lamp in her hand she found that the blood came from a small cut above his kneecap. Running across one of the roads a bullet must have grazed Tommy. The wound was not deep, it just bled quite a lot.

By mid-January the Soviet forces had advanced beyond Timár Street, and the bullets and shells whizzing by and exploding came from the retreating defenders. Slowly but relentlessly the Soviet soldiers encircled the Castle Hill area and trapped them in the Royal Palace itself.

People emerged from cellars and basements despite the fighting close by mainly because they were starving. The temperature never above minus five degrees, hungry men had cut to bits the corpse of a horse frozen solid in the unremitting cold with axes, hacksaws and knives. The unlucky beast had served the humans not only through his life but also after his death.

A baker stoked up his coal-fired oven and opened his shop. People queued patiently for bread, defying the risks. One by one the families sheltering in the basement returned to their homes, enjoying the comfort of them despite lacking electricity, gas or running water. Lack of water was the biggest problem by far.

People filled up all sorts of vessels at the start of the siege before the taps had dried up to provide themselves with water, but as time went by they had to give up washing themselves, saving the water for the purpose of drinking and cooking.

Cleaning and dusting the apartment that survived undamaged, Julia remarked how fortunate Irma had been. Irma made a startling comment,

'For what I have done God owed me this much.'

Julia was stunned but said nothing.

A new and different threat arose in the form of rampaging Russian troops. Some of them were life-term convicts released from jail on condition that they fight in the front lines – surviving the war would mean amnesty. The rest, the vast majority, had only basic education and had been accustomed to a simple lifestyle in the Soviet Union which in Europe would be regarded as poverty. They proclaimed anyone possessing a radio, or silverware, or carpet rugs on the floor as being *bourdghouy* (bourgeois) and helped themselves to watches, rings, anything they fancied. Objections gave rise to violence – at times the objector was shot dead.

Rapes and gang rapes took place with alarming frequency. Julia and most other women mixed soot into hand cream or lard and smeared it on their face to make themselves look unattractive. Eventually the Soviet Army had had to set up military patrols to catch and deter their marauding troops.

The fighting at Castle Hill ended on 12th February and the war at Buda was over. The lack of bridges divided Buda and Pest but the Soviet Army controlled both. Sounds of shooting and shelling had finally faded into the distance. The last stronghold of the German defence, the Royal Palace with some six hundred rooms lay in ruins and the destructive power of war was evident all round.

Damage to buildings varied from street to street, some partly demolished, some untouched, others flattened to heaps of rubble.

A section of the wrecked Royal Palace.

Early in the morning of 14th February, Julia and Tommy expressed their thanks to Irma and started the long journey home.

Apart from her concern for her husband, Julia was anxious about the rest of her family and her in-laws on the Pest side, so they took a slight detour to the river hoping that Russian sappers would be busy building a bridge.

There was no sign of any activity of that nature but the Danube had frozen solid. That is an infrequent but by no means rare occurrence, and they had spotted people actually walking across on the ice. Julia refused to take such a risk. Going home was her first priority but she did not know what lay ahead.

Burnt-out vehicles, tanks, troop carriers, cars and trucks littered the streets, some containing the frozen bodies of their occupants. Most of them had perished in hideous ways, some burnt beyond recognition and one could not tell whether before or after death. Vehicles hit by a shell or a building that collapsed on them contained crushed corpses. There were bodies lying around with limbs missing, and limbs with the rest of the body missing, in infinite varieties. The almost snowless but very cold winter prevented the decomposition of the innumerable corpses of humans and animals, mostly horses. Fallen masonry covered many roads and some were impassable. They walked by discarded ammunition on the ground along with weapons and uniforms thrown away by troops trying to hide their identity. Walking along deserted streets, skirting piles of masonry, vehicles and dead bodies, Julia didn't know where to look, more exactly where not to look. The sight of so many corpses revolted her and she felt nauseated. Tommy noticed her discomfort and frequently said to her, 'Look left Mum,' when he had spotted something gruesome on the right, or 'Look right,' 'Look up,' according to the location of corpses or human remains he did not want his mother to see. Yet all his efforts proved useless at times – for instance when turning a corner they had found themselves facing a barricade across the road constructed from the frozen corpses of fallen soldiers. Julia almost threw up and they had to make a detour.

A few yards from the main entrance of Lukács Thermal Baths, they came across the body of a German officer lying on his back in the middle of the road, seemingly uninjured. Going past they observed he was about twenty years old with a handsome face and a bullet hole in his right temple. From a larger opening on the other side, his brains had gushed out and froze onto the cobblestones.

Further on at Attila Road, a fighter plane had embedded itself in a sixth-storey apartment, with only the tail plane and the rear of the fuselage protruding from the building.

Attila út

A German 'Tiger' tank, motionless and abandoned, had the legs and lower half of a man's body protruding from beneath its caterpillar tracks. Was he dead or only wounded when the tank rolled over him?

Long after midday they at last turned the corner into the steep Berényi Street leading to their home. Half way up the road a horse was standing patiently at the roadside, blood dripping from its nostrils, presumably caused by the shockwave of an explosion. The animal's sombre gaze followed them as they walked past. Poor creature, Tommy thought, where did it come from, who does it belong to and what will happen to it?

Their once beautiful home came into sight. It was still standing but was uninhabitable. Judging by the thousands of small pockmarks on its walls it had been used as a defence post. The framework of the roof was largely devoid of tiles. Rendering on the walls was almost non-existent, exposing the brickwork, itself badly damaged in places. Only fragments remained of the front door and the window frames. Holding hands they walked in with apprehension. Rubble covered the floor but most of their belongings seemed to have survived. The reading room was different, half their library of over eight hundred books had disappeared and their fate was apparent when they glanced at the fireplace – the German High Command or their successors had run out of coal. They had also ruined the piano by pouring wine inside it and over the keyboard. There was a German officer's long coat lying on the floor. It was in perfect condition but all the carpet rugs had vanished.

The neighbouring four-storey apartment block, built shortly after they had taken up residence, had suffered top floor damage only. Tommy climbed through a broken window into a vacant ground floor apartment and opened the front door. They carried over furniture, bed linen, blankets and cooking utensils. There was no water to drink or to wash with but they found dried vegetables in the kitchen. Neighbours emerged with words of greetings but none of them offered help, probably because they were too busy cleaning and re-organising their homes or the remnants of them. Julia inquired about the nearest source of water and was told to go to the Turkish Baths at the bottom of Hegyalja Road, near its junction with Elisabeth Bridge.

The remnants of Elisabeth Bridge.

Next morning Julia carrying two buckets, and Tommy with a large mixing bowl, set off to the Turkish Baths. They walked past the horse lying dead on the road. Waiting for their turn at the natural spring, Julia discovered that she could barter for food. Most people brought items for exchange: clothing, candles, tinned food, butter, lard and other perishables the cold winter had preserved. Money was no use to anyone. Going home, uphill for half a mile and weighed down by the water was extremely tiring, but, being an absolute necessity, it had to be done every day.

Julia began to clean and reorganise their home as much as possible, making it ready for Sándor's return. She had no idea where her husband had been taken or of his fate. The thought of the future without him terrified her.

Tommy wandered around with other children having promised faithfully that under no circumstances would he ever touch any explosives like grenades, land mines, or the anti-tank device mounted on a tube with a triggering mechanism, the deadly Panzerfaust (Armour Fist).

The Panzerfaust.

Plenty of such devices had been left scattered around and several children have been crippled or killed out of sheer curiosity. However, the boys quickly found out that ordinary rifle, pistol, and other such cartridges could be safely dismantled by forcing the bullet out of the shell and pouring the cordite on a brick. There it could be set alight to burn away in a bright flash.

Scouring a vacant plot of land Tommy spotted a 'munitions bomb', a cargo-carrier designed for the replenishment of beleaguered German troops.

Parachutes dropped these huge and hollow bomb-shaped containers constructed of sheet metal.

Tommy was inspecting the open canister and noted that it must have been utilized to carry provisions because it had crushed tins of sardines inside its dented tip. Poking around with a stick he discovered a deformed but otherwise undamaged tin and took it home triumphantly, running all the way. Mother and son enjoyed two meals each out of eight sardines in the tin, savouring every bite. It was a real feast after they had subsisted mostly on boiled lentils, split peas and kidney beans.

Munition / supply bomb, a hollow, bullet shaped canister.

Julia noticed Tommy's troubled look, and when she asked him he admitted it was due to his friend Tibor's conduct. Tibor was avoiding him, not even saying 'hello' unless he had to.

'Can you think of something you had said or done which may have upset him?' Julia asked.

'No Mum, I cannot. I wasn't even here lately. He's behaving in an odd way ever since we returned home…'

The words stuck in his throat at the realisation that Tibor, his close friend not very long ago, did not like him any more because of his Jewish origins.

'Don't blame him Tommy,' Julia said, noticing Tommy's sudden grasping the truth. 'He only reflects the attitude of his parents.'

'Tommy, we ought to visit the Sisters of Mercy and thank them for looking after you,' Julia suggested and the following morning they strolled along Somlói Road to the convent.

Julia asked the nun answering the door if she could speak with Sister Zoé. The nun immediately ushered them into the small and austere office of the Mother Superior.

Sister Zoé had not met Julia previously, but recognising the boy her face lit up and then her expression changed.

'Young man,' she said in a stern voice. 'You have caused us a great deal of worry and concern. My Sisters and I have said many a prayer for you!'

'Your prayers did not go unheard,' said Julia and described Tommy's incredible escapade.

The smile returned to Sister Zoé's face. 'I can see that your guardian angel had an exceptionally busy day, Tommy.'

The ensuing conversation revealed that the Sisters still had some children in their care, unclaimed by their parents. These children, all Jewish, would never be claimed by anyone.

Throughout this period of time most smallholders in the vicinity of the capital had succeeded in augmenting their wealth. Aware of the scarcity of food they turned up in horse-drawn carts selling flour, lard, chickens, vegetables, salt, sugar, at greatly inflated prices. What's more, they seldom sold their wares for money; payment had to be made in gold or silver jewellery, or precious stones.

After a while when water and electricity supplies had been restored, a kind of normality returned and people became friendlier, smiling at each other. Julia and Tommy kept venturing out and found shops reopening one by one. Going on shopping and discovery trips they found something new each time. On one occasion they joined the main road leading to Franz Joseph Bridge, at the same spot Tommy had, after leaving the convent. They strolled along leisurely and opposite Gárdonyi Place, a tiny triangle not much more than a road junction, spotted a ladies' clothing shop with its door open.

'That's Eve and Rudi's shop!' exclaimed Julia and quickened her steps with Tommy in tow. The woman sitting behind the counter looked up as they entered and leapt to her feet. 'Julia!'

The two women embraced and had a gentle cry on each other's shoulder. They had first met on holiday in 1940, and after that the two couples visited each other on a regular basis, but the approaching war had put an end to activities of that sort. They spent most of the day chatting and recounting their stories, interrupted frequently by curious customers unable to resist the temptation to pop in but with one or two exceptions would not purchase anything. People had no interest in being fashionable so soon after the dreadfully violent times they had experienced.

One day, while at the shop, they heard rumours that the temporary bridge built by Russian sappers on the remains of Franz Joseph Bridge would be open to the public for a couple of hours every day. Julia and Tommy went there ahead of the appointed time and so had hundreds of people. When the last army vehicle rolled off the narrow structure, the route was opened to civilian traffic and people waiting on both sides rushed across.

With no public transport running, the first person on the itinerary planned by Julia was Klára Szabó because her home was the nearest. Both Julia and Tommy understood something had happened to her as when opening her front door she looked at them with a distant gaze before dissolving in tears. Klára hugged both of them in turn again and again. Her home was neat and tidy and sitting in the front room she had told them about her spell in hospital. Her speech was clear but slow and she paused before answering questions.

'Poor Klára has no one,' Julia explained to Tommy as they continued their journey to her in-laws. 'No parents, no siblings, no relatives or children.' Julia had no idea of Klára's profound loss of Sándor, the only man Klára had ever loved in her unselfish, undemanding way.

There was no one home at Lónyai Street and inquiries with a neighbour revealed that Sándor's family had recently moved to a large house in Stefánia Crescent, one of the most elite areas of the Pest side, unfortunately a very long trek, so the next person to visit was Julia's mother Hannah at Rottenbiller Street.

The sun was about to set as they entered the building and Julia's heart was beating fast. She was greatly relieved that the building had survived despite considerable damage, but had her mother and Aunt Helen? Would they be there or had they been sent to a concentration camp?

They went up the staircase to the third floor and around the gangway to flat number 35. With her finger trembling, Julia rang the bell. For some endless moments there was no response, then light filtered through the frosted glass as the door of the lounge opened and somebody shuffled along the hall. Aunt

Helen opened the door. She stood there like someone seeing an apparition. Then she quickly raised her forefinger to her lips while tears started rolling down her cheeks. 'Your mother is asleep in her armchair,' she said. 'Come in and wake her up.'

They tiptoed in and Julia noticed how much Hannah had aged in the last ten months. Ten months, she contemplated, less than a year and it feels like a lifetime. Everything before that seems to belong to a different existence. My past life appears to be a distant dream, or was it real, and what I have been going through recently just an awful nightmare?

Bending down she gently kissed her mother's forehead. Hannah opened her eyes slowly, looked at Julia without any sign of recognition and then sat up abruptly, threw her arms around her daughter's waist and wept. Julia kept stroking the old woman's hair, her own face awash with tears.

Talking late into the night they heard that Hannah, Helen and other Jews in the neighbourhood had not come to any harm because time had run out for their persecutors. Hannah had some vague information about Latzie being taken to a concentration camp in Dachau, but she had no idea of the fate of his wife and daughter or what had happened to Robbie. Julia told Hannah about her planned visit next day to her in-laws and then going back home, expecting Sandy to turn up.

At Stefánia Crescent, Paul was genuinely delighted to see Julia and Tommy. He ushered them into the large, elegant living room. Isabelle also seemed to be happy but Ibolya's smile was distinctly forced.

'Oh, well. Glad you have found your way to our new home.'

After a condescending and very cold greeting, nineteen-year-old Dávid departed with no excuse or apology.

At one point in the conversation Paul tapped Ibolya on the shoulder. 'Shouldn't we treat Tommy to some biscuits or a slice of buttered bread?'

'And what makes you think that we have got any?' Ibolya responded. She did not even offer Julia and Tommy a glass of water after their long trek to visit Sándor's family.

Julia and Tommy departed shortly afterwards and returned to their temporary home late afternoon, completely exhausted.

The following day, the conversation at Eve's shop turned to Julia's lack of income. Her last remaining piece of jewellery – her wedding ring – had been exchanged some time ago for a twenty-five kilo bag of flour and some sugar and lard, in the full understanding that she had paid fifty times the value of the goods she had actually received but she had no choice in the matter. Mentioning the bag of flour to Eve, she had come up with the idea that if Julia would bake small cakes and set up a stall outside her shop she could probably sell them at a profit. Julia agreed the suggestion was worth a try. She could hardly go wrong, if the cakes didn't sell they would eat the cakes themselves.

Meanwhile the fast advancing Soviet Army surged through Austria and entered Germany, liberating concentration camps in their passing. Inebriated by victory in their sight they paid scant attention to the needs or fate of the inmates. They forged ahead and met the Allies already on German soil at the river Elbe.

As a result, the Soviet Union gained control over the eastern regions of Germany, Austria, the whole of Central Europe, and Eastern Europe up to the Ural Mountain Range.

Germany capitulated on 7th May and the war in Europe was over. The infamous Third Reich ceased to exist, boosting Julia's hopes for her husband's return. She had no idea where he was taken or where he would come from but the yearning in her heart for their re-union was so strong that she was having daydreams about it, sitting by her little stall in front of Eve's shop.

Deep in thought one day, with Tommy reading a book by her side, she took some time to notice pedestrians slowing down and coming to a halt, staring at something in the distance. Due to the slight curving of the road she could not see what caught their attention so she moved to the kerbside to get a better view. The unexpected scene made her shiver. Pedestrians lined both the kerbside and the inside edge of the pavement giving clear passage to two men shuffling along slowly, dressed in rags. They reminded her of lepers she had once seen on the newsreel at a cinema. Watching their painstaking progress she recalled that this main road ran into the arterial road to Vienna, connecting the two capitals, therefore it was one of the most obvious routes for survivors of the concentration camps in Germany and Austria to follow on their way home. The slowly passing human wrecks looked dreadful and exuded an appalling odour.

These were the first of many more. No one witnessing the scene could have remained unaffected by their determination to walk hundreds of miles in extreme stages of malnutrition, infested with head lice, body lice and fleas. Tragically, having survived the horrors of the concentration camps, a large number of them perished on the way home.

The sight of the survivors pushed Julia's hopes for her husband's return to a positive belief. From early morning to dusk she and Tommy stationed themselves on the opposite side of the road at the small triangle of Gárdonyi Place, because the view on the outside curve of the road was much better.

The survivors came along in a totally unpredictable pattern in ones and twos or small groups, sometimes almost on the heels of each other while at other times not one turned up for several hours or even a day or two. Every time a survivor or a group of them came into view the excitement for Julia heightened and every time she suffered disappointment.

A survivor made his way in their direction one afternoon. The poor man did not just shuffle he also suffered from a substantial tremor in his arms and hands. Hobbling to the street bench where Julia had her little stall, he sat down. Julia placed one of her cakes in his hand.

The poor man attempted to eat it but missed his mouth at the first attempt because of his trembling hand. When he had eaten the cake Julia gave him another one. He looked at her.

'Thank you. You are very kind. Most people are. Some did not dare coming too close but they had left food for us at the roadside.' He ate the second cake and accepted the drink of water Julia poured him. She gave him only half a glassful to prevent him spilling it. He looked at the glass in his shaking hand. 'Look what they have done to me. I used to be a barrister.'

'Where were you?' Julia asked.

'Dachau.'

'I think my brother was there too, his name is László or Latzie Láng, did you know him?'

'I cannot recall. I'm sorry.'

The little food and drink reviving him a bit, the wretched man got to his feet and shuffled away.

'Will he find his family or have they perished elsewhere while he was in Dachau?' Julia asked Tommy, wiping away her tears.

The irregular flow of walking skeletons continued and each day brought sorrow for Julia. Her husband was physically fit and strong-willed yet he had not returned so far and that was a bad omen. She began to have doubts but kept telling herself that as long as survivors kept returning there was a chance that Sándor would be among them. To lessen the repeated disappointments, she forced herself not to look up the road trying to identify distant shapes of men but wait until they got nearer. After a while she moved her stall back in front of Eve's shop, putting a stop to the temptation of staring at distant survivors coming into view.

Tommy had been restless for some time now at Julia's side. He had read his way through lots of books. Sometimes, understanding the boy's frustration, Julia allowed him to stay at home so that he could be with other children. One particular afternoon however, Tommy was reading a book sitting on a folding chair by her stall. Being determined by nature, he had never left any book or story part read just as he would not leave anything half done, but he had found this one hard going. It was titled *Nana* by the author Emile Zola and Tommy decided to avoid the works of this author in the future. He put the book down, stood up and stretched himself.

'I'm going for a stroll, Mum,' he announced.

First he ambled down the road to the bridge where he turned around and coming back he passed the shop and the stall, wandering further in the opposite direction. A lone survivor was making his way towards him with slow and careful steps, one of hundreds he had seen so far. The gaunt and haggard face of this man triggered something in his memory. He hurried back to Julia.

'Mum, a man is coming down the road. I'm not sure, but he looks familiar.'

Julia stepped further out onto the pavement to have a look, trying hard not to hope for too much despite her quickening heartbeat.

Stepping gingerly with his feet covered in sackcloth the survivor came slowly into view. Despite his unshaven and wasted face Julia recognised him and rushed forward shouting, 'Latzie, Latzie!'

The familiar voice made the man stop abruptly in his tracks and he looked utterly bewildered. Yet he had the presence of mind to raise an arm and ward off his sister.

'Don't touch me! I am covered with lice and fleas.'

Julia grabbed hold of his outstretched arm and led her brother to the folding chair, tears making her blouse soaking wet.

'What is wrong with your feet?' she asked.

'Nothing much, I started in great haste and finished up with blisters. There is hardly any skin left on my heels and soles.'

The twenty-minute journey home took almost an hour. Julia boiled saucepan after saucepan of water to fill the bathtub until it was half-full. She placed an old tablecloth on the bathroom floor and told her brother to stand in the middle of it and strip off all his clothing. He did so, this was no time for modesty. When he was naked, Latzi stepped into the bathtub and yelled as the warm water enveloped his blistered, sore feet. He lowered himself into the warm bath, a simple luxury he hadn't had for a very long time, and silent sobbing rocked his frail body. He was back home and he was safe. He was soaking in a hot bath, which, only a short while ago he had never expected to enjoy again. He had survived horror at its worst. Had his wife and their little daughter survived? At that thought his sobbing became very intense. Julia tied the corners of the tablecloth together and burnt the bundle in the garden.

They spent the next day talking, reminiscing and expressing hope for the return of their loved ones. The sight of Latzie dressed in Sándor's clothing was rather painful for Julia. She had no qualms giving her brother Sándor's garments, Latzie had nothing else to wear and they were about the same height and size but seeing him in the outfits conjured up images of Sándor in her mind.

Latzie being in need of proper nourishment, Julia set off to find a job and a proper home. The house they had once been so happy to live in was in need of major repair and their present residence belonged to someone else. She returned in the evening totally worn out having walked from street to street looking for employment, leaving her brother in Tommy's care.

Next morning she was off again casting her net much wider. There was a tobacco-processing factory at the crossing of Verpeléti Road and Budafoki Road but they were just looking into restarting the works and did not need any employees yet.

There was a short street running parallel with Budafoki Road and also crossing Verpeléti Road, studded by a few modern apartment blocks with empty plots scattered amongst them. Beyond that the built-up area ended, abruptly changing into sparse wasteland, although Verpeléti Road with tramlines at its centre extended up to the nearby bridge and had been in use before the German sappers blew the bridge up.

Leaving the tobacco-processing place behind, Julia noticed the open door of a butcher's shop. The jaw of the butcher visibly dropped when she asked if he needed an assistant. He did, but due to the shortage of skills resulting from the loss of men who did not return after the war he had failed to find one so far. But a woman?

'Do you think it's easy handling meat all day?'

'No, I do not. I used to work in my father's shop. I know it isn't.'

The man was unconvinced. He placed a side of beef on the chopping block and said, 'Go ahead, impress me!'

It was a pointed challenge. Julia looked around, picked up a cleaver suitable for the job and got down to work. Watching her expertise the butcher said in utter disbelief, 'I have never seen a woman doing this before! You are hired!'

'Provided I don't have to lift and carry whole sides of beef, I'll accept the offer of a job.'

'No, you won't have to.' The man was laughing. 'They are bigger than you.'

A fortnight later Latzie was strong enough for the long journey on foot to Rottenbiller Street. Looking gaunt but smart in one of Sándor's suits he broke down as he arrived to the neighbourhood and the building where he grew up. By the time he got to the third floor he had composed himself but entering the lounge where his mother Hannah embraced him he could not hold it back any more.

By the beginning of July public transport was rolling, sporadically at first but improving daily. Julia found a small apartment in the short, little street crossing Verpeléti Road. From this street onward the road leading to the foot of the bridge had only wasteland either side of it. The other end of Verpeléti Road joined into a busy junction of five roads known as the 'Circle'.

The 'Circle'

The apartment was in a modern block, designed to have six floors with three dwellings on each and the ground floor with two. Belatedly, the architect had noticed the large loft space so he had two small flats built in there, one each side of, but not adjoining the lift mechanism. The lift ascended only to the sixth floor so residents of the two little flats on the 7th floor had two flights of steps to go on foot.

The accommodation had two medium sized rooms and a small one – just right for Tommy – a kitchen, a bathroom and a hall. One of the rooms opened to a balcony with a very good view, one could see part of Verpeléti Road leading to the Circle and some of the hills of Buda.

When the Hungarian National Bank re-opened its doors Julia, with the help of Klára Szabó, had managed to lay claim to Sándor's business account. It didn't amount to much because hyperinflation was raising its ugly head but it helped. The factory situated on an industrial estate had been demolished by bombing. Julia was left with only the badly damaged house with no money to put it right and no one interested buying it in the state it was in.

Shortly after moving into their new abode they became acquainted with a woman in the apartment directly below with a son of Tommy's age, called Gyula. The two boys warmed to each other in no time and through Gyula Tommy made other friends.

We are settling down at last, Julia contemplated, but why can't I have my husband back? Oh Lord, what have I done so wrong to deserve this?

Gyula's mother, Katie Kéry, and Julia had also formed a happy friendship. Discussing the future education of their offspring Katie strongly suggested the Cistercian Roman Catholic Grammar School, a quarter of a mile beyond the Circle, informing Julia of the strict entry examination the prospective pupils have to pass. Children of all ages had lost a year's education because most schools had declined to open their doors in the previous autumn and those that did had closed them soon afterwards.

The two mothers decided that their boys must go for the exam and in the second week of August they joined numerous parents, mostly mothers with their children, to enrol for the test.

Long queues formed in the Great Hall at four tables, with a Cistercian friar in his white habit with black vestment and sash sitting behind each. They were taking details of previous educational levels gained to select the boys eligible for the entry examination. Owing to the huge number of applicants, the queues extended from the Great Hall into the corridor outside. Moving slowly forward, Julia noted that the friar taking details at the head of their queue had spectacles on with the left lens painted black, signifying blindness in that eye. Just our luck to be in this line Julia pondered, observing the number of people still ahead of them.

At long last it was their turn and they approached the table. The friar placed the form he had just completed in a drawer, picked up a blank one and looked at Julia with an encouraging smile, 'It is an unexpected pleasure to see you Julia. This must be young Tottis.'

The blackened lens with a large facial scar below it and the short-cropped greying hair made recognition impossible but the deep, resonant voice was unmistakable. The friar behind the table was Zoltán Handsome.

'Zoltán!' exclaimed Julia surprised by the unexpected encounter, 'I wondered what had happened to you.'

'I am not called Zoltán any more. Entering the order one assumes another name. I am Father Udo, but tell me, how is Sandy?'

Julia's eyes moistened. 'He didn't return so far. I have lost hope Zoltán. Sorry, Father Udo.'

'I am truly grieved because he was an excellent fellow. I will say mass for him, but right now we must get on with your details.'

Gyula and Tommy had passed the entry examination and finished up in the same class. There were two classes of each year running on parallel courses, class A and class B, each consisting of almost 80 boys. This enormous number was the result of many schools lying in ruins and the shortage of teachers. The school provided excellent education and the children of this generation, having experienced the barbarity of the war, displayed an advanced maturity for their age.

Tommy did like the school despite the teasing he and another boy received for being the smallest in the class. The banter was never malicious though, the friars stamped on any sign of bullying or harassment. Due to the pupils selected purely on their educational standards, every class contained some boys of other denominations. High spirits the friars let pass, but any child who had gone beyond that would get a serious talking to. Upon recurrence, a note of caution would be given to the offender to bring back next day signed by his parents. In effect the school made the parents administer the punishment.

Tommy wrote a letter to Judy and was jubilant on receipt of the reply. She expressed her delight at his letter and her hopes for a re-union when circumstances permitted it. They carried on with the correspondence.

Katie's husband, István Kéry, returned home having been a prisoner of war. He was one of the lucky ones. Their Soviet captors had not released a large number of POWs for a very long time. The existence of these unlucky POWs had become known only by the escape of a few who had managed to walk and hitchhike hundreds of miles or more without being recaptured. This unjust, ruthless incarceration had far-reaching tragic results. Many of these POWs, escapees, or those eventually released years after the war had ended, returned to find that in their absence they had been declared dead and their wives had remarried.

The effect of this was a human disaster many times over. It was impossible to unravel, just like the legendary Gordian Knot that nobody could untangle. Men coming home full of hope and finding another man there who is married to their wife and is the stepfather of their children. The new husband and the wife are not guilty of anything but now there are two husbands and a state of check-mate.

Some of these encounters turned into ugly scenes, some ended in selfless and dignified outcomes even if very painful but suicides also took place, sometimes by the man who returned to his home to find it was no longer his, other times by a wife ridden with guilt or one who couldn't choose between husbands.

The approaching winter made the apartments in the block very cold. Built in 1941, time had run out to complete the central heating. The system was there but the boiler was not. Consequently, there was no hot water either. Julia and Tommy used a large washbowl in the bathroom with water heated in saucepans to wash themselves in the evening and cold water in the hand basin in the morning. It was a small inconvenience compared to their stay at Zápor Street where, having to economise with water, they had been unable to wash at all.

Julia was angry with God for not protecting her husband when by all accounts He had looked after some less deserving individuals.

I was brought up to believe in your justice, fairness and love, God, she deliberated. Or should I call you by your Jewish name, Adonai? I don't think it matters, you are one and the same. So if you are fair and just why did you take my husband away? Why are you penalising my son and me? What have we done to deserve this harsh punishment?

She felt guilty after each outburst against Him yet she did not regret any. She was convinced that God had let her down.

1946

The half term exams took place in early February in all subjects except music and physical exercise. A week later at the start of the two-week break each pupil received their results in a booklet recording half and full-term results all through the years to come. The grading was in a numerical system from one to four: one for very good, two for good, three for satisfactory, four for unsatisfactory. Tommy's report was a mixture of ones and twos with a three for Latin. Julia was most unhappy with his performance. The boy's reports in primary school had consisted almost entirely of top marks. She made no secret of her feelings, telling him in no uncertain terms that he must try harder.

Tommy was aware of not doing well and the reason for it, he found concentrating on most subjects very difficult. His mind kept wondering in two directions, one being the whereabouts of his father whom he deeply loved and greatly missed.

The other one puzzled him. Judy's pretty face kept coming up in his mind's eye. To top it all, a very unusual issue also existed and he could not discuss it with anyone: At the end of each month all Roman Catholic boys had to participate in 'Exercising the Soul', saying the Rosary and confessing their sins. It was an attempt to deter pupils of all ages from committing any. What the school had failed to visualise was that the younger boys aged eleven or twelve simply could not have committed so many transgressions that would necessitate or justify such frequent acts of remorse, asking for forgiveness and penance. Tommy could not go into the confessional saying he had not committed any sins so he invented some like telling lies, which he never did (except in the confessional). But he did truthfully confess more than once that he had used a pin to pierce the cellophane on jars of jam his mother preserved to make the top surface of the jam develop mould. Consequently, the jar had to be opened, the layer of mould removed and then the jam could be consumed.

Unable to confide in anyone about his cheating in the confessional, he did not know that other boys had also struggled with the same problem. His totally honest and truthful disposition was in conflict with this deception and the matter was playing on his mind.

Julia found a clerical job. She left home at the same time as Tommy but came home later at around six in the evening. After the evening meal, she prepared and cooked food for the next day or days and carried out other household chores such as cleaning, mending and ironing. She did the washing of clothing on Sundays – due to having to heat water in saucepans to fill the bathtub, a lengthy activity.

A year after the war had ended Julia resigned herself to widowhood, accepting that her husband would not return but she did not come to terms with it. Her emotional and physical desires remained with Sándor and she could not contemplate another man as a partner in any form.

László was received with open arms at Somosy International Spediteurs but they had to start again, like many other businesses, almost from scratch.

To keep in touch with friends and relatives, Julia had a telephone connected. She telephoned the orphanage making enquiries about Robbie and they told her that on his recent eighteenth birthday the young man had been released from the institute and they had no idea where he went.

The first post-war telephone directory appeared and the very evening of its distribution the phone rang. Julia picked up the receiver, 'Hello, this is 457-209.'

'Jutzie, how are you all?' a male voice asked. The voice distorted by the phone was familiar.

'I am sorry but I don't quite know whom I am talking to.'

'It is I, Ferie, Ferie Molnár. I've been trying to find you for a long time! I found no one at Mihály Street who could tell me where you have moved!'

'Oh Ferie, how nice of you to think of us. I am so sorry, I didn't recognise your voice.'

They had a long chat and Ferie Molnár asked permission to visit one evening. It was granted.

Tommy received a reply from Judy with a P.S. in tiny writing: *I think I love you.*

He replied instantly and his P.S. read: *I know I love you.* Sealing the envelope he had a strange and pleasant feeling in his chest and a yearning to see Judy.

Ferie Molnár came visiting and they enjoyed a very pleasant evening and brisk conversation. Discussing education at the religious establishment he asked Tommy if he believed in God.

'Of course I do,' Tommy replied. 'Don't you?'

'No, I don't.'

'Why not?'

'Because nobody can prove God exists.'

Tommy was shocked at the statement.

'What proof do you need?'

'Well, has anyone ever seen God?'

'God cannot be seen, but where do you think everything has come from?'

'Oh, you mean the so-called "Creation" God was supposed to have carried out in six days.'

'Yes, of course.'

'Tommy, you should read Darwin's *Theory of Evolution*.'

'I *have* read it and found it interesting. We have evolved from the primates but where did the primates evolve from and going back, the World, the Galaxy?' The boy stood his ground.

'The Galaxy and our globe are the result of a gigantic explosion – scientists have proved that conclusively.'

'True, something exploded but what was there before the explosion, Uncle Ferie?'

'According to eminent scientists the primordial mist.'

'Yes but they cannot explain where that came from or who created it.'

Ferenc Molnár turned to Julia who was fascinated by the verbal exchange.

'You should be proud of your boy. He knows his subject and conducts a discussion with conviction.' Turning to Tommy he proffered his right hand for a handshake, 'I consider it a privilege to have lost the debate to such a worthy opponent.'

'Uncle Ferie you are very generous.'

Julia was out visiting the Kérys when the telephone rang and Tommy answered it. The caller was Klára Szabó. Her speech was slower than usual.

'Tommy... can I... speak to your... mother... please?'

'Klára,' Tommy would never call her Auntie, he considered her too young for that. 'What's the matter? Mum is visiting neighbours.'

'Tell her... Mr and Mrs Roth... from Báthori Street... are taking me to court... They are accusing me of... embezzling their... jewellery... Thank you.' She hung up.

Tommy had no knowledge of the jewellery. He remembered the old couple being aloof and felt outrage that anyone could sink so low as to accuse Klára of dishonesty. He dashed downstairs and told his mother about the phone call. Julia excused herself and back home she rang Klára.

'Klára, I know what had happened to you, so must other people. There should be records in the hospital you were in, provided they weren't destroyed in the fighting.'

Klára replied that she herself had no knowledge of what had happened to her. She had been told what had presumably taken place.

'Anyway,' Julia asked, 'how can they prove they had given you the jewellery?'

'They can... I gave them... a receipt.'

'Did they ask for one?'

'No.'

'Oh, you poor, honest darling, please try not to worry. We'll find a lawyer to represent you. Would you like to come over and stay with us?'

Klára declined the offer. She was a very private person and had always lived on her own.

Tommy, Gyula and their friends would never play with toys or make-believe games. Even the favourite Shuco car Tommy carried in his pocket during his escapade to Zápor Street had remained in a cabinet, untouched ever since. The boys played dominoes, chess and *Capitaly* (Monopoly) and some boys played football and some preferred riding their bicycles. Tommy had been pestering his mother for a bicycle and had received the reply that money was in short supply and his school report would have to improve first before he could get one. At the end of the term Latin was still at grade three in his final report but there was only one grade two, an improvement he really sweated for. It was good enough for Julia because she was willing to buy her son a bike, being satisfied with his behaviour and attitude, apart from the occasional flare-up of his temper. Living at the edge of the city with the wide carriageway leading to the non-existent bridge offered safety from traffic. A bicycle was certainly in order but where was it going to be kept?

Julia confronted her son with the problem. Tommy replied that it would be parked in his room of course. He would not let it out of his sight!

'Tommy you know how tiny the lift is, you'll never get it in there.'

'I'll carry it up the stairs Mum.'

Julia pondered over that; Tommy is on the small side. If he cannot manage it I will have to do it but I must not break my promise.

The bike they purchased had twenty-six inch wheels, slightly big for Tommy but it had to last. The first time he carried it up the stairs he only managed to reach the landing between the first and second floor before aching fingers and muscles forced him to rest. He tried to hold it differently but his arm was too short to reach down over the crossbar and it was quite a struggle. Aided by his stubborn streak, he did not let his mother down. Tommy regularly carried the bike up to their home two or three times a day, setting targets for himself to go further and further up without stopping. He would not leave it unattended, not even in the lobby inside the gates. Some weeks later his perseverance paid off when for the first time, and puffing like a steam locomotive, he managed to carry the bike all the way up in one go. As time went by, the frequent effort helped to keep him fit and develop his muscles.

With parental agreement on both sides, Tommy was to spend a fortnight at Judy's place in August. Waiting for the day was sheer torment for both of them. They had not seen each other for two years.

When Julia and Tommy entered by the garden gate and proceeded down the long central path Judy, eagerly watching out for them, ran out of the house. Meeting half way down the garden the two youngsters faced each other with signs of embarrassment, taking note of the changes. Judy, almost thirteen was distinctly taller, her developing body giving a touch of feminine allure to her appearance. Apart from lacking height slightly, Tommy was a normal twelve-year-old boy. Neither of them knew what to do next and would have just stood there but for Julia coming to the rescue.

'Hello Judy, what an attractive young lady you are growing into.'

'Thank you Auntie Julia. Come in please.' She grabbed hold of Tommy's hand pulling him along, leading the way.

The house was small originally, built across the bottom of the garden with the main lounge-dining room at the centre, its French windows opening to the garden path. The kitchen was on the left with the bathroom behind it and the main bedroom on the right wing. After the birth of Judy an extension had been built in front of the large room, making the building T-shaped, the central stem being Judy's room, also with French windows. This was the place the two friends could hardly wait to go to, having to fare through lunch and polite conversation until Julia departed. At last they were there, seated on Judy's sofa with their hearts beating fast, holding hands and turning to each other with their knees touching, saying not a word. Judy was the first to break the loaded silence.

'I've got your letter, it was very nice.'

'So was yours, I was very pleased with it.'

'I've read yours many times, it made me happy.'

Tommy blushed. He also read and re-read the letter with the tiny PS but admitting it was not easy. Yet the truth had to be told.

'I did that too. I've never had such a nice letter before.' As the words came out Tommy conceded that he could not have because he did not correspond with anyone else. At this point however he got stuck and could not think of anything to say.

Judy was in a similar situation and embarrassed by it.

'I missed you a lot,' Tommy unexpectedly let slip.

'I missed you too. I was very lonely for a very long time.'

'Me too.'

They had found a common ground and the conversation gathered speed.

'Tommy, you are going to sleep on the settee in the lounge by the French windows opening into Judy's room,' Judy's mother said at the dining table after supper.

Judy insisted that she should sleep on the settee and Tommy on her sofa. Her parents exchanged amused and understanding glances and agreed.

Tommy went to the bathroom first, brushed his teeth, washed himself and changed into pyjamas. He carried his garments from the bathroom into Judy's room, deposited them on a chair and slipped under the blanket.

Judy went next, her mother tucked her in bed. Shortly after that Judy's parents turned off the lights and retired to the bedroom, closing the door behind them quietly to let the children sleep undisturbed.

In the silent semi-darkness Tommy was staring at the ceiling without actually seeing it. His mind was elsewhere, contemplating the last few hours and the fact that Judy was still fond of him and not bothered by his lack of height.

'Are you asleep?' he heard Judy whisper from the other room.

'No, I am not, but I am dreaming.'

'What about?'

'I can't tell.'

'You must tell. I need to know.'

'We have to be careful not to wake your parents, talking.'

'Come over here and then we can talk quietly.'

His heart pounding Tommy slipped off the sofa and tiptoed over to the settee. Judy was looking up at him with her head on the pillow and the blanket rolled down to her waist. She was also in pyjamas, the jacket buttoned up to her neck. Tommy knelt on the floor and Judy moved herself to the edge of the settee.

He placed his right arm over the rolled-down blanket and Judy got hold of his hand. With his other hand he was stroking her hair. Gazing at each other without words they were experiencing emotions as yet unknown and savouring them. Time went by. The boy's knees began hurting on the floorboards but the delight of his closeness to Judy made him ignore them. All of a sudden he heard himself saying, 'Judy, I love you.'

'I love you too,' she said and letting his hand go she pulled Tommy towards her. Their lips met with a gentle touch and moved no further. Captivated by the magic of their first kiss they held on to each other, spellbound. Tommy felt with some alarm Judy's developing breast pressing against his chest through their pyjamas and a strange and pleasant sensation in his loin he had never felt before. I wish this could last forever, he thought.

Judy being older and more mature realised that her overpowering sensations could be in breach of what she believed to be proper and acceptable. Gently she pushed at Tommy's shoulder. 'You must go back to bed now.'

Holding each other the following night, they repeated their creed of pure and genuine love. Both of them yearned for another kiss and were about to embrace when the floorboards creaked in the main bedroom. Tommy darted back to the sofa in the belief that, if caught, he would never be allowed to see Judy again. The bedroom door opened silently, someone went to the bathroom and returned a few minutes later. They were not found out. No one had ever learned of their nights of adolescent passion but they did not dare to try again. They had no way of knowing that the memory of their first tender kiss would never leave them.

At the farewell a fortnight later, despite the perfect manners displayed by the children, the three adults did not fail to notice the attraction between them.

Shortly after Julia and Tommy had departed, Judy's mother looked at her husband and said, 'The way things are going the two of them will be married within ten years.'

'It wouldn't be a bad thing,' her husband replied. 'They are very well matched.'

Back home in his room Tommy could not go to sleep. Judy, Judy, I love you so much why do we have to live so far apart? he pondered. Long past midnight he fell into a deep sleep. Eventually he was at Judy's place and although it seemed vague and unreal Judy was real, she was in his arms whispering, 'I love you. I always will.' Their lips met and her breast was against his chest once more. The sensation was exquisite… ethereal… but the dream abruptly evaporated and he awoke with the shocking realisation that his pyjama trousers were wet. His mind was in turmoil, he had not wetted himself since babyhood. Then it dawned on him that it was a different kind of wetness.

He made up his bed in the morning, a standard procedure, and gave no more thought to the matter.

Stripping the bed on Sunday morning Julia noticed the stain. When Tommy returned home after attending Holy Mass she asked him about it. The boy's face turned red.

'I don't know, Mum.'

'Tommy, you know something. What did you do?'

'I didn't *do* anything!' Tommy replied angrily.

'Tommy, I am not accusing you of any wrongdoing and I am not angry. Just tell me what happened.'

'I don't know, Mum. I had a dream and woke up in the middle of it, wet.'

'What was the dream about?' Tommy blushed again and bit his lips, saying nothing.

'Tommy, you know that there is absolutely nothing you cannot tell me. What was the dream about?'

'Judy.'

Julia cupped her son's face in her hands. 'Remember how babies are conceived in the mother's tummy, the process starting with the seed from the man's "thingy" entering her?'

'Yes, I do.'

'Well, Tommy, that's what has happened to you. This was your first step to manhood.'

Tommy's eyes widened with amazement and Julia smiled. 'Don't let your imagination run amok. You have a few years to go yet.'

Julia accompanied Klára to the court hearing, not only as a friend but also as a character witness. In the chaos of the siege of Budapest, Klára's hospital records had been lost. The lawyer representing her traced a nurse in attendance during her stay and she testified that Klára was brought in bleeding from the back of her fractured skull and had remained unconscious for the five days she was on duty. The nurse had no recollection of the handbag.

Referring to a seldom-applied prerogative the judge asked Klára to take the witness stand.

'Miss Szabó. Do you admit that in the summer of 1944 you were given items of jewellery by Mr and Mrs Roth?'

'…Yes… I do… And I gave… them a receipt… for their… jewellery.'

'Miss Szabó. Why did you not leave the jewellery at your home, why carry them in your handbag?'

'My home… could have been… hit by a bomb… I considered them… safer with me.'

'Thank you Miss Szabó. Please return to your seat.'

The judge faced the court. 'While I sympathise with Mr and Mrs Roth for their jewellery that was stolen by someone the accused, Miss Szabó, is eminently innocent of the charge. Case dismissed!'

Ferie Molnár came visiting regularly and kept asking Julia if she needed assistance in any way or form. He really tried his best to repay her for Sándor's helping hand in his hour of need. He asked to take her out frequently with or without Tommy, but Julia explained that Sándor's memory was still very strong and declined the offers.

Tommy and Gyula joined the scouts. The school had its own group named after St Bernard. To gain entry, certain levels of education had to be achieved: no grade four in any subject and no major breach of discipline. If the mother or parents of a new member could not afford the cost of the uniform the rest of the group, numbering hundreds, had been asked to contribute. No one had ever been left without a uniform.

Having figured out how to use his father's Rolleiflex camera, Tommy took a picture of himself with the aid of the self-exposure attachment and sent the picture to Judy.

Judy's reply was full of admiration. She was keen to become a Girl Guide but there were very few groups for girls and the nearest was in the capital, too far away.

1947

At the general election early in the year the communist People's Party had failed to gain the majority vote so they set about using underhand methods to entice, coerce, or destroy leaders of other parties. For youngsters the Pioneer Movement was launched based on the Soviet version, implanting Socialist doctrine into their young, untainted minds. It was a mixed sex project with branches springing up everywhere. Apart from the uniform parents had to pay for, the state sponsored the movement along with all activities, fares, entry fees, etc.

Julia sold the house on Gellért Hill for just the value of the bricks, a pittance, but she was glad that someone was interested buying it. She had neither the capital to have it rebuilt, nor the desire to move back into it without her husband.

Tommy's school reports remained the same, a mixture of ones and twos with Latin at a permanent three. Julia kept telling him that his father had better marks at school which was not true, but Tommy did not know that and the comparison hurt him because he was really trying hard.

In the summer break, the St Bernard Scout Group went camping in the Bükk Mountains. They set up camp in a valley miles away from the nearest habitation, by a stream some twenty-five feet wide and two to three feet deep at the centre. They pitched their tents and dug a foot-wide trench around each to prevent rainwater running under them.

The cooking range was partly dug, partly built for the large steel plate with removable sets of rings to fit safely and securely over it. Each day a different platoon had to cook for the rest, guided and supervised by their leaders – friars wearing scout uniforms. The boys stripped to their underpants every morning to wash themselves in the cold stream, pretending to enjoy it at first but by the end of the week they really did.

At evening time they sat around the campfire with stories of heroism, courage, self-sacrifice and other noble acts narrated by the scout leaders along with the history of their country, instilling in them a sense of pride for their origin and homeland. In between stories there was a lot of singing.

The boy sitting next to him at the campfire one evening Tommy only knew by sight because he was a year older, hence in a different class at school. His name was Vince Dorkossy and once they had started chatting they rapidly warmed to each other. While his own shyness centred on his lack of height, Tommy quickly realised that Vince – tall, slim, with dark brown wavy hair and with a handsome chiselled face – was also very shy. He wondered why.

Tommy stayed at Judy's place in late August for a week. Something was different, very much so. He felt drawn to Judy, his desire was stronger than ever yet he did not know what to do about it. Judy was in the same predicament. She really wanted Tommy to touch her, kiss her, but was unable to encourage him. Both of them expected and yearned for the other making a move. Not once through the week did they hold hands or declare their love for each other. Perhaps it was the burning all-consuming love that they had in their young hearts that made them afraid of spoiling the cherished memory of the previous summer.

School started and little did Tommy know that this would be his last year in the school he loved so much where, regardless of mediocre grades, he had learnt a great deal. The methods and quality of teaching triumphed over the huge number of pupils.

He frequently visited Vince who was a bit of a loner and would not join his group of friends. Vince had his mother's photograph pinned to the wall of his room. She had died when Vince was six years old. Tommy noticed that she was indeed a beautiful woman. Vince's father remarried and had a daughter from his second wife whom Vince felt certain was the favourite. He had the impression he was not wanted, never mind loved. Tommy had tried hard to reassure his friend with very little success.

1948

The communist-dominated People's Party having eliminated all other parties but the largest, the Social Democrats, coerced them into a coalition leaving no party in opposition. Gaining absolute control they embarked on creating a totalitarian regime. First they confiscated all cars, vans, and trucks, making them the property of the State. Only some doctors and of course the Party's officials were allowed to have cars. To a large number of communist Party officials (promoting equality for all) having a car was not enough. They also awarded themselves chauffeurs, making the state to finance the running cost of the car and the wages of the driver.

The next step was the seizure of property: farms, land, factories, apartment buildings, houses, with the exception of extremely small, single-room dwellings, had all been confiscated without compensation. Even people living in their own, fully-paid property had become tenants of the State. The State turned into the one and only property owner; rent had to be paid to the State but the State did not maintain the buildings to the standard the original owners had been compelled to.

The last blow was the nationalisation of all private enterprise. Small businesses like bakers, butchers, builders, solicitors, tailors, etc., had to cease trading. Only a very few specialist firms remained in existence but they were State owned and controlled. Tradesmen and professionals joined State-run co-operatives or found employment in other occupations.

The lack of shops, small businesses and skills made normal essential services and items unobtainable.

People had to wait several months for spare parts becoming available or any task or repair carried out by a 'co-operative' workshop.

There was a saying not far from the truth that, one must never have children's clothing dry-cleaned in the State-run setup because by the time you get the garments back the children had grown out them.

Any form of work undertaken privately such as the repair of a radio, a clock, or a pair of shoes was proclaimed illegal 'capitalist enterprise' and carried a jail sentence.

In their zeal, the communist leaders had failed to heed the warning of one of their heroes, Vladimir Ilyich Ulyanov (Lenin). He had said that the margin was very narrow between Socialism and State Capitalism where the only employer was the state, that being the worst form of capitalism there was.

For the second year running Tommy visited Grandmother Isabelle on her birthday at the end of March with a bunch of flowers. Julia persuaded him to do so, explaining that despite the strained relations between them the old lady was Tommy's grandmother and he also had to represent his father. Tommy could not argue with that aspect. The reception he received, just like the previous year, was one of indifference. Isabelle looked happy to see him, yet his cousin Dávid talked to him like a member of royalty dealing with a lowly servant. Paul was genial but Ibolya's friendliness was evidently forced if not false. Tommy departed after half an hour.

The Government repressed faiths and religions albeit rather covertly, discouraging people from attending services. They abolished the Scout movement on the pretext that it was 'clerico-Fascist'. Judy joined the Pioneers and was very excited about it in her letter.

Tommy replied by return post pointing out that the Pioneer Movement lacked the noble, virtuous, worthwhile activities and directions of the Scouts and advised her to be cautious.

At the end of the last term in July, teachers in church schools regardless of denomination had all been dismissed. The government banished friars, nuns, rabbis, teachers of any faith to small rural communities. Actually, they had to live in exile. Julia panicked at the news and made a serious mistake by enrolling her son in a school someone recommended to her on the Pest side of the river, a long way from home. Gyula and Vince remained at the old school – only the teachers were going to be different.

The summer break had passed without a chance of seeing Judy. She was away most of the time on various Pioneer activities. Her bright and keen young mind rapidly soaked up Communist ideals and propaganda, the vision of a future where everyone would be equal and live happily ever after, not wanting for anything (An idealistic Utopia because without distinction there would be no ambition either). The correspondence drew to a halt. Tommy felt hurt. Unable to lavish his love and affection on Judy it was now choking him.

In a crowded tramway on her way home from work Julia found herself standing next to her nephew, Robbie. The unexpected encounter embarrassed both of them but they started chatting even if in a slightly strained fashion.

'Robbie, I don't know what to say, too many things have happened since we had last met.'

'I am aware of that.'

'I didn't forget you, Robbie. I telephoned the orphanage in 1946 but they told me that you had been released from their care. You're twenty years old, aren't you, what do you do?'

'I'm training to be a primary school teacher.'

'Robbie, I would like you to have dinner with us, Sunday after next.'

The young man seemed visibly uncertain but accepted the invitation.

Robbie duly turned up on the pre-arranged Sunday and was well mannered throughout but also very quiet and distant. Although he did not have a grudge, in effect his family abandoned him and he had to spend all his youth in an orphanage.

Julia insisted that they should keep in touch and Robbie agreed to visit again. He kept his promise, even though turning up rather infrequently but, with the passing of time, his initial reticent attitude gradually disappeared.

Joining the new school Tommy promptly befriended a boy called Karl Vasas. Karl was a lively fellow who also lived at the Buda side, not too far away, with his parents and younger sister. He also had a bicycle and was delighted to join Tommy's group of friends on their jaunts.

1949

The land that had been confiscated from landowners and distributed among the peasantry in the previous year was now being organised into large co-operatives. The recently established smallholders offered their plots 'voluntarily, according to the newspapers, also owned and controlled by the State. The government then issued a diabolical ruling for the advancement of the working class at the cost of all others. The directive classified people by their origins or backgrounds and the category, (the 'cadre'), they fell into determined their prospects of higher education, promotion, better housing, holiday entitlement and vacation resorts and so forth. Anyone who had employed or whose parents had employed ten or more people before the war, or before the recent nationalisation, the scheme classified as 'capitalist origin'. There was only one category worse than that: Aristocrat.

Julia and Tommy fell into the 'capitalist' slot, because Sándor had employed twenty-three people. People with 'working class' or 'farm worker' backgrounds the system placed into responsible, managerial jobs despite lack of experience replacing those who had it.

Entry examinations for universities had nine questions for students from that kind of origin, thirty-seven for all others. A large number of students of the working or farming category, most of whom had no wish to enter university at all but were pressurised to do so, had fallen by the wayside within the first year. The zealots in high places suppressed this dismal failure and continued with the totally arbitrary and unjust method of selection. All the population regardless of 'class and origin' considered it wrong.

Visiting the Vasas' home for the first time, Tommy noticed that Karl's fourteen-year-old sister Suzy was very pretty indeed with a lovely figure. He ignored the temptation. According to unwritten rules the sister or girlfriend of a close pal was taboo.

At the end of March, Tommy paid the customary annual visit to Grandmother Isabelle with a large bouquet of flowers. As in the previous years he received an indifferent reception. Only Isabelle seemed happy to see him. His cousin Dávid tried to impress him with his 'unparalleled operatic successes', unaware that Tommy knew that he was only a member of the choir and at the back row of that. Paul didn't say much and Ibolya kept tapping the tabletop with her fingers on and off. Tommy could hardly wait to get away from the supercilious atmosphere.

Judy wrote, very proud of herself having been promoted to the rank of troop leader. Tommy congratulated her in his reply, adding his concern about the aims of the Pioneers. He was aware of an invisible wall descending between him and Judy, but his love and physical desire for Judy was as strong as ever.

Judy pushed her feelings for Tommy into the backyards of her memory. She was a brilliant scholar, her brain soaking up information readily. Along with other Pioneers she had learnt about the harm caused to society by the churches and religions, the scouts, and the like. People following or believing such doctrines were enemies of the Socialist principle and obstructing the glorious future only Socialism would bring. There was no room for sentiment, regardless of the dissenters being friends or family they had to be denounced!

Twenty-two year old District Commander Adam Bodor, a very handsome chap, delivered the lectures on the subject with fire and conviction.

Tommy tried to keep away from the Vasas household as much as he could. He was flattered by Suzy's attention yet not only was she 'out-of-bounds', but should they start dating the friendship with Karl would be over and then he couldn't go on dating Suzy any more.

Gyula had already been dating one of the girls in the neighbourhood. Tommy was tempted to ask one out, but partly out of his devotion to Judy and partly because the girls were at least his height he did not make a move.

Ferie Molnár turned up on one of his occasional prearranged visits. When Julia went to the kitchen to make coffee and fetch some cakes he asked Tommy in a hushed voice, 'Tommy, how would you feel if I were to ask your mother to marry me? I must know before I ask her.'

The question was unexpected but Tommy replied without hesitation. 'Uncle Ferie, I still miss my father a lot but if Mum accepts your offer I will not object.'

'Thank you, Tommy. I am very fond of you both and I hope she will accept. She is not only a nice person but also a very attractive woman. If I had to guess I would say she couldn't be more than thirty-eight years old at the most.'

Julia seemed ill at ease later that evening. 'Tommy, you ought to know that Ferie asked me to marry him. I will have to consider his offer because he is a very pleasant and kind man and also because he has a good job at the Ministry of Health while we are just about making ends meet. I told him I would think about it. What do you think?'

Tommy had wondered whether his mother would accept or decline the offer. He replied, 'Mum, I really like Uncle Ferie but I still miss my dad. I cannot tell you what to do, you are the one who will have to decide.'

Julia declined Ferie's offer of marriage as gently as she could, telling him he was the best friend she had ever had and that she hoped the friendship would continue.

It did not. Ferie Molnár never called again.

Tommy and Gyula had become virtuoso cyclists over the years, spending most of their free time in the saddle. Apart from long tours to places like Gödöllő and Esztergom they had become experts on the wild terrain that was right on the doorstep beside the unused main road leading to the bridge foot. The vast overgrown area on different levels was pitted with bomb craters offering all sorts of gradients. Only people walking their dogs, and lovers trying to be out of sight, went there. The boys were adventurous and daring, coming croppers time and again and collecting cuts and grazes. They had also become very experienced at bicycle repair. A bigger challenge was sought for. Gyula and Tommy enrolled in a State-run motorbike club with grudging agreement from their parents.

Seated on a street bench the youngsters used to gather at, Tommy seemed to have waited in vain. No one turned up. Dusk was falling when one of the girls popped out heading straight for the bench. Eszter was also fifteen, dark-haired with a round doll's face befitting a buxom young girl. She sat there chatting for a while and then suggested going for a walk.

They strolled slowly to the bridge foot a quarter of a mile beyond the built-up area. By the time they reached the railing across the width of the structure preventing people from falling to the embankment below, darkness enveloped them. Only illuminated windows glistened far behind and on the other side of the river encircling them in a myriad of distant, tiny flickers. Looking around Tommy said, 'I've never been here before after dark. What a lovely view.'

The response was quite unexpected. Eszter wrapped her arms around his neck and kissed him fully on the mouth. Caught unawares Tommy failed to react instantly and she pulled her head back. 'Didn't you like it?' she asked in a whisper.

'Of course I did,' Tommy replied with a touch of humour. 'All through its one-second duration.'

He returned the kiss with passion, pulling Eszter's well-rounded body against his. Tommy enjoyed the intimate episode, feeling elated and aroused, yet he was aware it was not the enchantment he had experienced previously. The wonderful unique spell was missing.

Holding hands they walked back in total silence and parted at the corner of the street by the empty plot. Tommy's home was adjacent to it on the left, Eszter's just beyond it straight ahead. A pleasant, warm feeling enfolded him all evening but Eszter received a thrashing from her mother for being out with a boy after dark. She did not tell Tommy at the time but she was not seen out after dusk any more on her own.

A friendly neighbour explained to Julia the quandary she found herself in, owing to what she had heard being said about Tommy. A woman seated exactly opposite her at a wedding reception was telling someone in a snobbish fashion that her nephew, naming Tommy, turned up in March every year shortly before his birthday hoping for a handout. Admittedly it could be someone else with the same name but she had found the woman's manner obnoxious and decided to inform Julia about the episode.

Julia thanked her, explaining that grandmother's birthday falls on 31st March and Tommy's on 10th

April, therefore the visits had nothing to do with an expectation of a handout. The woman said that she was glad to hear it because she had found the story hard to believe.

When Julia told him, Tommy was furious. Julia had never seen him so incensed before but clearly understood that the boy's pride was hurt. He had found himself accused of something he would never contemplate doing. Ibolya's accusation had found his 'Achilles' heel'.

'I'll never ever go there again!' he roared. 'I don't want anything from that rotten lot and I'm going to let them know!'

Julia waited for him to cool down before responding.

'You will only make them happy by revealing that they have succeeded in annoying you.'

Tommy stared at her contemplating the wisdom of her words. 'What do you think I should do? Nothing?'

'We'll think of something. Never act in anger, Tommy.'

The school break was over and he had not heard a word from Judy. Tommy has had to accept that their long and happy love affair was coming to an end. The wound was still there, healing very slowly.

One of the two ground floor apartments changed hands. The family moving in consisted of a middle-aged couple with two daughters, Adele aged twenty and Edith only fourteen. The young girl caught Tommy's eye the first time he saw her. She was petite, slightly shorter than he was, slim and yet very feminine. Apart from Judy, she was the first girl Tommy felt genuinely drawn to.

1950

Following a heavy January snowfall, the trainer of the motorbike club told the best of his team to meet him at a deserted part of Margit Island, accessible by the slip road at the centre of Margit Bridge. He arrived on a tatty old bike for the lads to use and gain experience on, in really slippery conditions. The idea was a brilliant one. There was no chance of a collision and one by one the lads skidded and fell, to the hilarity of the others watching. No bones got broken but they finished up with lots of bruises by the time they had mastered the skills to ride around in a figure of eight and other tricky formations.

Tommy's feet did not reach the ground sitting on the powerful 250cc motorbike, so Gyula steadied it for him every time he got on and he brought the bike to a halt where fellow members, motivated by camaraderie, stood waiting to steady the bike while he dismounted.

Tommy did not miss his grandmother's birthday or forget his aunt's venomous accusations. He left the flowers with a note attached at the door of the house without ringing the bell.

The friendship between Tommy and Edith had flourished quickly. At the very beginning, Edith's parents declined letting her go out with Tommy in an area that was entirely new to them. As time went by they recognized Tommy's good manners, and the occasional neighbourly chat with his mother had also helped. Edith was happy in Tommy's company and they always returned home by the stipulated time.

Consequently, her parents accepted Tommy as their daughter's boyfriend.

'Tommy,' Julia said, 'I have no objection if you wish to bring Edith home and close the door of your room behind you. You are growing up but you must control yourself. On no account should she become pregnant.'

'Mum, she will be sixteen in November. I would not dream of touching her before that.'

'All right, but stick to it. If you find yourself in need of advice don't be afraid of asking me.'

'Thanks, Mum, I'll do that.'

He had a great mother, Tommy really appreciated that, but the offer of the privacy of his room was hardly ever taken up. He preferred to walk out to the wasteland with Edith and there, out of sight, he gathered the slender girl up in his arms. With her arm around Tommy's neck, Edith enjoyed being carried along. Both of them loved the tender intimacy of this harmless affection.

A letter came from Judy, disclosing her recently found happiness. The man she was so much in love with was twenty-three years old with a great future, *'...a wonderful person, tall, handsome and decisive.'*

She didn't need to mention that she had been seduced, Tommy could read that between the lines. He accepted that Judy would not hurt him deliberately but the contents of the letter tore the wound open and the word *'tall'* made it bleed. Judy, in a state of adoration of her first lover, could not see the difference between decisive and dominant.

The school term about to end, Julia and Tommy got involved in prolonged and very serious discussions.

Julia would have preferred to keep her son at school and get him to university but this idea was doomed to fail. To start with, the 'capitalist' tag or background

198

made it almost impossible to gain entry and added to this was the likelihood that Tommy, an average scholar, would not manage the thirty-seven test questions successfully. Secondary education to the age of eighteen was essential for going to university; if that were not forthcoming he would be left without a trade or any other qualification. The only other option was to leave school for an apprenticeship. Supporting this course of action was Tommy's aptitude for things of a technical nature. His ability to figure out how things worked and how to correct faults in them, helped him to mend their chiming clock that the local watch and clockmaker co-operative declared beyond repair.

The motorbike racing season being in full swing, Tommy and Gyula attended to their older participating team-mates in the 'Depot', the equivalent of pits. Motor racing events in the capital took place either at the City Park or on the steep and winding roads of Castle Hill, demanding great skill and courage, each area closed to vehicular traffic for the duration.

Both lads were good at cross-country races due to their long experience on the wild terrain on bicycles, but they had to wait for the annual Beginners' Race and qualify by their performance for the issue of the much coveted Motorbike Racing Licence.

Karl was showing off his girlfriend, Éva. He certainly had something to boast about. The girl was a real beauty, a natural blonde with an alluring voice and perfect figure. She was also very chic and friendly, her inherent egotism disguised by her charm.

The oppression was growing relentlessly. A dictate by the government prohibited the forms of address, 'Mr', 'Mrs', and 'Miss', and replaced all three with an untranslatable genderless word, 'elvtárs' akin to 'comrade'. Anti-government comments, articles, even jokes, carried jail sentences.

Because only one party existed, the communist People's Party, the media referred to it as 'The Party'. The People's Party also controlled the one and only trade union in the country, 'The Union'. Everybody over the age of sixteen had to carry an identification booklet at all times, containing a photo and itemised personal details.

Officers of the ÁVO, the State Police, frequently raided public places. Anyone caught without their identification booklet would be taken into custody and seldom released before enduring terrifying methods of interrogation. There was no need for such drastic measures but some of the officers in the ÁVO enjoyed exercising their power to the extreme.

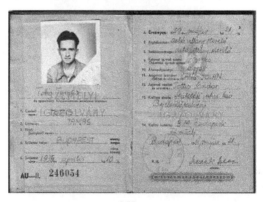

To stop the movement of labour, the government introduced Work Passports. It had to be passed on to the employer at taking up a new job. The employer had to retain the booklet and was obliged to record details of how and when the employment terminated, whether by the employer or the employee, i.e. *'Transferred on the request of so-and-so Company'*, *'Dismissed for habitual late arrival'*. The worst comment was: *'Quit on his/her own accord'*. No one could gain employment with that statement in their Work Passport within six months of its date, by law. The person concerned would also lose all social and pension credits. Only an absolute imbecile would chuck their job in, regardless how awful or unpleasant it might be. Out of shared hardship, camaraderie grows. Someone in need of changing jobs turned to a friend, who had a friend, who asked another friend, and so on, to help with a transfer.

Tommy enrolled for an auto and vehicle electrician apprenticeship at a small establishment of specialists, once a private company, now nationalised. Situated at Dráva Street on the other side of the river and at a diagonally opposite part of the city, it took him just over half an hour on his bicycle which he had turned into a quasi-racing bike over the years.

He left home at seven sharp in the morning and got back home around ten minutes to six in the evening, six days a week. Changing in and out of overalls and washing hands had to be performed outside working hours in the employee's time. Anyone not at their workstation at eight in the morning or away before five more than once a month, faced disciplinary procedures.

Despite her parents' pleading and warnings, Judy married Adam Bodor at a registry office. No invitations had been sent or announcements made. Only the two witnesses attended.

The telephone rang. Julia called out, 'Tommy, it's for you!'

Taking the receiver Tommy recognized the caller as Éva. She sounded fretful and troubled, saying that Karl was neglecting her, not paying much attention. Tommy told her that he had no idea how he could be of help, the matter being rather personal. Éva begged him to meet her, him being Karl's best friend, to pour her heart out. Tommy said he would have to ask Karl first. Éva objected, saying that if Karl learned she had spoken of a private problem he would chuck her. She suggested the portals of the Eastern Railway Station as a meeting place, away from prying eyes. Very reluctantly Tommy agreed.

Decked out in a smart jacket and tie, at the appointed place and time, he spotted Éva strolling towards him and looking absolutely gorgeous with a bright smile on her face. Tommy wondered that she didn't look unhappy at all when a man's voice from close behind said,

'I couldn't believe that you would commit this sort of treachery, trying to steal my girlfriend. I had to see it myself.'

It was Karl. He looked at Tommy with contempt and, holding Éva's hand, the two of them turned their backs on him and walked off. Tommy stood there humiliated and in shame. He retreated to the men's toilet and stayed in a cubicle for a long time trying to calm down and think of a way out of the poisonous, spiked trap he had fallen into. He realised that if this episode became known he would have no friends left. Enticing a friend's girl was by far the most serious breach of the Unwritten Code. He would become a dishonoured outcast and his friends would keep their distance from him. There would be no chance to explain.

Returning home he wrote a letter to Karl informing him of the events leading up to the unfortunate episode. Karl did not reply and ceased to join the activities of the group. Owing to that, thankfully, Tommy's friends did not hear of the incident.

On Julia's insistence, Tommy started taking lessons in the English language. The tutor was an elderly lady, risking a jail sentence for private enterprise, but she had little else to live on.

The arrival of the first snow made Julia worried about Tommy's long journeys to and from work but using public transport would have taken him more than an hour each way. She had to trust his cycling skills to keep him safe.

With his keen, inquiring mind Tommy enjoyed the apprenticeship. Once a week, along with a fellow apprentice, he attended Vocational Trade College with emphasis on mathematics, physics and electrical theories. With his previous educational background he found it quite easy. Working on cars, vans, trucks and motorbikes fascinated him, giving him new and more detailed knowledge to boast with at the motorbike club.

1951

He left the customary bouquet at the door of his grandmother's home but did not ring the bell. The phone rang shortly after Tommy arrived back home. It was Karl.

'Tommy, I owe you an apology. I hope you will accept it.'

Tommy was curious but also cautious. 'Why do you owe me an apology?'

'I shouldn't have misjudged you on the allegations of somebody else. Also, I should have accepted your explanation instead of ignoring it.'

'That was last year, Karl! What made you see the truth now, after all this time?'

'Bear with me and I'll explain. Some time ago we met another couple at a party, Árpád and Rosie, and began going out in a foursome. Árpád phoned me recently saying that Éva asked him to meet her, just like you had explained in your letter but he told her he wanted to think about it and rang me. I told him what took place before and asked him to agree to a meeting with her. Éva told me the same story as before, that some men cannot resist her and I ought to know that Árpád asked her for a date. I must admit I was really hurt by her deception and the realisation of how unfairly treated you must have felt. When the two of them met up I came up behind Árpád but instead of reprehending him, I told Éva that my friends mean more to me than she does. By the way, I told my family the whole story so they know that you are not guilty of any wrongdoing. Can we be friends again, please?'

Tommy perceived the request was genuine and he missed Karl. 'As far as I am concerned we had never stopped being friends. It is up to you.'

Julia, nicely dressed and made up, went out on one of her occasional jaunts leaving Edith and Tommy alone. Outside, the rain was coming down heavier and heavier. Standing side-by-side at the balcony door they gazed at the deluge in silence as darkness slowly enveloped the view. In the comforting security and atmosphere of his home Tommy turned Edith towards him and kissed her gently. The young girl responded eagerly. With his passion rising he placed his hand over her small breast. Edith didn't object, it wasn't the first time she had allowed him to go so far. Moments later she became aware of buttons of her blouse being undone one by one. She could have and should have stopped him, yet somehow she did not want to. This was new and thrilling. Tommy's warm hand cupping her breast and the anticipation had eliminated her misgivings. She kissed him with passion and they made love silently and a bit clumsily on the parquet floor. It was the first time for both of them. Holding on to each other afterwards Tommy said, 'I couldn't stop myself, I am sorry.'

'Don't be, it was wonderful.' As Edith gave him a long and gentle kiss, he remembered the one and only time he had kissed Judy and felt some wetness behind his closed eyelids.

Judy was preparing a special meal, it was her first wedding anniversary. Her husband Adam had left the Pioneer Movement for the Ministry of Interior but would not reveal in what capacity. Judy had hoped it was not the dreaded ÁVO. She had become an ardent socialist but recent directives of the Party and some events troubled her conscience.

Arriving home and confronted with the beautifully laid table with candles either side and a bottle of wine at the centre, Adam asked what it was all in aid of. Her husband, forgetting the significance of the day, had hurt Judy but she tried not to show it.

'It's our wedding anniversary. We got married a year ago today!'

'Oh what a load of garbage, stinks of religious upbringing. Come on, serve the nosh!'

Adam ate hurriedly, poured himself a glass of wine, drank it and said, 'I am going out. Don't wait up for me.'

When she heard the front door closing behind her husband, Judy pushed away her dinner plate and resting her head on her arms, wept.

The day of the Beginners' Race approaching, most of the lads spent all their free time improving the performance of their second-hand motorbikes, the only sort the State-owned club could provide for riders with no proven record.

The first task, to improve the performance of the two-stroke engines, was the polishing of the inlet and outlet ports of the cylinder to a mirror finish. After that the carburettors and the exhaust system had to be modified and different sprocket ratios experimented with. Running short of time, three pals, Tommy, Gyula, and Veres (it was his surname but as it meant a certain shade of red, and he had ginger hair, the name stuck) decided to carry on building their bikes through the night. Tommy telephoned his mother who informed Katie Kéry. The two mothers looked at each other with what-can-we-do-to-stop-them expressions.

Helping each other all the time, the three lads had their bikes ready for road trial at the City Park.

'Let's get going,' said Veres.

'Not yet,' Tommy objected, 'our bikes have no lights fitted.'

They sat chatting, waiting for dawn to break. The City Park was quite close to the club's premises, a straight run along Szondy Street just around the corner. Finally, it was time to go.

Deemed to be excess weight, the kick-start leavers had been removed so they push-started the bikes, Gyula in front, Tommy next, Veres behind him. Turning right into Szondy Street with the engines still cold Tommy's bike almost stalled and he fell behind. Veres slowed down in case Tommy needed help but after some spluttering the engine recovered.

Gyula in the meantime approached Isabella Street, the first crossing and a main thoroughfare, unaware of the gap that had opened up between him and his two pals. He slowed almost to a halt and looked both ways because it was expected from the leader of a convoy to give signals, warning others behind of approaching traffic. Apart from a bus waiting at the bus stop there was no other vehicle in sight so he crossed over without signalling.

The bus driver swore. Well behind schedule due to an unavoidable late start and belting along his route to catch up, he had to stop here for just a single passenger. He pulled away from the stop, changed into second gear and pressed the accelerator pedal to the floor. With only three people on board the powerful diesel engine responded with immediate acceleration.

An incredible scene unfolded for Veres. Entering the crossing ahead of him Tommy suddenly let go both handlebars and raising his right leg over them tried to turn sideways in the saddle. Then a speeding bus appeared from the right hitting the bike and sending Tommy flying beyond the corner out of sight. Veres almost ran into the side of the bus as it sped across his path with tyres screeching, coming to a halt at the left-hand side of the crossing.

Gyula heard the sound of the collision and stopped at once. Glancing over his shoulder he saw the rear end of the bus sticking out at the crossroad behind him, a woman at the corner of the road screaming hysterically, and Veres dismounting from his bike. His heart almost stopped. He turned around and arriving at the scene found Veres kneeling beside Tommy's body on the road, not knowing what to do. The conductor and a passenger alighted from the bus and ran to his injured friend. The driver remained in his cab with his head buried in his arms across the steering wheel.

Gyula kept his head, rode back to the club and called an ambulance. Then, with his hand shaking, he dialled Julia's number.

The telephone ringing shortly before seven in the morning, at her habitual and regular time in the bathroom, could not be Tommy. Must be a wrong number, Julia assumed. Let it ring. But it kept ringing relentlessly. Annoyed by the shrill tone she went to pick up the receiver while still in her underwear.

'Hello, 457-209.' She took several seconds to identify the caller because Gyula was close to tears.

'Gyula, what's the matter?"

'Tommy was involved in an accident.'

'What sort of accident?' Gyula was unable to reply.

'Gyula! Answer me! What sort of an accident?'

'He collided with a bus.'

'For God's sake, is he badly hurt?'

'I think so, I am not sure.'

'What do you mean you are not sure? Didn't you *look?*'

'No, I didn't. I called an ambulance before calling you.'

Julia realised that the young lad has done the right thing and was obviously shocked. She tried to calm her fears.

'Can you tell me what happened?'

'He was hit by a bus.'

'Is he conscious?'

'No, he isn't.'

'Tell me Gyula, is he alive?'

Gyula's reply was hardly audible. 'I don't know.'

'Calm down, Gyula. I know you must be very upset. Has the ambulance been yet?'

'I don't think so, I have only just called them.'

'Gyula, go back and find out where they are going to take him and ring me immediately. Will you do that?'

'Of course I will.'

Julia replaced the receiver of the telephone, her whole body shaking. My son, she reflected, my only son, the son I adore is injured or dying and I cannot be with him. First you robbed me of my husband, God, and I believed that you had punished me unjustly. Now you are after my son! This is not just punishment. This is merciless torture. What sort of a God are you? How can you call yourself just?

Two older bikers, also working through the night, had heard Gyula returning and calling for an ambulance. When he put the phone down they followed him to the scene of the accident. They found Veres holding Tommy's wrist, checking his pulse. Blood was trickling out of Tommy's nose and ear and his left arm was badly grazed by sliding along on the road. Other than that he seemed to have no obvious or visible injury.

Gyula walked over to the bus. The motorbike jammed underneath and dragged along by the huge bumper was a crumpled wreck. The aluminium radiator grill above it bore the impression of Tommy's head and body and the sight of that made Gyula tremble.

'I saw him raising his right leg over the handlebars,' Veres told Gyula, ashen-faced. 'Had he not done that he wouldn't have it now.'

The ambulance had arrived. The ambulance men surveyed the scene and examined Tommy, thrown so far away by the impact.

'He's had it,' said the older one. 'Transporting cadavers in an ambulance is strictly forbidden. I'll send the Corpse Carrier over when we get back.'

Veres stood up. 'He isn't dead yet! Feel his pulse.'

'If he isn't he will be, any moment now. I should know, I have tried to save quite a few like him during my twenty-three years in the service.' He was unaware of the two older bikers standing behind him.

'Take him immediately!' said the taller one of the two menacingly. 'Or the pair of you will finish up with numerous fractures and I will drive you to a hospital a hundred miles from here, choosing the roughest roads I can find.'

'All right, all right, no need to get excited! If you insist on making him a cripple for the rest of his life, *should he survive that is*, we'll take him to the Accident Hospital.'

Listening to the details from the ambulance men, the young surgeon at the Emergency Unit asked a more experienced senior surgeon, also on duty, for assistance. Carefully they undressed the unconscious lad and placed him under the X-ray equipment. The senior surgeon, looking at the image of the young man's head, observed, 'There is no obvious damage to his cranium, although I think I detect a crack.' He pointed to the X-ray picture on the screen. 'There, can you see it? Good. Right then, let's see the rest.' He pulled at the machine, making it glide along the overhead rail and positioned it over the ribcage. 'Shoulders fine, spine and ribs fine, no bleeding in the lungs.' He pulled the machine further along.

'Good heavens!' exclaimed the surgeon. 'He would break all his bones where we can't reach them. Start taking notes, will you please?'

'Yes, of course.'

'Here we go: The right pelvic bone has fractured in two places. Femur undamaged but the head smashed through the *acetabulum* and fragmented it so the cup does not exist any more. The *os pubis* and *os ischii* on the right are both in bits. One wrong move and a fragment will pierce his bladder causing deadly *peritonitis*… Oh dear, this boy will need a miracle…. What a waste of a young, healthy lad… Let's have a look at his legs… No, I can't see any damage.'

As he was pushing the machine back to the top end he added, 'Apart from that nasty cut below his ankle, but that will not be much of a problem. Did you write it all down?'

'Yes, I did. What shall I do with the patient?'

'Nothing just yet. I'll telephone our "Resident". He has no qualms about treating hopeless cases. This young man has sustained serious damage and I wouldn't like him to die while I'm trying to save him.' He picked up the phone and rang the internal number of the Resident Surgeon.

The 'Resident' was about to have his breakfast in the kitchen of his 6th floor lodgings when the phone rang at a quarter to eight. Having heard the details, he asked his colleague to leave the patient under the X-ray machine so that he could examine the fractures himself. Leaving his breakfast uneaten, he decided not to wait for the lift, and ran down the stairs instead taking them two at the time to the ground floor.

The Resident, Dr J. Manninger, was thirty-one years old. Doing his last term at university in 1942, studying surgery at the Medical Faculty he received his call-up papers. Sent immediately to the Russian front he had gained his surgical skills there with no one to help him or ask advice from, relying on his own judgement when removing bullets and shrapnel, treating burns, mending broken bones. On occasions, amputating a finger or limb when no sutures were available he had no other choice but to heat a piece of metal, a spoon, red-hot to seal off arteries with, like surgeons used to do over a century before him. After his regiment was captured he found conditions in the POW camp just as bad. He had to operate with meagre instruments and use sewing cotton when sutures were unavailable. There was nothing he would not try to save a life. He returned from the POW camp with a wealth of experience and the same attitude, when life is ebbing away there can be no harm in trying to save it.

Taking over from his colleagues in the X-ray room he observed the fractured, fragmented bones. Due to the location and the number of fractures an operation was not feasible. The patient was in shock. Fortunately his heart was still pumping hard. The surgeon then requested a bed be rolled into the X-ray room, fitted with a Kirschner-type traction device, a surgical trolley, and a nurse to assist him.

With the arrival of the equipment, the surgeon and the nurse carefully transferred the lad to the special bed, his leg on the injured right side placed on a purpose-made rest. While the nurse held the leg steady Dr Manninger drilled right through the top of the leg, an inch below the knee. He pushed a shiny metal rod into the small opening until it emerged on the other side and attached to the protruding ends the legs of a U-shaped bracket. A rope connected to the centre of this bracket went over a pulley on top of the high framework at the foot of the bed and had nine kilos of cast iron weights attached to it. The undamaged femur had to be pulled away from the damaged area to allow the bones to heal and to prevent fresh bone tissue from bonding to it.

Aided by the nurse, the surgeon then tried to realign the fractured bones by massaging and manipulating them back to place and away from the bladder, constantly watching the screen of the X-ray machine and ignoring the perspiration running from his brow. Having done all he could, he requested a porter to transfer the bed with his young patient on it to a small, two-bed ward.

Julia took a taxi to the Accident Hospital and was shown into the waiting room. To the young surgeon entering the room her immediate question was, 'Can I see my son?'

'I am afraid not just yet. The Resident, Dr Manninger, a very experienced surgeon is with him, doing all he can.'

'How badly is he injured?'

The young man swallowed before answering, a fact that did not escape Julia.

'Very badly. I'm sorry to say his chances of survival are very slim.'

A seemingly endless and agonising time later a nurse came to take Julia to her son's bedside.

Tommy was in a two-bed ward, his face washed and his hair combed, looking very peaceful. Sitting there all alone she was glad the other bed was unoccupied. It was better to be on her own at a time like this.

A tall fair-haired man in a white coat and with a reassuring presence entered.

'I am Dr Manninger.'

'Tell me, Dr Manninger, what are my son's chances of survival?'

'I cannot make any promises,' said the surgeon and explained the possibility of a bone fragment piercing the bladder. 'The next ten or twelve days will be critical.'

'What condition will he be in if he survives?'

'There is no sign of brain damage. As for the fractures he sustained I think he will be confined to a wheelchair. I will not deceive you with false hopes. He might, just might, progress to move around on crutches. There are a couple of things in his favour, the physique of a young bull with a heart to match.'

Tommy was in a coma for ten days, occasionally saying incomprehensible things as unconscious people tend to do.

'Once or twice he called out for Judy,' a helpful nurse said trying to reassure Julia. She burst into tears thinking, he is not asking for me, his mother. He wants Judy!

The nurse who had assisted the Resident Surgeon in saving Tommy's life was one of the team looking after him. She described to her colleagues the various fractures she had seen on the X-ray machine and Manninger's efforts to save the boy. Most of them had witnessed the young Resident's attempts to save not only lives, but also limbs that some other surgeons would have amputated. The small team of nurses looked after Tommy with added vigilance, probably because he was at the age of seventeen not much more than a child in their eyes and almost all of them had children of their own.

Consciousness returning gradually, confused Tommy a great deal. Strange images appeared in his mind but not for long. Eventually the mental confusion diminished and he became more and more aware of his surroundings and agonising pain. Acknowledging that he was in hospital, he had no idea why or what had happened to him. His last memory was of the three of them push-starting their motorbikes. Something obviously had gone wrong afterwards but what? Had Gyula and Veres been injured as well?

A nurse entering the small ward to monitor his pulse rate and temperature saw his eyes open and a faint smile on his face.

'Hello Tommy, nice to see you coming out of your coma! How do you feel?'

Tommy took a deep breath and his face contorted in pain. His expanding chest moved the lower part of his body and that hurt. The nurse saw the light fade out of his eyes as he lost consciousness again.

Julia, visiting later in the evening, heard the good news and she hoped Tommy would come round while she was there, but in vain.

Next morning Tommy was awake when two nurses entered to help him with his bodily functions and then wash him. So far he was given fluids only with the aid of small, teapot-shaped vessels, the long curved spouts designed for the purpose. The liquid nourishment passed through his system easily, minimising abdominal muscle activity.

The nurses saw his unease and explained that he had no need to be embarrassed, it was part and parcel of nursing to deal with bodily functions and if he tried to do it on his own he could seriously damage himself.

He was fully awake when Julia arrived and she had to stop herself from cuddling him. She kept stroking Tommy's hair, unable to speak. Tommy spoke slowly to avoid taking in too much air.

'Mum, I've been told that I was in a collision with a bus. I have no recollection of it. I'm sorry for causing you more problems.'

'Never mind that, just get better. Are you in a lot of pain?'

'Not a lot, I can bear it.'

Julia was holding his hand when Tommy fell asleep again. She left quietly, contemplating the prospects of Tommy in a wheelchair in their seventh floor home, with no access to the lift.

Tommy gained strength rapidly and had many visitors but not Judy, she did not hear of the accident. One very talkative visitor made a remark that it would not be long before Tommy could leave hospital and roam around in his wheelchair.

Visiting time over, he had a lot to mull over and reflect on. Tommy refused to contemplate life in a wheelchair – he would rather die. The more he thought about it the more resolute he was. He would not be a burden on anyone and he had no wish to go on living if he could not ride his beloved bicycle.

His leg was on a leg rest, the thigh in an upward angle aligned with the rope going over the pulley, the leg from the knee down lay on the horizontal part. The shiny rod through his leg did not really bother him any more, provided the pulling force was equal at both ends. It only caused excruciating pain when only one end got accidentally pushed or knocked. He had been like that for three weeks and never moved his leg. He tried to pull the leg towards his shoulder carefully, fearful of pain. The shiny rod caused only slight discomfort but the pelvic area objected strongly and the thigh muscles, having been stretched non-stop by the weights produced no movement. He tried again, helping the muscles in his thigh with both hands placed behind his knee joint, determined to ignore pain. Perspiration saturated him but the leg moved a little. Resting for a few moments, he had another go and yet another when the sound of metal striking metal stopped him. Tommy burst out laughing, the cast-iron weights dangling at the end of the rope had struck the framework of the bed.

Dr Manninger came in the following morning on his routine visit and looked at the charts. Temperature, pulse, blood pressure remained normal and steady for over a week. The worst must be over by now.

'How are you, young man?' he asked with a big smile.

'I'm fine, thank you, or so I had been until last night. Is it true that I will spend the rest of my life in a wheelchair?

The surgeon's smile turned into a concerned expression. 'Tommy, I cannot say for certain but that is more than likely. Your injuries were extensive and serious. I cannot give you an accurate prognosis. We shall see how you progress after the traction is removed in about three weeks' time. By the way, after the weekend you will be under the supervision of Dr Árkos for the next two weeks. I'm going on holiday.'

His friends from the neighbourhood, bikers from the club and other visitors meaning well made Tommy dread visiting time. Too many people, some with banal questions, some with forced merriment, some asking him to recall the accident despite being told he had no memory of it. Tommy appreciated the effort and kindness of many but at times it was too much.

Katie and István Kéry proved themselves true friends in the way they supported Julia in her distress. István, a quiet, reserved man was a pillar of strength.

Klára telephoned, telling Julia that some time ago, by an odd coincidence, she had met one of Sándor's clients in a library. The man, older than her, was a widower and had asked her out several times in the last eight months. Recently he had proposed to her and after careful consideration she had accepted. She asked Julia to be one of the witnesses at the registry office. Naturally she agreed and said nothing to Klára about Tommy's accident.

Three days after Dr Manninger started his holidays, Tommy noticed the skin around the shiny rod emerging from the right side of his leg was swollen and tender. Next morning the swelling was larger and pressing it produced pus. He mentioned it to Dr Árkos who said there was nothing to worry about and instructed the nurses to drain it daily. The following day the same thing happened on the other side, so day after day the nurses drained both sides. Tommy was perplexed by it. He had collected countless cuts, grazes, all sorts of injuries during his daring cycling days yet none of them had ever turned septic. He was feeling better and better, had carried on doing the exercises, so this inexplicable nuisance annoyed him.

Judy began to realise that her happiness after marrying Adam had all but disappeared. He worked unusual hours and spoke in gruff sentences.

'Adam, you are pushing yourself too hard. Try to relax a bit.'

'I'm fine. I know what I'm doing. Just leave me be.'

'But you come home so tired that you don't even say "Hello" to me.'

'Is that important? Would you expect me to bow as well?'

The coldness displayed in Adam's replies was enough for Judy. Tears began to emerge.

Dr Manninger returned from his holiday and found his young patient in good spirits.

'Hello Tommy! How are you getting on?'

'Let me show you,' Tommy replied with a mischievous smile and removed the blanket covering him. Grabbing the side rails of the bed to anchor himself he pulled his thigh away from the leg rest as far as he could, three times in a row, pulling the weights up in the process.

'How long have you been doing this?' The surgeon asked with genuine curiosity.

'Since the day you told me that I'll be in a wheelchair.'

The surgeon looked at him with a relieved expression. 'I don't think you'll need one.' His eyes detected the swollen areas surrounding the shiny rod.

'Tommy, how long have the exits of the rod been inflamed?'

'About ten days, the nurses drain them daily.'

'How long? TEN DAYS?!'

'Yes, about that.'

The surgeon pressed the emergency bell. Seconds later a nurse came rushing in.

'Nurse, would you fetch the surgical trolley, hurry please.' The nurse left in a hurry and soon the rattling of the small trolley loaded with surgical apparatus was audible in the corridor. The surgeon held the door open for her.

'Thank you, Nurse. Stay here please, I'll need assistance.'

He looked at the young lad with concern, 'Tommy, this is going to hurt.' Tommy nodded.

Despite being very careful, the clamps of the U-shaped bracket gripping the shiny rod could not be undone without the rod being pushed about. Tommy was grinding his teeth and perspiration formed on his forehead. Finally the clamps were loose and the painful experience was over.

'Nurse, would you please lift up the weights so I can remove the bracket.'

The nurse did as she was asked bringing to an end the lengthy and incessant stretching of thigh muscles. The abrupt ending of the traction gave Tommy the sensation of a steamroller pushing his thigh into his pelvis with ever-increasing pressure. His eyelids squeezed tight, his fists clenched, he let out an almighty agonised scream.

The surgeon had expected the painful reaction to the contracting muscles. He quickly removed the U-shaped bracket and whipped the rod out of the leg.

Opening his eyes as the pain slowly subsided, Tommy observed the surgeon inspecting the rod, his normal amiable expression transforming into an angry one.

'Now take a look at this, Nurse. We are trying to save lives yet we are supplied with substandard material that could kill. This rod had not been manufactured to our specification, the nickel plating is obviously not the required thickness and the steel is not rustproof. Given time, the plasma attacks the nickel and corrodes plain steel. I am amazed that the patient hasn't succumbed to septicaemia!'

'May I have a look please?' Tommy asked.

'Of course you may.' Manninger passed him the rod.

The cause of the surgeon's anger was evident. Both ends of the rod were shiny but in-between only small patches of nickel remained. The section of the rod that was inside his leg had a blackish-brown and uneven surface. Tommy was fascinated. 'May I keep it?'

'Of course you can keep it. We can't use it again, and the rest of our stock will have to be checked.'

As soon as they had left the room Tommy attempted to scratch the sole of his itching foot. Out of action and the circulation restricted by the leg propped up for weeks, the skin on his sole was peeling off like parchment. Immediately he suffered an unexpected, shocking setback; the movement of his hip joint was indeed limited. His knee would not move to his shoulder by a long shot. Despite struggling hard he could not reach his foot, his fingertips could just about reach the middle of his leg. Supporting himself on his elbows Tommy positioned his legs side-by-side and compared them. The difference was quite a blow. Whilst his left foot was at a slight angle leaning to the left, the right foot was pointing outward at forty-five degrees and seemed to be an inch beyond the left foot. Looking at his knees he observed the same dissimilarity. He realised with quite a shock that since his leg and thigh bones had not been fractured the shattered pelvic bones must have rejoined in an incorrect position. The apprehension that he would walk with a pronounced limp for the rest of his life was difficult to accept. Yet walk he would, and reach his foot he would – he was certain of that! He sat up and swung his legs over the side of the bed. Blood rushing into the right foot caused a sharp stab of pain below the ankle on the outside. He was surprised to see a three-inch long scar there, out of sight until now and turning purple from the first real pressure of blood inside it.

The nurse returned to treat the inflamed exit holes below his knee and seeing Tommy sitting at the edge of the bed exclaimed, 'What do you think you are doing, trying to ruin all our efforts and damage yourself? The traction had to be removed ahead of time due to the infection caused by the rusty rod. Don't you dare get out of bed!'

Tommy laughed. 'You don't think I would really do that, do you?'

'Yes I do, and you must not take this lightly. Any damage at this stage could be irreparable.'

A fortnight later, in the last days of October, Tommy walked out of the Accident Hospital on crutches. Julia was overjoyed to have him back home in a better shape than expected and she presented Dr Manninger and his young wife with a set of liqueur glasses and a matching tray. The gift was greatly appreciated and the surgeon told her not to hesitate to contact him for advice.

Following some initial improvement, the rotation of Tommy's hip joint had become more and more restricted despite his exercising it vigorously. By the end of November he had problems sitting down and standing up. Julia telephoned Dr Manninger and he advised her to ask their family doctor to refer Tommy to Rheumatology because his thigh muscles were contracting excessively.

The Rheumatologist concurred with the diagnosis and said Tommy should go to one of the spa-hospitals with natural hot water springs and specialising in the treatment of the joints. The therapy involves immersion in the hot, soothing water for a prescribed duration, combined with exercise and medication. The problem he said was the waiting list in the Social Health Service because Tommy ought to undergo treatment within a week or so. Asked about the consequences if treatment would not be available in such a short time, his reply was horrifying, 'The hip will lock solid.'

The family doctor had tried and failed to have Tommy admitted as a case of emergency. The earliest chance was in March, four months away. Julia dialled Ferie Molnár's home number but it was no longer in existence and his name had disappeared from the telephone directory.

'Asking for help would be preferable on his private line,' Julia said. 'Since I can't do that I will have to telephone him tomorrow at his department in the Ministry of Health, from my workplace.'

Next morning she rang Ferie Molnár's office.

'There is no Comrade Molnár here,' a gruff male voice on the phone said.

'There ought to be. He used to work there at least until two years ago.'

'Oh, you mean *that* Comrade Molnár.'

'I don't know what you mean by saying *"that Comrade Molnár"*. I would like to speak to Comrade Ferenc Molnár about an extremely urgent matter.'

'Yes, I know the person you want but he is no longer at this department. He was promoted to the position of Chief Executive of the Social Health Service quite a while ago. I'll give you his number.'

Julia rang the number. A woman in a callous tone answered and refused her request to speak to the Chief Executive on the grounds that he was a very busy man.

'I appreciate that,' said Julia, 'but the matter is extremely urgent. I am certain that he would find time to talk to me.'

'Oh yes, and three thousand other people,' came the sarcastic response. 'Tell me what you want and I'll try to fit you in.'

'I must talk to him urgently about a private matter.' Julia was curbing her anger, well aware that this was the typical style and standard with which the majority of the regime's rapidly-promoted officials treated the population. 'I'm begging you to put me through to Comrade Molnár.'

'He is extremely busy. I'll tell him you rang. What's your name?'

'Julia Tottis.'

'Thank you. Good bye.' The line went dead.

Julia realised that the woman did not take her telephone number or her address. Evidently, her message was not going to be passed on. Tears of desperation flooded her eyes. Writing to him would be futile, it would be the same hostile woman opening his mail.

At five o'clock the secretary knocked and entered the office of the Chief Executive who was immersed in paperwork. 'I see you are still at it Comrade Molnár.'

'Yes I am and I will be for a couple of hours if not more. I must advise you not to apply for this post should it become vacant,' came the good-humoured reply. 'Anything you wish to discuss?'

'No, nothing I couldn't cope with. Just that I fobbed off a woman who insisted on talking to you. I wonder how she has managed to get hold of this ex-directory number.'

'How do you know it was not something important? We are supposed to *serve* our people. *That is what* socialism *is about*!'

'I can tell when people are wasting our time Comrade, believe me.'

Ferenc Molnár knew that his secretary could be a 'plant', an agent of the ÁVO. The general atmosphere with the population terrorised and afraid to express themselves was not the kind of Socialism he had hoped to see. Even a Chief Executive had to be careful what he said or did.

'I am sure you are right but as a matter of interest what was the woman's name?'

'Julia Tottis.'

The Chief Executive did not react at all to the familiar name. His facial expression did not change and his eyes indicated no sign of recognition.

'You did the right thing, Tilda. The name means nothing to me.' He smiled at his secretary. 'Thank you, I'll see you tomorrow.'

'Good night, Comrade Molnár, I am off home.'

Ferenc Molnár listened to the receding footsteps. The moment he had heard the main office door closing behind his secretary, he reached for the telephone on his desk.

A bed was found for Tommy in a spa-hospital within forty-eight hours. There were hospital beds, and many other things in short supply, available to people willing and able to pay large sums of money to those who expected payment for them and maintained reserves under false pretences for the purpose.

Ferenc Molnár did not pay a penny – he knew the system and its weak points, he only had to put his finger on one.

1952

Tommy made the most of the treatment at the spa-hospital and did not spare himself when exercising the painful joint. He walked out of the hospital in February with a pronounced gait but without crutches, proud of his achievement but not yet satisfied with it. The need was there for further improvements.

Studying for a degree Judy admitted to herself that Adam was not a good husband anymore and her marriage was failing, but she tried to repair the damage. She mentioned on a Sunday morning that they did not go out as a couple any more. Adam came and went at odd times, away for days sometimes. Where has he been on those occasions?

'Why do you need to know?'

'Because we are married. I am your wife.'

'I will remind you of that one day,' Adam said with a sneer. Judy dropped the subject.

Tommy was eager to return to work but the family doctor insisted he would need more time to recuperate. This proved to be a blessing in disguise. While Julia was at work and his friends also, or attending school, he set off for longer and longer walks and tried to run, which he found very awkward on uneven legs. The next challenge would be a critical and important one.

On a bright sunny morning he rolled his bicycle down the fourteen flights of stairs. Then he encountered another disappointment – failing to mount the bike because his hip joint had virtually no movement sideways. He thought he could do it a certain way and was determined to succeed. Positioning the left pedal just beyond the top of its circular path, he stood on it, bent forward to an almost horizontal posture and swung his right leg deftly over the rear wheel before the pedal with his left foot on it descended too far. It worked, but only just.

Although Tommy was not expecting miracles, he found to his regret that pedalling the bike was intensely uncomfortable and painful. Steering the bike to the foot of the bridge he planned to stop at the stone parapet there, leaning against it. That was easier said than done. By the time he arrived there, perspiration ran down his sides in rivulets.

I did not sweat like this after a forty or fifty-mile round trip before, Tommy reflected, resting by the stonework and panting. I have been crippled! What I wouldn't give to wake up from this horrible dream and find myself as I used to be! Tears ran down his face for the first time since the accident. This was no dream.

Collecting himself, he let the bike roll down the sloping road. At the bottom of the slope he turned round and pedalled up again. It was not any easier. He did it once more and arriving back home he put his foot down at the kerbside to steady himself before trying to dismount. Having done that he had a pleasant surprise, he found walking a lot easier. The effect lasted only a few minutes but it encouraged him. He encountered just a little discomfort carrying the bike up to the seventh floor and only stopped once, halfway up. His cycling ability improved bit-by-bit, except getting on and off the bike, and every day he went a little further or covered a route more than once.

Katie kept glancing out the window, waiting for Julia to come home from the office. She intercepted her getting out of the lift at the sixth floor.

'Julia, I must talk to you. Come in please.'

With no idea what the urgency was about, Julia followed her to the kitchen where they sat down. Katie appeared tense and anxious.

'I've been thinking for days whether to say something or keep quiet. The matter is very delicate, but I would feel guilty if something were to happen I could have warned you about.'

'Katie, we have always shared our problems. What could be so unpleasant you and I could not deal with?'

'Well...' she hesitated, '...it's about Tommy.'

'What about him?'

'Julia...' she paused again and then continued, 'I don't know when it started, but several days ago I spotted him on his bike. He's been out on it every day since.'

Julia's eyes widened and the colour drained from her face.

'Julia, please don't punish him,' Katie said, watching her.

'Punish him? Wasn't he punished enough? I just don't know what to do about it. I can't tie him down.' They sat there gazing at each other in silence, both of them aware of the possible and fearful consequences.

Julia stood up. 'Katie, may I use your phone?'

'Of course.'

Julia knew the Accident Hospital's telephone number by heart. She dialled it and asked the switchboard operator to call Dr Manninger. Within two minutes the surgeon answered.

'Hello, Mrs Tottis. What can I do for you?'

'Dr Manninger, I must apologise for this inopportune intrusion, but I am in urgent need of advice.'

'No need to apologise, what's the problem?'

'I have just found out that while I am at work my son is riding his bicycle, apparently every day. Then he carries it up to our home on the seventh floor. I think I must put an immediate stop to this, don't you?'

'No, I do not,' said the surgeon. 'I am aware of the risks and understand your fears and concern but he is pursuing the best exercise there is. I must admit that I would not recommend it to all my patients with his type of injuries but your son is tough. You should be proud of him.'

'Thank you Dr Manninger. I am grateful, you are very kind.'

'Don't mention it, any time. His improvement is very significant for me.'

Julia went home and didn't mention the subject. She was glad she didn't have to because of the changes she had noticed in her son's behaviour and temperament. The good side of his nature remained, he was considerate, helpful, undemanding, and his sense of humour remained just under the surface, ready to pop up. It was the other side that had deteriorated. What used to be his occasional flare-up of quick temper, even if never violent, became frequent. His impatience with himself and his imperfection made him irritable and angry. Julia understood the problem, or so she believed. Her love of Tommy, the son she wanted so much that she risked her life bringing him into the world, would never be affected by his appearance. The true and pure love of a mother prevented her from seeing the real problem.

His lack of height Tommy grudgingly accepted. The pronounced limp, combined with his short stature made him feel sub-standard, damaging his self-confidence. He had suffered another blow – during his stay in hospital Edith and her family moved away.

His friends rallied around coming to play cards, dominoes or a game or two of chess. They often took him to a particular café in the evening where a pianist played modern numbers, or to the cinema, but Tommy could not go on long bicycle tours and he wouldn't go dancing or to the swimming pool where his defects would be far too apparent.

Julia began to shield and protect her son as any mother would, unaware that her protective attitude amounted to curtailing his movements. Robbie noticed this at one of his infrequent visits and asking Julia to have a word in private, admonished her.

'How long are you going to keep your almost eighteen-year-old son tied to your apron strings? What sort of a life is he going to have sitting by your side each and every evening?'

Shortly afterwards Robbie introduced Tommy to his circle of friends and then, on numerous occasions, took him to all sort of events. Some of the parties lasted into the early hours, so, instead of going home Tommy slept in Robbie's tiny, one-roomed lodgings until morning. Bit by bit, as the passing of time diminished the age difference, a deep and genial bond developed between them.

On one of his cycling jaunts Tommy came across a chap working on a motorbike in front of a small workshop. They knew each other slightly as he had been four classes ahead of Tommy at the Cistercian school and for some unknown reason had the nickname of Kleff.

Kleff worked on his own at the tiny company of specialist instrument makers. The man running it, a brilliant designer who used to be the proprietor of the nationalised business, was known as Mr Boss affectionately and Comrade Boss jocularly, although 'Boss' was not his real name.

Kleff did everything himself, producing interesting constructions and pieces from drawings. He invited Tommy to watch him working on a lathe, milling machine, grinder, horizontal planer and a pillar drill, the only one Tommy was familiar with having used one often in his short-lived apprenticeship. The action fascinated Tommy and he asked Mr Boss at the first opportunity to let him drop in and help. Permission granted, he spent several hours there almost every day, sometimes late into the evening when pressure of work made Kleff to stay on. It didn't take long before he was allowed to perform simple jobs on different machines, helping him learn new skills.

The daily cycling routine and lugging the bike up the stairs built up his fitness and improved his mobility. At the end of March, Tommy returned to work and resumed the apprenticeship. He had little difficulty catching up with lessons missed at college by his absence and carried on commuting on his bicycle. The journey took longer than before but not by much.

He placed a bouquet of flowers at his grandmother's door just as he had in previous years.

Adam returned home long after midnight. Judy, tired and sleepy, heard him entering the bedroom. Lying on her side she was facing the other way when he climbed into his bed adjacent to hers, and started making advances.

'Adam, I am sorry. I am very tired. I hope you don't mind but I really don't feel up to it.'

Adam took his hand away and she heard him getting out of bed. A moment later she had the blanket ripped away from her, then she was grabbed by the ankles and dragged face down across the twin beds in one violent movement. Instantly, she felt his knees between hers, forcing them apart.

'Adam, what are you doing?' she pleaded.

'A short while ago you made an issue of you being my wife,' he replied harshly, 'and now I am going to remind you of that fact.'

'No Adam! Please no! NO! NO-O-O!!!' Her piercing scream gave way to silent, tearful torment.

When Adam rolled off her Judy staggered to the bathroom and threw up in the bowl. Then she ran a hot bath. Waiting for the tub to fill, she wanted to cry and relieve the hurt, but no tears would come. Instead of relief, a horrifying prospect occurred to her, having done this once he was bound to try again. How could she prevent it? How could she defend herself?

Immersed in the hot water she felt traumatized and so humiliated, degraded, de-humanised and dirty that she had failed to notice the red hue of the bath water. And when she had noticed, the physical injury was insignificant compared to the emotional harm inflicted on her.

Returning to the bedroom she slipped into bed slowly so not to wake her husband. He had changed a lot but examining the past Judy was aware that, at the time she had refused to admit that there were signs of his ruthless personality. Too late now, having missed her last period unexpectedly. What sort of a father was he going to be? What if he objects to a family? Would he agree to a divorce? Judy remembered her parents begging her not to marry so young. Why had she not listened to them?

Normally, she would fall asleep as her head hit the pillow but now she could not. She kept her eyes closed but sleep would not come. Opening her eyes she could see the dim outlines of the furniture. Being awake in the middle of the night, she pondered, really unusual. No it was not! Not quite. Memories came flooding back; the dining room in the summer of 1946, hoping Tommy had not fallen asleep. Their one and only kiss, with his chest pressing against hers. The Night of Enchantment. She slipped out of bed and going to the bathroom sat on the toilet. Overwhelmed by memories of a pure and genuine love, Judy buried her face in her hands and cried her heart out.

Tommy was stuck with the limp and had to accept that, but his fitness had fully returned. He joined his pals on infrequent bicycle tours. Scarce they had become, because all of them had girlfriends and the boys-only activities progressively diminished. One of Tommy's good traits was his total lack of jealousy of anything or anyone, but the anguish of not having a girlfriend, coupled with the enforced celibacy, was hard to endure.

He spent most evenings at the little workshop. There was plenty to do and he thoroughly enjoyed working on the lathe and the miller. He attended motorbike meetings again with Gyula, and his fellow club members gave him all the encouragement he could have hoped for. When the trainer allowed Tommy to ride again he was thrilled. Julia was unaware of this. Tommy realised that she would be out of her mind with worry if she knew.

At the age of eighteen, all young men received their call-up papers for a couple of years' service in the Army. The only exceptions would be students enrolled at university who only had to serve two months, and individuals unfit for duty. Tommy failed his army medical which was a relief, yet the label, 'Unfit for service' he deemed very distressing.

Eszter remained very friendly every time they had met. Tommy did not know that the pretty young girl was yearning for him to ask her out. He was tempted to ask her for a date but would not dare, he was scared of the likelihood of a rejection.

Shortly after lunch one day in mid-summer, the secretary/typist girl at Tommy's workplace called him to the telephone in her small office.

'It's your mother,' she said. Tommy, concerned about the call, picked up the receiver.

'Hello Mum, is anything wrong?'

'Not with me Tommy, but with a colleague of mine. Seven months ago her husband left her for another woman and just now she was informed that the apartment above hers caught fire this morning. Partly due to the fire, mostly to the amount of water the firemen had doused the flames with, her home is now uninhabitable. I hope you don't mind but I invited her to stay with us for the time being. We're going to her place now to collect some of her things.'

'Fine with me Mum. See you later.'

When Tommy arrived home they were already setting up a bed in the room where Julia had hers. The woman was called Anna. She was of average height with a striking figure, a lovely oval face, auburn hair and nicely formed lips, her grey eyes barely visible due to eyelids puffed up from crying. She hardly touched her food at supper and kept dabbing her eyes to stop the tears emerging.

Next morning Tommy went to the bathroom first at half past six as usual. At seven he set off for work, giving Julia a peck on the cheek as she was coming out of the bathroom.

Anna kept breaking down in tears all morning. The office manager suggested a visit to her doctor before she suffered a total breakdown. The doctor gave her a certificate for nine days to the end of the following week, a prescription for sleeping tablets, and told her to rest as much as she could. In the evening the Kérys invited her to accompany Julia for a game of cards.

Starting early and finishing late, Tommy worked through his lunchtimes almost in a frenzy. He had his first great challenge, rewiring an elderly Opel Olympia. He was expected to find the route of each and every cable and make a diagram of them to help him reproduce the harness, and then reconnect each lead to the part they were supposed to serve. He also had to take note of the thickness, or rating, of each cable. The job had to be finished by Saturday evening, because 'The Union', arranging everyone's holiday period (providing holiday resorts only to people in the favoured 'cadre'), organised his fortnight to start on the following Monday.

At the final test, apart from the reversed connections on the indicator switch and an unconnected interior light, both easily remedied, everything worked. His tutor patting him on this back said, 'Neat job and well done.'

Sunday afternoon, smartly dressed, Tommy went strolling in the Inner City, an area about half a square mile adjacent to the Danube on the Pest side, between the Chain Bridge already reconstructed, and Elisabeth Bridge still in ruins. This elegant quarter, the equivalent of London's Bond Street, Oxford Street, Regent Street and Knightsbridge all rolled into one, had been a popular meeting place on Sundays for friends and strangers for many decades. Tommy was hoping for a chance meeting with a young woman.

Walking past Gerbaud, the confectioners and cafeteria serving all sorts of exquisite cakes, parfaits, sundaes, gateaux and such, at extravagantly high prices even in their nationalised state, he heard his name called. Looking around he failed to spot the caller in the midst of many tables spread out on the wide pavement in front of Gerbaud's, until he heard the call again.

The caller was Ibolya, in the company of her husband and another couple. Ignoring them would have created the impression that he had no manners, so Tommy had no other option but to respond. He was greeted with huge smiles and compelled to take a seat.

After introductions to the other couple, Ibolya ordered a slice of cake and coffee for him, against his protestations. They fired questions at him non-stop, at times even before he had managed to answer the previous one.

The overflowing affection Ibolya had demonstrated, Tommy found repulsive. At a suitable moment he excused himself creating the impression of going to the 'Gents'. Actually, he went searching for the waiter who had served him and he settled his share of the bill. Giving the waiter a generous tip, Tommy pleaded with the man not to forget when calculating the total amount that he had paid for his part. Returning to the table he carried on chatting for a while and then thanked his hosts courteously and departed. With only small change left in his pocket he went to visit Vince.

The telephone rang later that evening. Julia answered it, surprised to hear Ibolya's voice and totally unaware of the episode at Gerbaud's.

'Julia, I don't know what to say.' The sweetness in Ibolya's voice was over-affected. 'At long last we met your son, invited him to our table at Gerbaud's and had a very enjoyable time with him. Settling the bill we have found to our dismay that he had paid the waiter for what *we had ordered for him*. Most peculiar!'

Julia was more than pleased hearing this.

'Ibolya, Tommy is self-reliant and proud just like his father was. He would not accept *handouts.*' She put emphasis on the last word.

'But Julia, my dear, it doesn't make sense! We are his family!'

'I don't think he is aware of that. Since his father died you've never given him a birthday or Christmas present, or his share from his grandfather's legacy.'

The phone was slammed down at the other end. Julia was delighted, the account had been settled.

Tommy's natural in-built alarm clock woke him at half past six, but remembering that it was the first day of his holiday he went back to sleep. He woke again shortly before eight o'clock and took off his pyjamas ready to go to the bathroom, when he recalled that Anna must be around because she was on sick leave. He slipped the trousers back on, opened the door and stepped into the hall just as Anna, unaware of Tommy being at home, came out of the bathroom. She had a pale blue combination slip on, concealing her knickers but providing inadequate cover to her well-formed, ample breasts. She dived back in the bathroom and was so embarrassed that later on when properly dressed she still did not want to leave her room.

Tommy kept calling her, 'Anna, I am sorry if I embarrassed you, it was unintentional. Come into the kitchen I've made you a cup of coffee.' … 'Anna, please come and drink your coffee, don't let it go cold.'

Seated at last in the kitchen, Anna was unable to look at the young man sitting opposite her.

Tommy broke the silence. 'Anna you are very alluring.'

Embarrassed by the genuine compliment of an 18-year-old she blushed to a deep red. 'Tommy I had no idea that you did not go to work.'

'I am glad you didn't, otherwise I would not know how alluring you are.'

'Tommy I beg you to forget it. Should your mother find out she will be offended. I cannot repay her kindness by upsetting her.'

'First of all I cannot forget what happened, it is not possible. Secondly, I am not going to tell Mum about it and I doubt that you would either.'

Anna had to laugh. 'No, I certainly won't tell her but you must pretend it didn't happen. You are eighteen I believe and I am thirty-four. I am too old for you.'

'Your being thirty-four doesn't make you less attractive – and attractive you are. Really!'

Anna blushed again. Tommy's convincing style and his reasoning found their target. Being desired made her feel good, particularly after the rejection she suffered by her husband who had found another woman more appealing. Yet it just wasn't on, it was unthinkable. Propriety had to be observed.

'Tommy,' she said after a short pause, 'you are more than generous with your compliments. Let us agree that what has happened should not have happened.'

'But it did. My only regret is that you are upset about it. That is the last thing you need right now.'

'You are very sweet, very considerate, and very mature.'

Next morning Tommy stayed in bed until he heard Anna coming out of the bathroom and walk down the hall.

Passing her a cup of coffee later on in the kitchen he grinned, 'I didn't wish to embarrass you again but it took a lot of self control.'

Anna giggled. 'You wouldn't have. I wore my dressing gown.' Nevertheless she welcomed the compliment, a boost to her self-confidence.

Tommy spent most of the day at the little workshop. Returning home in the afternoon he found Anna sitting in an armchair by the balcony with the doors wide open and the sun shining in. She didn't stir hearing him enter. Tommy wondered if she was all right and tiptoed over to her. She seemed to be asleep but her face was wet, tears emerging slowly from the corners of her closed eyelids. Tommy sat on the side of the armchair.

'Anna – why the tears?'

'I have some problems. Please do not worry about me.'

'I am not worried I am concerned. I don't like to see you so unhappy.'

'I do not enjoy being unhappy but I have nothing to be happy about right now.'

'I do understand, but your home will be restored, it is just a matter of time.'

'That is only one part of it.'

'What's the other part?'

'The other part is rather personal, it is a problem only I can solve.'

'I assume you remember the proverb: "Shared happiness twice the happiness, shared grief half the grief"?'

Anna opened her eyes and gazed at the young man watching her with a concerned expression. His anxiety is genuine, she concluded.

'Will you promise me to keep it to yourself?'

'You have my word.'

Anna sat silently for some time before unburdening herself. 'I was twenty-three when I married my husband and unaware of his aversion to children. He told me on our honeymoon in no uncertain terms that he did not want any. I had learnt to live with his demand for ten whole years. Then he left me for a woman slightly older than I am with a seven-year-old daughter. I must be very repulsive for him to do such a thing.'

Placing his hand under her chin, Tommy tilted up Anna's head making her look at him.

'You are definitely not repulsive, just a bit silly if you really believe that. I'll make some coffee.' To finish the sentence he bent down and gave Anna a quick kiss on the lips. A quick kiss it was but Anna had the impression that her lips received an electric charge and found herself trembling.

The Kérys came to play cards that evening. Tommy went to see Vince. The young man was too shy to make friends with the opposite sex and was always glad to see

Tommy because Tommy understood his dilemma. The two of them had become firm friends.

The following morning Tommy was waiting for Anna to finish in the bathroom. His imagination was running amok, he could not get Monday morning's scene out of his mind. He heard the bathroom door open and Anna walking along the hall. Her footsteps stopped at the door of his room. There was a pause and then she knocked twice, but before Tommy could respond she had entered, closing the door behind her promptly as if she was afraid of being spotted by someone outside. She was wearing a very seductive, very short combination slip and nothing else. Lifting up the blanket she slipped in beside Tommy.

Their first encounter was explosive and as such it did not last long. Anna had no fulfilment yet she had no regrets either. By the time they dozed off in each other's arms much later she had contentment to justify the gamble she had taken. The young man had proved that she was desirable more than once. She had no reason to question her femininity any more – without it they would not have had the ecstasy and gratification they had enjoyed. She slept with a smile on her face and was the first to wake. Supporting herself on her elbow she gazed at her young lover's muscular arms, the smooth skin and nicely formed lips. Lowering her head she kissed those lips softly in a gesture of thank-you. Tommy responded by pulling her close and returning the kiss with passion arousing her desire. Tenderly she changed her place and made love to him.

Sitting in armchairs side-by-side and holding hands in the warmth of the afternoon, they enjoyed that particular sensation of tiredness that can only be described as a haze enveloping both body and mind. They were deep in thoughts. Anna reflected how keen she had been to marry her fiancé in 1941 just before his call-up in the army and his recent departure humiliating her completely. She was certain she would not have had the courage and confidence to go out with and trust another man for a long time, if ever. In spite of that, this young man seduced her. Or did he make *her* seduce *him* by using gentle words and just one tender kiss? Her husband was never rough, he did not harm her but he was not very gentle and as he was the only man whose bed she had ever shared she could make no comparison until now. She appreciated that the affair could not be described as love, yet it was not just plain lust either but something in between – the tenderness in their touch, the concern for each other during the moments, minutes, hours of passion proved that.

Tommy's reflections were similar. He experienced a heady attraction mixed with compassion drawing him to Anna. He could not help comparing it to the night in 1946 with Judy. That was truly exceptional. Making love for the first time with Edith also had its allure. The passionate yet tender nature of the last few hours provided yet another kind. What makes it so amazing he asked himself, concluding it was not just the act but also the situation, the individuals and the emotions involved. He turned to Anna, 'I must thank you for a truly wonderful gift.'

'I didn't give you anything you couldn't have had from another woman or girl.'

'You are mistaken. What you gave me nobody else could have given, only you. To me it is very precious.'

The following days could only be described as an idyllic honeymoon except they could not go out and be seen together. They were painfully aware on Saturday, the last working day of the six-day week, that their short and sizzling affair had run its course. Anna would go back to work on Monday. An unexpected chance for a few extra hours offered itself in the evening when Julia went out nicely dressed and made up. Tommy assumed that she was going to a theatre or a concert.

Sunday evening Julia was off to the Kérys to play cards. Anna asked to be excused, she was going for a walk. Tommy was reading a book.

'What are you reading this time?' Julia asked.

' "*My Son, My Son*", by Howard Spring.'

'That is a fascinating story about too much love given to a child, ruining his personality and character.'

'Is that why I get virtually no love at all?' Tommy asked with a laugh.

'The result justifies the means and methods,' came the riposte, giving Anna a glimpse of the bond between mother and son.

They went off together, but Anna returned within a short time to spend her last evening with Tommy.

'I haven't seen much of Gyula lately,' Julia said. They carried on with small talk during card games.

'He is head over heels in love with a fifteen-year-old girl,' said Katie. 'He can't leave her alone.'

'They are growing up fast, they aren't children any more,' her husband remarked.

'Do you think Anna is well enough to go back to work?' asked Katie.

'Yes, I think so. She is quite relaxed now. I spotted her a couple of times on the balcony looking around with a smile on her face. Having a break seems to have done the trick.'

'Nice to hear.' István was rearranging the cards in his hand. 'Has Tommy also got a smile on his face?'

The implication hit Julia hard. Her love for the son she had risked her life for and almost lost in 1944, and once again in the previous autumn, turned possessive. She could not face losing him to another woman.

'István, what are you saying? She is almost twice his age!'

He looked at Julia. 'She also happens to be a very attractive woman.'

Julia's mind was in confusion by the possibility and impropriety of the supposed affair.

'Are you implying the likelihood that Anna would seduce my son?'

'I am not implying anything, but tell me, how long is it since Tommy had a girlfriend?'

Julia found herself confronted with an issue she deliberately avoided and ignored.

'Well, with the accident and recuperation he didn't have a chance. But him and Anna, really, that would be wrong.'

'It would do him no harm. On the contrary. Matter of fact, it could be to her benefit as well.'

Like it or not, Julia had had to admit that István had noticed something she should have – Tommy was at the threshold of manhood. She was torn between her overwhelming maternal love and common sense telling her to control it and accept the fact that Tommy was no longer her little boy.

Sunday morning Anna moved back into her renovated apartment. Having seen no sign of unusual affection displayed between her son and Anna during the week, Julia considered that either there was nothing going on or it was all over and finished.

Judy could not delay telling Adam about her pregnancy any longer, it was beginning to show. She had no idea how he would respond.

Adam did not show any sign of delight in the prospect of becoming a father. Actually, quite the opposite. 'You should have asked me whether I wanted to have children.'

On the first anniversary of his accident Tommy had sent a thank-you note to Dr Manninger and resolved to do that every year.

'Mum, would you mind if I were to leave you on your own tomorrow night?' Tommy asked on a Friday evening, in a tone indicating that there should be no objections to the idea.

'What do you mean by leaving me on my own? Are you going to stay out late?'

'No, Mum. I mean yes Mum, I might not be back before Sunday evening.' Tommy was blushing.

'Are you going to stay at Robbie's?'

'No, Mum.' Tommy said softly.

Julia's heart missed a beat at the realisation that István was right. Tommy had never stayed out overnight before except when staying with Robbie. Images of Anna's contented, happy demeanour at the office since her recent breakdown suddenly made sense. The two of them were lovers after all! Her maternal instincts urged her to say NO! and stop the affair but her conscience warned her of the harm her objection would cause. On the other hand she could see no happy ending or outcome for either of them.

'Are you going to stay with Anna?' she asked with a concerned expression.

'Yes Mum,' Tommy replied still blushing and looking right into her eyes.

'Have you considered the implications of your association?' She was unable to say 'affair'.

'Don't worry Mum, I won't make her pregnant.'

'I sincerely hope not! What I was thinking of was the age difference.'

'Mum, I know it's not an accepted thing but we really get on so well – where is the harm in it?'

'I admit there is no harm in it right now, but with time passing one or both of you are likely to get hurt.'

'You mean one of us may get tired of the other?'

'Either that, or in the event of one of you falling in love with someone else.'

Tommy deliberated the point made before responding.

'Mum, I accept that is possible but tell me, should we break up a happy "association" as you call it on the basis of what might or might not happen in the future a long time from now?'

Julia could not dispute the logic of this. 'No, I'm not suggesting that. I'm only trying to protect you from getting hurt.'

'I appreciate that, Mum, but life is full of hurt and we must accept that.'

He is speaking from experience, Julia had to admit to herself.

'My darling,' Anna said on a Sunday afternoon as the time to part was drawing near. 'I am afraid I cannot see you next weekend.' Her eyes revealed genuine regret.

Tommy looked at her with alarm. 'Why ever not?'

'Don't look so worried! We have been very lucky up to now but next weekend I will be out of action. You do understand that, don't you?'

The relieved look on Tommy's face delighted Anna. She lived with the constant knowledge of having to lose him one day to another, younger woman and was dreading the thought of it.

'Annie, it doesn't matter. We don't have to *do* anything. I enjoy being in your company it is a pleasure just to be with you. We'll go out somewhere.'

She was enthralled by his words. They had started venturing out recently to restaurants and to the occasional show or cinema ignoring the curious glances from other patrons. Actually, they had fun out of the covert looks and furtive whispering by some people when they spotted such.

'Don't look now,' Anna would say, 'but the middle-aged couple at the table on the right are trying to figure out whether we are brother and sister or could I have given birth to you at the age of twelve. They might just conclude that we are lovers and then they could be virtuously disgusted.'

They always found it difficult to stop themselves laughing.

Anna looked at Tommy, cherishing his genuine feelings for her but a line had to be drawn.

'Tommy, I hope you don't mind but I'd prefer to be on my own. It is a very private thing.'

Tommy was late coming home from work on Saturday and Julia was already in the bathroom.

She is going out again, good for her he mused.

Julia, elegantly dressed and looking a lot younger than her age appeared.

'Your supper is prepared. All you have to do is warm it up.'

'Thanks, Mum, enjoy yourself.'

He went to bed early, read a book and eventually fell asleep thinking of Anna. Late in the night Tommy heard his mother returning and making more noise than usual but he went back to sleep. Voices spoken very softly woke him sometime before dawn. One was a male voice, the man was leaving in the darkness of the November morning and Tommy was aghast at the recognition of it. His shock turned to anger as he felt affronted by actions of his mother. Tommy understood and accepted that Julia was not only his mother but also a woman with feelings and emotions. If she had needed a man he would not have objected but doing *'it'* with the father of his best friend was truly unacceptable.

He was in an awful predicament. How was he going to face Gyula and his parents without giving away this terrible secret? His anger was building up fast. Julia's advice: not to take action in anger, was easier said than done. His mother broke the rules and let him down. He wanted to shake her by the shoulders and shout at her, *What have you done*!?

He tried to calm himself but it wasn't easy. Better go for a walk and cool down. He went to the bathroom. Julia in her dressing gown was waiting for him in the hall when he emerged.

'You heard us.' It was not a question.

'Yes, I heard you and I am disgusted by what you have done!' Tommy shouted.

'Calm down Tommy, please. There is no need for you to be hurt and angry.'

He looked at Julia with piercing eyes. 'But *I am* hurt. What did you expect?'

'Please try to understand—'

'Understand what,' Tommy cut her short, 'that you are having an affair with the father of my best friend? What is there to understand? It is totally wrong!'

Julia paused before responding. 'Remember the Latin saying *"Audi alteram partem?"* – *"Listen to the other party"* before making judgement?'

'Yes Mum, I do,' he said with less anger in his voice.

'Well then, listen and I'll explain. I trust you not to reveal it to anyone.'

'I won't.'

Julia inclined her head and, looking at her angry and fuming son, took a deep breath.

'We have been friends for many years but you know that. István started making advances a long time ago and I kept rejecting them despite my own feelings as a woman. Some time later Katie said that she knew of her husband's yearning for me and I was deeply embarrassed. She told me not to be and explained that she loves her husband but she had to give up making love a long time ago because it causes her a lot of pain. She was in tears telling me that she could cope better with her dilemma knowing her husband was having an affair with someone nice instead of the possibility of him visiting prostitutes.'

She paused. 'Tommy, would you object if I were to enjoy a personal, private life on random infrequent occasions?'

Tommy, slightly taller than Julia cupped her face between his hands and kissed her furrowed brow. 'No Mum, I would not object. I'm sorry.'

Acquainted with the situation his anger subsided. The hurt did not.

During the two-day Christmas break, renamed 'Father Winter Days' as everything religious was oppressed and thwarted, Judy asked Adam of his choice of names for their baby.

'I never thought of it,' Adam said. 'Not much point when I didn't even want children.'

Judy was deeply hurt that her husband was not bothered about his child. The child she was carrying.

1953

Judy gave birth to a healthy boy in January but there was no husband pacing up and down in the waiting room anticipating the arrival of his son. She had the baby's name registered as Tamás Bodor. His friends would call him 'Tommy'.

Later that year Judy had a nightmare. In her dream she seemed to have been a patient in hospital and visitors kept coming up to her bed, one by one, looking at her and saying nothing. One was her father with a sad expression on his face, then some strange characters, and then her mother crying into her handkerchief but not talking. Suddenly there was Tommy kissing her on the lips and saying, *'Judy, I love you'*, and then walking away. She wanted to hug him, to return his kiss, and she cried out, 'Tommy! Tommy, please come back!'

She woke up in pain. The pain was real. Adam holding her hair was shaking her head.

'You effing whore! Who's Tommy? Is he the father of your brat? To think I married a trollop like you. I must have been mad!' He slapped her face several times then let her go.

Judy did not cry. She was beyond that by now. To explain would be pointless. He would not believe or understand that something exquisitely beautiful happened to her a long time ago, part of it appearing in her dream.

In the morning Adam packed his belongings and departed without a word. The present situation was for him most advantageous. He had an affair going with another woman for quite a long time and had made a decision recently to leave Judy for her sooner rather than later.

As the weeks passed by following his departure Judy had no idea whether Adam would return – he had taken his door key with him. When a couple of months had passed without Adam making contact she had the locks changed. In the meantime she was contemplating her next step. She did not know what the outcome would be but she had to give it a try.

Tommy recognised Judy's handwriting despite the changes over the years. He stared at the envelope with mixed feelings. Then he slit it open and removed from it the folded letter.

My Dear Tommy,

I know I have no right to ask anything from you, I must have hurt you more than I can imagine.

I am also aware that saying sorry will never be enough, it will not rectify the mistakes I have made. Should you have any feelings left for me would you please come and visit me and my six months old son named after you. I would understand if you chose not to.

You need not worry about my husband, he moved out some time ago.

Judy.

Reading the letter, Tommy truly wished it had not come. The delight and ecstasy of their one kiss was a treasured memory and it was precisely that: a memory. Something in the past that could never and would never come back. Like a beautiful jewel or painting hidden in a buried vault never to be seen again.

He took a deep breath, knocked on the door and Judy opened it within seconds. She must have been waiting in the hall. They looked at each other in silence just like in 1946 taking note of the changes.

She is a trifle buxom, Tommy noticed.

He is smart but still lacking height, observed Judy and stepped aside to let him enter. Noticing Tommy's uneven gait she asked with genuine concern, 'What has happened to you?'

'Nothing much. A motorbike crash two years ago.'

'Oh Tommy, I am so sorry. I had no idea.'

'I know you hadn't. Don't worry about it.'

She made coffee and sat close to him on the settee, giving a chance for their knees to touch, just as they had in 1946. They talked quietly, telling each other the main events and ups and downs of the last few years with total frankness. Tommy had become anguished to the point of being hurt by her account of her disastrous marriage. Had he been given the chance he would have treasured her, body and soul.

Judy sensed Tommy's concern and yearned for him to hold her hand or for any act of tenderness.

Tommy had to fight the temptation to caress her and give Judy a sign that there was a place in his heart for her but he regarded an act like that as cheating on Anna. He could not do that.

Their parting was poignant, lacking a kiss or a caress. They stood facing each other at the open door of the flat, neither of them willing to make a move. Both of them sensed the finality of the last farewell. Tommy noticed that Judy's eyes misted over. Then, with a slight click the door closed.

The reunion saddened Tommy. He would have been more than happy to give Judy another chance and for his feelings to blossom if he did not have his present state of happiness and contentment with Anna.

Judy wept uncontrollably. She had tried to rekindle a flickering flame but she had failed to get it going. The fire of the genuine pure love, once so cosy and warm, her reckless act had snuffed out.

1954

Tommy finished his apprenticeship but did not stay in the trade for long. With the skills he had acquired in the little workshop, he applied for a transfer to Geophysical Measuring Instruments, situated in the vicinity of his previous job at Dráva Street. The 'network of friends' arranged the transfer and he started working there at the beginning of summer as a precision instrument maker. He settled in quickly and enjoyed the work. It was more creative, a lot cleaner, and offered a new challenge.

All went well until the arrival of another unexpected letter. Tommy paid no attention to the handwriting and slit the envelope open, unfolding the letter with curiosity.

Dearest,

I have attempted to talk to you several times recently but lost courage each time to discuss the matter. I am really sorry because I know it will hurt you. It is hurting me more than I can tell.

The purpose of this letter is quite simply a request that you forget me and never visit or call me again. Please do not jump to the conclusion that I have found someone else, that is most unlikely for quite some time having shared my life with you.

The problem I have had to face was that I could no longer deny that I had fallen in love with you and the longer I let it go on the more it will hurt me in the end. You will, I am sure, get over it even if you feel badly hurt right now because you are young.

The time was going to come anyway when you would feel compelled to find someone younger to start a family with, a very natural desire.

*There is nothing left for me to say except to ask you
again not to seek me out in any way or form.*
I have had to do this because I truly love you,
Annie.

Reading the last line Tommy cried out loud, 'I love you too!' realising he had never said it to her and now he never would.

He left work early the following day, pretending to be unwell, bought a beautiful not fully open dark red rose and dropped it through her letterbox without a note of any sort. There was no need to write anything.

Julia asked him after supper whether he had had a disagreement with Anna.

Tommy looked at her with apprehension, 'What makes you think that?'

'The sudden change in her. She has the appearance of living death instead of the bubbling, happy woman she has been for the last two years.'

Tommy left the table and returned with the letter. Julia read it and looked at her son with great understanding.

'What a pity she is so much older. You will be hard pushed to find a nicer person.'

She did not say: I told you so I knew it will end in tears and for that Tommy was profoundly grateful.

The so-called Socialism had turned into a tyranny. Every office and workshop had a person planted there by the State Police, most often under duress to report anyone 'reactionary', meaning critical of the socialist system or the government. Many of those reported had been the victims of personal dislike, nothing else. Fortunately, the volume of information flooding in from this gigantic spy ring was so huge that actually very little got acted upon. Even so, despite lack of evidence, sadistic members of the hated and feared ÁVO had quite frequently tortured people to death. Unable to supply information expected of them because they had no idea what they were supposed to have been guilty of, they either confessed to trumped-up charges or perished.

István Kéry fell foul of this awful practice. His immediate superior, the Chief of Accounts, disappeared with a huge sum of money. The ÁVO arrested István at his home in the middle of the night and after that he was not heard of. His family had not been told where he was taken and why and they cried their eyes out in fear of never seeing him alive again.

Twelve days later he unexpectedly turned up at his own doorstep. He didn't say a word for about three weeks, just sat around all day. There was no sign of maltreatment on him, not a bruise, not a scratch; but when anyone touched him, however gently, he screamed.

This form of torture became known by the general public through a number of people who had experienced it and had never revealed the slightest detail about the kind of ordeal they had endured. István was one of the lucky ones who had survived the 'treatment', although he never ever disclosed what had happened to him either.

The arrests invariably took place after nightfall. Owing to this almost every home had a telephone – no one would go visiting in the evening without announcing their intention beforehand. People committed suicide by jumping to their deaths from fourth or fifth floor windows or by other means just because somebody was knocking on their door or ringing the bell after sunset. There was an underground joke that went:

"Following unexpected knocking on their front door at night, the inhabitants heard somebody shouting through the letterbox, 'This is the concierge! Do not be afraid! There is nothing for you to worry about only the building is on fire!'"

For telling jokes of that kind the ÁVO, the State Police, arrested people and charged them with spreading anti-state propaganda.

Only members of The Party had well-paid jobs. A large number of people joined the Party against their principles just to provide a better existence for their families. From nurseries to universities youngsters were indoctrinated with socialist propaganda. Adults had to attend all sorts of seminars, praising the regime and its directions at their workplace, after hours, 'voluntarily'. In many ways the whole set-up was strangely similar to and no better than the Nazi regime.

The dissent of the population was approaching a crescendo.

1956

In the early hours of 1st January, a bus driven by a man who celebrated the New Year all through the night failed to take the bend at the centre of Margit Bridge, by the slip road leading to Margit Island. The bus crashed through the cast iron railings and plunged into the shallows of the river, instantly killing the driver and conductress. Shortly afterwards a mild earthquake shook the capital and some other parts of the country, a very uncommon occurrence. Bad omens, people said.

Everyone dismissed rumours flying around in October about university students planning a protest march. No sane person would dare take such action in an oppressive regime with methods comparable to the Gestapo. The authorities had the same impression apparently and expected only a small turnout whose participants could easily be dealt with and so they made no effort to intervene or stop it. Their miscalculation became evident on Tuesday, 23rd October, when a huge number of marchers set off carrying national flags with large holes cut in their centres where for many years a Soviet style, hammer-and-sickle style image replaced the 'Shield', the centuries-old emblem of Hungary.

The students intended to deliver a list of fourteen demands to the Houses of Parliament. The marchers proceeded peacefully and in total silence, adding dignity to their action. Their number increased rapidly by people joining in and onlookers kept cheering them on.

By early afternoon the column was so long that the number of people in it was inestimable. The authorities, confused and baffled, had no idea what to do about it so the Deputy Prime Minister made a live broadcast from the central Main Radio Station, denouncing the march.

Residents along the route watching the unusual event from their windows placed their radios on windowsills and turned up the volume so the marchers could hear the broadcast. The Deputy Prime Minister described the marchers as enemies of the socialist state, either Fascists themselves or being paid by Fascist masters from abroad.

This single word was the spark that lit the fuse leading to the powder keg. A large number of marchers enraged by being labelled Fascists, quickly advanced to the radio station trapping the Deputy Prime Minister inside.

The machine-gun-toting bodyguards ordered the crowd to make way, but that was not possible because of the mass of people spreading either way in the narrow street. Someone issued a command and the bodyguards opened fire on people with no weapons other than casual penknives in their possessions. Dozens were injured and some died on the spot before the crowd dispersed, reformed, and then converged at the large army barracks half a mile away on Üllői Road. There they forced their way in as the soldiers within had no intention of shooting their fellow countrymen and armed themselves.

Along with thousands of other people who were at work during the day, Tommy had no idea of the aftermath of the march. Having finished his supper he was sitting by a window reading Louis Bromfield's passionate story, *The Rains in Ranchipur*, when he heard the once-familiar sound of machine-gun fire. Glancing at the peaceful scenery outside he dismissed the possibility of it. The sound of firing was audible again and another burst was heard loud and clear coming from another direction. Tommy closed the book and went out to the balcony, totally unaware that the events unfolding would drastically change the course of his life.

The spontaneous unplanned uprising was successful. By the first week in November the country was free and the fighting ceased. The Soviet army leaders asked for talks at a neutral location to resolve the situation peacefully and the Hungarian army chiefs agreed. The 'talks' lasted as long as it took to have all of them arrested and their leader, Colonel Pál Maléter, executed. While the Hungarian Army and people waited for the outcome of the negotiations, column after column of Soviet tanks poured into the country, just like their German predecessors in March 1944.

The might of the Soviet armoured divisions failed to quell the rebellion of people quickly who, even if only for a few days, had tasted freedom. During the following weeks thousands died on both sides and the damage to Budapest was said to have exceeded the ravages of the siege in 1945.

Destroyed Soviet tanks and damaged buildings

Although the bridges had not been blown up (at this point in time the suspension-type Elisabeth Bridge had not even been re-built), a vast number of apartment blocks had been shot up and burnt out. Many lay in ruins making streets impassable. Some narrow streets like Práter Street had become clogged-up by different means. Convoys of Soviet tanks drove along them to their peril. The defending Hungarians ran up to the one in front and threw Molotov cocktails inside. Some gave their life doing that. The tank stopped and the crew clambering out of the turret in a panic were shot like sitting ducks. The convoy came to a halt. In the meantime the tank at the end of the line received the same treatment. When the crews of the tanks in between emerged from their immobilised vehicles, the furious Hungarians shot them all from second and third floor windows. They took no prisoners.

The abandoned column of tanks remained motionless in those narrow streets for a long time.

People of all ages and in ever increasing numbers risked life and limb at the border with Austria, the only neutral neighbour, in their attempt to escape from the resurgent Soviet tyranny; among them Gyula with his girlfriend and Vince with his first. Tommy refused to leave his mother behind but she kept persuading him that he must give himself a chance for a better future, perhaps in Britain.

On the bright but cold morning of 27th November Tommy made his way to Kelenföld Railway Station hoping a train would show up. Hoping was the right way of describing it – everything was either in chaos or in ruins. The fighting in the capital was over but still raging in some parts of the country.

A train pulled in at around ten. This was its first stop from the Southern Terminal yet defining it as 'full' would have been an understatement. Passengers stood shoulder to shoulder, not only along the passageways but also in the narrow spaces between seated travellers. Some stood on the steps of the carriages hanging on to the handrails. The packed state of the train indicated its destination: Hegyeshalom, a border town just a few miles from freedom in Austria.

His boy-scout haversack dangling from his arm containing change of underwear, shirt, socks, soap, shaving accessories, needle and thread, scissors, his English dictionary, and half a bottle of apricot brandy to keep him warm, Tommy strolled along the train trying to board it somehow.

A sturdy fellow watching his progress from the open window of a carriage jokingly called out, 'What are you looking for? First class?'

'Not really,' Tommy answered cheerfully. 'I can't afford the fare.'

'Give me your haversack.'

Tommy did so and the man passed it on to someone behind him and then leaning out he got hold of Tommy's arms and dragged him through the open window. A good-humoured cheer went up at the unusual method of embarkation and people shuffled to create yet another space in the jam-packed area. Tommy noticed the wide luggage racks holding only small bundles and cases. He asked this helpful friend if he would mind giving him a leg-up. Shifting the luggage, he climbed up and deposited himself on the rack above the window in comfort. To people making fun of his small stature, he said that being short did indeed have its advantages.

The few radio stations still free warned the population that the watchtowers at the border with Austria were manned again and travellers on journeys to border towns intercepted. The Iron Curtain was rapidly descending once more. As the train moved closer and closer to the border region, large numbers of passengers alighted at every stop, starting long journeys on foot along country lanes steering clear of towns and villages to reach the border and freedom. Tommy suspected that people trying to escape in groups would be easily spotted so he decided to go for 'double or nothing' and stay on the train all the way to Hegyeshalom. Even then he would face a five or six-mile trek to reach Austria. The carriage emptying, he descended from the luggage rack.

By the last leg of the journey the carriage contained only three passengers, Tommy being one of them. One of the other two, a man about the age of forty, wandered over for no obvious reason and sat down opposite him observing his tiny haversack. Looking at Tommy he asked straight out, 'Are you trying to cross over?'

Tommy stiffened and replied with defiance, 'What if I am?'

'Have no fear. I live around here and know the area. I'm only trying to help.'

'Sorry.'

'That's all right, I do understand,' said the man and carried on describing a route in detail: how to by-pass the town, which way to go, advising Tommy not to follow the old railway tracks to Austria, the easiest route, because they were under observation. He added that Soviet troops guarded the railway station and told him what he would have to do to avoid arrest. Tommy had no way knowing if the advice was genuine or not but thanked the man for it. The train already decelerating, the man pulled the window down. 'Look out and tell me what you see.'

Sticking his head out into the darkness, Tommy spotted the illuminated station in the distance and a line of soldiers along the platform. 'I see what you mean.'

'Come! There is no time to waste!' Going to the door of the carriage the man opened it and told Tommy to get down to the bottom step. Tommy was scared but did as he was told. The brakes having been applied, the train was slowing down rapidly, the engine far ahead edging into the illuminated area.

'Jump!' the man commanded.

Tommy did, expecting to get hurt but landing on a slightly sloping grassy embankment he only rolled once.

The man had indeed been helpful; everything on the route was exactly as he described it. Plodding across ploughed fields, the town was soon behind Tommy but walking on soft soil was tiresome. The man said he would soon see the lights of the Austrian border town of Nickelsdorf in the distance but a mist had descended. He had to be careful not to wander around in circles so he kept glancing back at the lights of Hegyeshalom behind him. Here in the open the silence was absolute. Trekking across ploughed fields made him feel safe; he could not be seen by anyone he could not see himself except when approaching hedgerows he had to cross.

Infrequently, as time went by he heard gunfire, dogs barking and people shouting in the distance. There was no doubt about the border being guarded again.

Crossing yet another hedgerow he found himself on an unploughed piece of land with stalks of sweetcorn heaped in small scattered piles. Walking on firm ground was a happy relief but short lived. All of a sudden the blinding beam of a searchlight lit up right across his path. Throwing away his haversack, Tommy dropped onto the ground with arms stretched sideways to make himself less visible. The narrow beam of light about three feet above ground level swept over the small piles of stalks moving away from him. A machine gun opened up on his right no more than two hundred yards away. The air was filled with screams of human beings and dogs barking viciously. The beam of light then started to move back. It passed over and above Tommy's prone body, going further back and then returned to its original position just in front and went out. He was not spotted. The words of Sister Zoé sprang into his mind about his guardian angel. I have had quite a few close shaves in my life, perhaps I really do have one, Tommy meditated. In anticipation of the searchlight being switched on again he crawled across the field to the hedgerow at its far side, dragging his haversack beside him.

Some time later Tommy realised that he was spot on guessing his direction in the mist because he had arrived at the actual site of the Iron Curtain. Ahead was a strip of fallow ground, approximately thirty feet wide, covered with freshly dug holes about eighteen inches in diameter, in a zig-zag pattern. Landmines used to be buried there not long ago. The barbed wire fencing had been removed as stated by the free radio stations but they did warn about the minefield – there was no guarantee that every one of them had been found and lifted.

There was no point being scared, he concluded, danger was all around. He took a deep breath and ran across, trying to step near the holes in the ground assuming that there wouldn't have been two landmines buried next to one another. Reaching the other side he stopped and said a short prayer.

Trudging across ploughed fields again for quite a while he detected faint lights in the distance. It took about another hour for Tommy to reach the outskirts of a village. The time on his watch he could just about make out was a few minutes past eleven o'clock. Not knowing where he arrived to, made him fearful that walking in the mist he could have wandered back into Hungary. He had been slogging over rough and muddy ground for about five hours and now he had no idea if it was worth it. However unlikely, he might have gone around in a circle, so he stayed out of sight walking around the village. A wide road and an office block came into view with light coming through some of its windows. Was it the local police or a border guard station, he wondered. He had to find out where he was and so approached carefully, observing a sign of a sort fixed to the wall but with no streetlights to illuminate it Tommy could not make it out without getting closer. Seeing nobody around he cautiously sneaked up to the building.

The oval sign displayed a two-headed eagle and one word: *ZOLL*. Customs. He was in Austria. He kept looking at the sign on the wall and kept asking himself if it was real. Tommy knew it was but it was hard to believe.

He felt liberated and free from a tyrannical regime that enslaved him and attempted to break his spirit but his joy was tinged with sadness. He had paid a high price for liberty having to leave everyone he loved and everything he ever had, behind.

Next morning with the help of the local Red Cross geared up to help the fleeing Hungarians, Tommy was on a train free of charge and taken to a refugee camp in Eisenstadt on the outskirts of Vienna. Before settling down there he exchanged his small amount of Hungarian currency for Austrian schillings and then travelled to Vienna and reported to the British Embassy. His details were taken and they promised to notify him at Eisenstadt.

His next and most important task was to get in touch with Radio Free Europe because they were broadcasting messages of the safe arrival of individual refugees, identified by a codeword or phrase. Leaving Hungary illegally was a serious offence and if the culprit was unavailable the next of kin had had to endure a spell in jail, losing all social and pension credits. Tommy summoned up a certain saying he knew his mother would identify as coming from him and deposited his written message at the radio station.

Two days later in the company of other refugees a train took him to Ostend, where they boarded the ferry *Prince Albert* and landed at Dover on 2nd December at 2 a.m. in the morning. The Army was away at the Suez Canal and, as a temporary measure, the garrison of Connaught Barracks opened its doors for the refugees.

In an unprecedented move the British Government waived immigration rules but Tommy soon found out that the intelligence service was hard at it. His command of the language was good enough for him to become the interpreter of the camp and carrier of information supplied by the man in charge, Brigadier Thompson (Rtd).

Tommy visited the barracks scattered around Dover Castle daily, as a passenger in a military vehicle equipped with a loudspeaker system, carrying information and news for the refugees. He also listened to their problems and needs. In the meantime Home Office personnel interviewed all the refugees and requested that they did not leave the premises before the issue of the identification certificates, booklets actually.

After a week of carrying information, Tommy said to the Brigadier that he was baffled by the disappearance of a man who had approached him at one of the barracks without fail in the first few days, each and every time he went there. The Brigadier asked Tommy to describe the man and he did so.

'You are very observant,' he said with a wry smile, 'I am afraid you will not see him again.'

'Why not?'

'He was not a genuine refugee. He was the commanding officer of a hard-labour type punishment camp for political prisoners in Hungary. Keep this to yourself.'

'What will happen to him?'

'That I am not authorised to tell anyone. Rest assured he will not be harmed.'

Meanwhile, in Budapest the Kérys and Julia listened in a rota system to the constant, endless broadcasts of Radio Free Europe relaying the messages of those who had made it across the border. The large number of them, and because every message was read out twice on two consecutive days, created a huge backlog. Gyula's message was received first as he had left earliest and the Kérys listened to relieve Julia because a week had passed since her son's departure and she was in total despair. Late one night, nine days after Tommy had left home, Julia heard the unmistakably coded message, Tommy's favourite description of himself: *'From the cut-in-half giant to his mother. Destination Great Britain.'* Julia collapsed in her armchair.

Before the identification certificates could be issued, the refugees had had to vacate the barracks due to the British Army's hasty return from the Suez Canal debacle. Quickly and efficiently they had been dispersed to several locations. Tommy, in a group of two hundred and forty refugees finished up in Broomlee Camp, a mile outside the tiny village of West Linton, twenty miles from Edinburgh. It was mid-December and a thick layer of snow covered the Scottish countryside. Broomlee Camp was a summer school camp with no heating except in the communal washroom and the common/dining room. The group of refugees contained a cross section of everyday folk, single men and women, couples and families. Unsurprisingly, nobody complained about the harsh conditions, they didn't seem to matter compared to the feeling of being free from tyranny. Tommy and some other young men made a sport of running in the thick snow from the cold dormitories to the heated washroom every morning, clad only in underpants.

1957

The National Coal Board offered jobs to miners among the refugees, subject to a spell of learning the language at the NCB's expense. Having worked with geological measuring instruments in Budapest, they offered to send Tommy to college provided he would be prepared to work in a coalmine for six months, gaining experience. Consequently, in January they relocated a number of men to a miners' hostel at Falkirk-Laurieston.

The hostel comprised of an office building, a large dining room, a communal washroom and the dormitories – unheated Nissen huts. Just as before, no one complained.

In February the refugees received a bolt from the blue. The National Union of Miners refused to accept foreign labour. The NCB advised the refugees to find jobs and lodgings for themselves.

By way of correspondence, Tommy discovered that a former classmate from the Cistercian school, László Pápay, was already working in West Hartlepool. Tommy got in touch with him and László arranged lodgings. Tommy moved there in early March and found employment as an auto-electrician at Ewart-Parsons Garages.

Julia found life without her son unbearable. She made enquiries about emigrating and discovered that she could leave the country on the grounds of approaching retirement age and because she would vacate her home leaving it fully furnished. The shortage of accommodation, a legacy of the war and the recent fighting was truly chronic – whole families living in each and every room of an apartment or house, sharing the kitchen and the bathroom.

The Kérys implored her not to leave, pointing out how hard it would be at her age to start a new life in a different country without speaking the language, leaving everything and all her friends behind, to no avail. As a last resort István told her that since Tommy had just started creating an existence in England she would be a burden on him. Julia refused to see the logic of this. She could not endure being separated from her cherished son.

With the permission from the Home Office, Julia arrived in October by train, with precious few belongings, hardly more than she could carry. The strict Hungarian emigration rules forbade her to leave with anything more.

At the end of November Tommy, Julia and László Pápay left West Hartlepool for London. Tommy and Julia rented a room in West London and Tommy found a job in a factory, earning wages barely enough to make ends meet. The company of his mother pleased him but being a realist he could see the difficulties and problems he would have to cope with.

He was up to the challenge of creating a new life and existence but even after a year in England the change was rather drastic. He had left behind the country he loved along with all the familiar places he used to go to and effectively lost all his friends. László Pápay was an excellent chap but not one of his circle of long-standing, close friends. Last but not least he missed his bicycle, the one he had modified so many times that it was really special by any standard. No other bike would ever replace it.

Julia for her part also understood, albeit far too late, the enormity of the change she had run headlong into. Sharing a room with her son left her with little privacy.

She had no job to go to and no one to talk to all day. Full of regret for leaving her comfortable home and all her friends behind, her frustration was evident by her daily instructions, arguments, criticism, and demands on Tommy.

Despite their desperate need of income she objected to Tommy working overtime, criticised their accommodation for being digs with shared kitchen and bathroom, and the lack of social life among other things. Determined by nature to succeed she found herself imprisoned by the language barrier.

Searching through newspaper advertisements they came across a vacancy for a lady companion to an elderly spinster, *'Applicant must be educated to a high degree and fluent in French or German language.'*

Julia applied by writing a letter in German, and received a request to make an appearance at an address in Hampstead. Tommy took her there for the interview and three days later a letter arrived addressed to Julia offering her the job that included a room for her, all meals and a good salary. This was a bit of luck, not just financially, but for her personally. As for Tommy, he had to accept that living with his mother was not like it used to be.

Eventually, he gained better employment with higher wages at the Strand Electric & Engineering Company in west London. He also found more suitable lodgings, a room with a built-in kitchenette, in a house converted for the letting of such with three rooms sharing a bathroom on each floor. His fellow tenants were sociable and the house was in a quiet, pleasant location.

Romance was nigh impossible. Even when Tommy had managed to secure a date it did not last long. This was the age of rock'n'roll, way out of his league. Occasionally a girl's parents objected but most of the time the attraction was purely physical. Emotionally he felt nothing, memories of the past kept him tightly shackled.

1959

A tenant moved out of his room and a young woman in her mid-twenties, slim and on the short side, dark hair tied back, dark eyes, accompanied by a frosty demeanour, moved in. She kept herself to herself to the point of being unfriendly, saying 'hello' only if she could not avoid it. Leaving home in the morning about the same time as Tommy, she would walk at a fast pace leaving him behind. When coming up behind Tommy she would cross over to the other side, making it obvious that she did not wish to get acquainted or chat.

She was struggling with a large parcel one morning and Tommy offered to carry it for her. She declined the offer. This was the first time they had actually spoken to each other and her foreign accent was quite pronounced.

Tommy persevered, 'May I ask your name?'

'Maria Rozdonyi.'

Tommy smiled at her. 'Nice name! Shall we carry on speaking English or would you prefer Hungarian?'

She stopped on the spot and stared at him.

'You Hungarian?'

'Me Hungarian.'

For the first time her face broke into a smile, giving Tommy a chance to introduce himself.

Maria was a dressmaker, a very good one at that, employed in the rag trade and in her spare time she undertook alterations and making complete outfits at home, she was always busy. Work seemed to be an obsession with her. Emotionally she would not let anyone near her – she surrounded herself with an invisible brick wall and that in turn had entrapped her own feelings and emotions. She would not ask questions and would not answer many either. Tommy had the impression that he was wasting his time but he liked Maria and persevered.

Bit by bit, by taking her out and listening to her patiently Tommy succeeded in removing some of the 'bricks' and a companionship built up between them. Maria told him that she had left Hungary only because she needed to escape from her domineering mother, yet she regularly sent parcels for her containing many expensive items she could hardly afford. She claimed to have been a laboratory assistant, making Tommy wonder why she was not seeking employment along those lines but trying not to offend her he didn't ask. By simply letting her talk about her past Tommy heard about her father in the army, a casualty of the war.

'My father was such a warm, loving person,' she explained, 'I can't remember him ever being upset or angry. He was the exact opposite of my mum. Mum was often furious and doling out punishment. I was twenty years old when I told Mum that I was going to the theatre with two of my friends, both of them girls. The show finished after ten o'clock and I should have been home by then. I found myself locked out and had had to spend the night in the garden shed.'

Her harsh, strait-laced background demonstrated itself by her turning her face sideways when, several weeks into their friendship Tommy tried to kiss her. Accepting his gentle kiss sometime later, she did not return or respond to it. Tommy had become fond of her, feeling obliged to protect her from harm and he tried to drive away the dark clouds of her past.

In the fullness of time when Julia visited him Tommy introduced Maria to his mother.

At long last they made love, or rather Maria let him make love – she did not participate beyond providing her body. Tommy was intrigued because he certainly was not her first lover and, according to Maria, with her mother insisting on chaperons, she had never had a boyfriend. Prudently, he made no comment and asked no questions. On the second occasion he was in for a surprise because once into the act Maria turned passionate and active. She was a bit of a mystery, Tommy acknowledged.

1960

Tommy visited his mother at the Hampstead address and disclosed that he was considering asking Maria to marry him. Julia had no objections. On the contrary, she said it was time for him to settle down. As an afterthought she asked, 'Are you in love with her?'

'No Mum I'm not but I do like her a lot and there is no one else on the horizon.'

Regarding real love he reflected it had happened only twice in his life: Judy and Annie. From here on he considered the chances of falling in love being nil.

They married in a quiet civil ceremony and went on honeymoon along the South Coast in a second-hand car Tommy had bought, staying in bed-and-breakfast accommodation. It was a happy time for both of them.

Shortly after returning from honeymoon Maria found a nice unfurnished third-floor apartment in a quiet tree-lined street at the Chiswick-Acton border. Tommy opted for the seven-year lease of rental, the longest available. They furnished their first home bit-by-bit with good quality second-hand furniture.

Promotion was offered to Tommy; the Strand Electric & Engineering Company was expanding opening new premises in Kennington, South-East London and he was given the task to help setting it up and training new personnel. A substantial rise in wages covered more than the cost of travelling.

Maria's irregular mood changes perplexed him. Smiling happily in the morning, Tommy found her unfriendly and not willing to communicate in the evening or vice versa. It made no sense. Asking her what the matter was she answered with a single word, 'Nothing.'

'Did I upset you? Have I said or done something wrong?'

'No, just leave me alone!'

The more he tried to find the underlying cause of her unhappiness, the more aggressive she got. Leaving her alone didn't help either. She remained withdrawn and unfriendly for a day or two and then all of a sudden when Tommy got home, or in the morning, she was her happy self again. There was nothing Tommy could do about it but accept her as she was.

To make matters worse it had become increasingly difficult to persuade her to make love. Tommy could not think of a reason for her frequent refusals because she did enjoy the act, on occasions so much that she lost control of herself. Yet she seldom let him share her bed more than once a week, sometimes less. Tommy was getting more and more frustrated by her behaviour and by his own unfulfilled state of desire.

Julia was no help, more like a hindrance. On her visits she went from room to room, kitchen and bathroom included, looking into cupboards and wardrobes. Finding nothing to criticise or very seldom she inundated Maria with advice and instructions even when there was no need for any. Tommy also got his share. Her way was the best and only way. It was an attempt whether she realised it or not to stay in control.

The first sign of the political situation easing up in Hungary, apart from the unrestricted correspondence, was that people could travel to countries outside the Iron Curtain provided a letter of invitation had been sent to them guaranteeing all expenses. However, a next of kin (wife, husband, children) had to stay behind to guarantee the traveller's return.

1961

A letter came from Aunt Helen in February. Hannah had dislocated her ankle several weeks before and a locum doctor put it in plaster. The edge of the plaster rubbed up and grazed her skin. Having suffered from diabetes for over twenty years, the small wounds would not heal.

Tommy had kept his promise and did write to Dr Manninger every year on the anniversary of his accident and sometimes in between. He posted a letter right away asking if it would be possible for the surgeon to visit Hannah to see what could be done.

Dr Manninger, by this time one of Hungary's most respected surgeons, did not reply but another letter arrived from Aunt Helen:

'...there was someone ringing the doorbell at around eight o'clock in the evening. I found a tall and nice-looking man standing there who introduced himself as a doctor somebody, coming to visit Hannah because his friend Tommy asked him to.

Examining the wounds he said that Hannah should be in hospital. The following morning an ambulance turned up and took her to hospital. Latzie is going to visit her every day, the journey is too much for me...'

A fortnight later, Dr Manninger's letter arrived reporting in detail what the problem was and the treatments tried without success. Because the wounds would not heal, the foot was bound to become gangrenous and he would have to amputate. Consequently, it was expected that the stump would not heal either. Tommy replied immediately, thanking the surgeon for all he had done and expressing total confidence in his decision of a suitable course of action.

Four weeks later Hannah was laid to rest. Uncle Latzie with his second wife, and Great Aunt Helen, represented Julia and Tommy. Apart from Robbie who could not be contacted in time – there was no other living relative left.

Dr Manninger wrote, expressing his regret at not being able to save Hannah's life. He concluded his letter: *'There are times when our limited knowledge can go no further.'*

Taking her holidays, Julia came to stay with Tommy and Maria. Tommy sensed the tension at home within a couple of days. By the end of the first week the two women hardly exchanged a word and each of them complained about the other, placing him in a most awkward situation. He tried to reason with each of them to no avail; neither would admit making any mistakes or to make amends.

His exasperated mother and his angry wife confronted Tommy in the hall as he got home from work one evening, both of them speaking at the same time their voices rising, accusing each other. Tommy could only make out that the cause of the quarrel was trivial and he did not want to get involved in the argument. His frustration mounting, he asked himself; How can they do this to me? They must be aware that I cannot possibly take sides. How can they be so selfish? *Selfish.* He shocked himself by grasping the truth. Both his wife and his mother wanted him for themselves only! No sharing or compromise and no apprehension or concern for his feelings.

'Shut up the pair of you!' he heard himself shouting a lot louder than intended. 'I've had enough of your bickering. Both of you running to me for help and protection with only your side of the story. You have started it, you sort it out.'

Maria got into her mood on the spot, her tightly closed lips and facial expression said it all.

Julia retired to her room in a foul mood. Next morning she was up early, packed and ready to leave as Tommy came out of the bathroom.

'I am not staying in this place one moment longer,' she announced with the face of a martyr and walked out without a kiss or a hug for her son.

His mother's behaviour failed to make Tommy feel guilty but it did make him feel awful. His wife did not talk to him for several days which did not help either.

Maria answered the telephone one evening almost two weeks later. 'Tommy, it is your mother.'

'Hello,' he said, taking the receiver.

'Have you no concern for your mother any more?' Julia's tone was grumpy.

'Of course I have.'

'Then why didn't you ring?

'Mum, you left our home with a most discouraging attitude. I had no wish to make you more upset.'

'I was badly hurt and offended.'

'Did you consider how I had felt, constantly being asked for judgement between two people I am equally devoted to? Not even King Solomon would be prepared to offer *himself* to be cut in two halves.'

Peace was restored between Julia and Tommy but he was aware that the tension between his mother and his wife was far from over.

Maria announced in September that she was expecting. The news delighted Tommy. He was looking forward to becoming a father and hoping the baby would have a beneficial effect on his wife. Julia was overjoyed and kept giving advice and instructions what to do and when. She meant well but was oblivious to the effect her overbearing attitude had on the young couple, mostly on Maria.

1962

Tommy received a letter from Dr Manninger, apologising for burdening him with a request. As there were no official channels in Hungary to do business with other than Socialist countries within the Iron Curtain, he had no other option but to ask Tommy for help. He had become involved in surgery of hands and fingers, looking for improvements. The problem he tried to overcome was that rejoining the ends of cut tendons makes them shorter, consequently reducing the movement of the hand or fingers. He had heard about a braided wire developed in Britain, slightly thicker than human hair, which is attached to the ends of the cut tendon bridging the cut, thus the length of the tendon remains the same. He wondered if Tommy could get hold of some.

With the help of the family doctor, Tommy purchased two metres of the wire and posted it hoping it would not get lost en route because it was very expensive.

The reply from the delighted surgeon assured him of the safe arrival of the consignment.

'I am now enabled to restore people's hands so that they can continue working and not left crippled by their injuries,' he wrote.

The Sunday lunch was delicious – Maria was an excellent cook. The salt cellar was out of Tommy's reach. 'Would you pass the sodium chloride darling?'

She looked at him curiously, 'I beg your pardon?'

'Would you please pass the sodium chloride?'

She looked confused. 'I'm sorry, pass what?'

'The sodium chloride,' Tommy said with a grin.

Maria had an uneasy, scared look on her face. 'I don't know what you want.'

'Sodium chloride. *Salt*. I am sorry, I didn't expect that an ex-laboratory assistant would find identifying the substance difficult.'

Her face turned deep red. 'Oh no, of course not. I was just not listening properly.'

There was no doubt that she was telling a lie and Tommy was shaken by it. He had suspected her of lying before and this was positive proof. Something is wrong with my wife, he reflected, and she is carrying our child.

They had applied to the Home Office for naturalisation. The reply informed them that it would take approximately six months before they would know if their application had been accepted for further processing or not. Six months, Tommy pondered, just to find out whether the application could be processed any further didn't seem warranted.

Maria gave birth to a healthy and perfect baby girl in Queen Charlotte's Hospital at the beginning of May – they decided to call the baby Jacqueline. Tommy said that he would like baby Jacqueline, Jackie, baptised into the Church of England instead of following the Roman Catholic faith of her parents. Maria had no objections but when told that preferably both parents but at least one would have to become members of the Church she pulled out. Tommy had spent many hours at the vicarage studying the difference between the two branches of Christianity. In due course, after a blessing by a bishop he was accepted into the Church and shortly afterwards young Jackie was baptised.

The baby had a beneficial effect on the relationship between his wife and his mother he was pleased to see, but Maria's moods kept returning time and time again. Tommy accepted them but had never learnt to live with them. The periods of gloomy silence coupled with not sharing her bed frustrated him increasingly.

'Some days you are happy, other days you are in a mood I cannot bring you out of despite asking and trying to help. I am not keen coming home from work to be confronted with a gloomy face and attitude. At other times it is a pleasure to be with you. Sometimes I think that there are two of you in one body.'

Tommy did not know that his comment was in fact a perception. He lost his patience with Maria more than once and arguments and quarrels started to occur.

With no overheads, Julia saved almost all her salary and offered a sum of money to help with the baby's expenses. Tommy declined her offer saying that young she may look for her age but she would need the money one day because her employer would not live forever.

The notification from the Home Office required all three applicants for naturalisation to be present on the day and time given for a visit from an Inspector by the name of Barlow.

The doorbell rang precisely at the appointed time. The Inspector was tall, smart in appearance and his manner was reassuringly friendly.

'I'm Inspector George Barlow from the Home Office. I believe you are expecting me.'

'Yes we are Inspector, this way please.' Tommy showed him into the living room. 'Would you like a cup of tea or would you prefer coffee?

'Not at the moment if you don't mind. First I would like to have a chat with all three of you.'

The Inspector opened his attaché case and removed three large folders from it containing the particulars of Tommy, Maria, and Julia. He explained that the interview would be informal. Each of them would have to recount their life starting from childhood.

'Where exactly would you like us to start, and at what age?' Tommy asked.

'That's up to you, but start at the early years.'

He turned to Julia first. While she recalled her life in broken English, the Inspector was leafing through the loose sheets in his file. At one point he stopped her.

'Can you tell me which regiment your father served with in the Great War?'

Julia replied that she could not recall the name of the regiment but she remembered that the regiment was garrisoned at the town of Győr.

'That is absolutely right,' said the inspector. 'For your interest your father served with the "21st Jägers" in the then Austro-Hungarian Army.' He asked one more question and closed the folder.

Tommy was next. The Inspector put questions to him too such as the location of the Roman Catholic Cistercian Grammar School he had attended, the name of its headmaster and the name of the trainer at the motorbike club. The questions asked indicated that the Inspector was validating their identity, checking their answers against the information on his files. The vast amount of detail assembled in regard to their past lives and the accuracy of it was incredible. It clearly demonstrated why they have had to wait six months just to get to this point.

'We are doing well,' said the Inspector, 'may I now take up your offer of a cup of coffee?'

'Of course you may. We could do with one too.'

Coffee cups in hand, it was Maria's turn to recount her life, they did not stop for a break. She answered questions confidently at first. In response to whether she had ever been a hospital patient she had become agitated. By gentle prodding the Inspector made her admit that she had been.

'But it was nothing serious,' she said.

He asked her the name of the hospital but Maria could not remember it. He asked her the location of the hospital. She said her memory of it was vague, somewhere in Buda.

Very patiently the Inspector enlightened her, 'It was the József Attila Hospital,' and told her where it was. Maria's face turned deep red and the Inspector asked Tommy if he had any objection to leaving him alone with her.

Out of the room Tommy said to his mother, 'I wonder why Maria was so edgy about that hospital. I've never heard of it,' contemplating that Maria may have had an abortion she did not want him to know about.

'I know why,' Julia said, 'and I am very concerned. The József Attila Hospital is a psychiatric institution for nervous disorders.'

In next to no time the Inspector asked Tommy and Julia to rejoin the interview and everything seemed to be in order with Maria. Then he passed over a newspaper and asked each of them to read a few sentences aloud and explain the meaning of what they have read. He also examined their income and expenditure and thanking the family for the hospitality he received, departed.

Later that day Tommy asked his wife what the inspector wanted to know.

'He was wondering why I keep so many names in my address book.'

Tommy had to accept that his wife was telling a lie. This one was blatantly obvious because the Inspector wouldn't have requested to speak with Maria privately, just to ask about names in her address book. Tommy had caught her telling lies before, most were borderline, difficult to nail down. Lies made him unhappy and distressed. If there is no trust, there is nothing to build on.

In due course, after taking the Oath of Allegiance, they were granted British nationality.

1964

Julia moved in following the death of her employer the old spinster. The tension built up in no time and arguments became frequent. Julia kept complaining about Maria's behaviour, the way she looked after Jackie, the way she dressed and just about everything. While some of her criticism was appropriate the majority of her allegations were exaggerated.

'Mum, would you please stop undermining my marriage.' Tommy asked her many times in the most genuine manner, 'I know Maria has faults but she is my wife and the mother of my daughter. You are not helping with your constant interfering and critical comments.'

Tommy was deeply distressed and hurt by his wife's unexplained moods, her lies, and her playing hard-to-get in the marital bed. He was also troubled by his mother's conduct of not listening to reason and let them be.

Time and again, unable to sleep he was haunted by the memory of that wonderful night in 1946 and the happy times he had had with Anna. They seemed to belong to a different life in another non-existent world.

As for Julia she was only trying to protect her cherished boy regardless whether he needed it or not.

Help came from an unexpected quarter. In her will the old spinster had left Julia a considerable sum of money, the rest of her estate she bequeathed to charity. Financially independent, Julia moved into a small apartment in central London. His mother living on her own played on Tommy's conscience, despite the awareness that it was the best solution for all concerned.

1967

The slow liberalisation of Hungary was gaining momentum. The border with Austria had been opened in the previous year, although strictly controlled. Gyula who had settled in Vienna to finish his university studies visited his parents in Budapest on a regular basis.

Tommy received a letter from Dr Manninger informing him of his forthcoming visit to Great Britain, arranged by the World Health Organisation. He replied immediately offering his hospitality and the surgeon gladly accepted, sparing him from lonely evenings in a hotel.

Day after day the surgeon visited hospitals. The evenings and weekends gave him and Tommy a chance to really get to know each other and the surgeon insisted on being addressed by his Christian name, Jenő.

Tommy had been searching for a property to buy for almost two years without success. Either the deposit asked for was beyond his means or the building was in a very poor state, in need of a large investment. This being the last year of the lease on the apartment, they were facing a sharp increase in rent to renew it. The only solution to the problem was to find employment outside London, away from large towns and cities where property prices would be more affordable.

In the autumn he landed the job of Foreman at Astralux Dynamics, an electrical engineering company in the small rural town of Brightlingsea, about seventy-five miles from London. During his three-month trial period, Tommy travelled back to London on Friday evenings and returned to Brightlingsea where he had lodgings paid for by his new employers late on Sundays. House prices being a lot lower he found a property he could afford to buy in a nice, quiet street and the family settled in quickly – the fresh air, the garden, and rural surroundings suited them well.

Maria was happy with the new place and worked hard to make it a home. Tommy was more than glad about that but painfully aware that the novelty would wear off. Maria quickly grew tired of everything she started or had purchased and once her interest waned she abandoned the matter. There was one exception, Jackie. Maria was a good and caring mother. She loved her daughter, taught her good manners, helped with her homework, and Jackie was always smartly dressed.

Tommy, in contrast, fell out of favour with young Jackie. He asked her to stop spending her pocket money on comics pointing out *Little Women*, *Black Beauty*, *The Famous Five*, *Swallows and Amazons* and Beatrix Potter's books they had bought for her.

'Comics are far from real life and the language they are written in is a nightmare for spelling. If you keep reading them you will never be able to spell properly.'

Yet the comics kept coming. When young Jackie ignored his request for a second time he put his foot down and withdrew the pocket money. Jackie stopped talking to him and two weeks went by with father and little daughter at loggerheads. However, curiosity made Jackie sneak a look at the books on her shelf and she started reading *Black Beauty*.

She lost interest in comics after that, despite the eventual reinstatement of pocket money (including the period of suspension), to the satisfaction of her parents.

Julia visited every fortnight but refused to move out of London. The two women seemed to get on quite well but could not refrain from criticising each other when alone with Tommy.

1970

Plans to visit Hungary finalised, they set off by car in July. The first stop was Aachen in Germany to visit Vince with whom Tommy kept in touch just as he had with Gyula. The next stop was Vienna to spend the night in the home of Gyula and his family before the last 200-mile stage of the journey to Budapest.

In Budapest they stayed with Maria's mother, Margaret, at her small house on the outskirts of the city. She was very talkative and hospitable but her forceful, overbearing character was evident at the first meal by placing more food on their plates when asked not to and frowning when they could not cope with it. Mother and daughter hardly stopped talking and got involved in a heated argument before the day was out.

The following day Margaret introduced them to her neighbours, a couple in their late thirties. The woman, Anikó, had actually grown up there next door to Maria and over cups of coffee they reminisced over old times.

Taking their leave, Tommy allowed the ladies go first and Anikó held on to him.

'You have done a marvellous job. I had never seen Maria so contented. She was always a bag of nerves.' The statement or compliment came as a shock to Tommy, making him wonder how much damage had been done to his wife in her formative years.

Next on the list was Maria's aunt Ilonka, her mother's younger sister, a very bright, lively, straightforward person Tommy enjoyed talking to. She had similar impressions of him and urged them to visit her again before returning to England.

The rest of the holiday they spent almost entirely by visiting. The Kérys received them with genuine affection. Being in their home brought back many memories for Tommy but he declined asking the occupants of the flat on the seventh floor to let him see the place he used to live in with his mother. He realised also that the pangs of homesickness he had experienced many times over the past fourteen years had been relevant to his memory of the area as it used to be. Changes that had taken place in his absence had made the picture in his mind obsolete. The roads were busy. The vast field with the bomb craters had eight and ten-storey apartment blocks built on it, and at the roadside where the well-trodden path leading into its depth had once been an automatic car wash was in operation. It was a bit of a blow finding that the terrain where he had spent so many happy hours on his bike with his friends, and where he used to carry Edith in his arms, had been buried like a corpse and covered with concrete.

They visited relatives, the Manningers, Karl and his wife. Suzy, also married, had a little boy.

They went to see some places out of pure nostalgia. Cousin Robbie was most hospitable. He had a car, an East German Trabant, and insisted taking them to wherever they wished to go.

Robbie took Tommy to the cemetery where, on huge white marble slabs forming a colonnade are the names of those who had perished in the Holocaust.

When Tommy found his father's name carved in the cold white marble under the heading: BUCHENWALD, he wept. Robbie placed an arm around him, but his tears kept flowing.

He recalled the time when as a small boy he watched his father repairing his scooter. He remembered the two of them pedalling hard on the steep gradients of Gellért Hill and then rolling downhill gathering great speed. Then his memory focused on their last time together in the company of Corporal Sulyok and Klára.

At the thought of his father's remains buried in a mass grave somewhere in Germany he sobbed his heart out. He picked up a large smooth pebble from the ground and put it in his pocket to take home to Brightlingsea. A memento. A symbolic gravestone.

The only unpleasant aspect of the holiday was the daily quarrel, often furious, between Maria and her mother who insisted on their permanent re-settling in Hungary.

On the return journey they stayed the night again at Gyula's place before the long drive to the ferry at Ostend.

1975

As the year wore on, Maria had become increasingly irritable to the point of hysteria. She was cross with everyone and everything and even untidy. Items of clothing had been dumped all over the place, shopping not put away, crockery and cutlery left unwashed.

Coming home after working long hours Tommy often found the place in disarray and his gentle questions were met with her curt and angry responses. Unable to fill the kettle on a Sunday morning because the sink was full of unwashed pots and pans he expressed concern about the state of their home. Maria responded by screaming abuse and attacked him, gripping his neck. Tommy could only free himself by slapping her face to stop the fit of hysteria. She collapsed in a heap sobbing. Tommy tried to console her but she repeatedly shoved him away. Hearing the commotion 13-year-old Jackie ran to the kitchen and witnessed the incident.

Next morning, unusually calm and collected, Maria packed a suitcase and announced that she was going away for a while. She refused to disclose for how long or anything about her destination and turned down Tommy's offer to take her to the railway station ten miles away. She went away on her own.

Julia, at the age of seventy-five still very active, offered to take over the household chores. Tommy declined her offer explaining that it would cause more problems by making Maria feel that she was no longer wanted.

Five days later Maria telephoned speaking very quietly. She would not divulge her whereabouts but promised to return soon and two days later she did.

For a week or two she was easy to live with and then her moods returned. Everything was back to 'normal'.

1976

Shortly after their annual summer holiday Tommy received a telephone call from the director of a local company inviting him to his home for a chat. Tommy turned up at the appointed time and after a short chitchat the man offered Tommy the position of Production Manager in his factory. Next, the two of them visited the company's premises. In fact Tommy was being 'poached', industrial slang for being enticed, and that appealed to his self-esteem.

Tommy discussed the offer with his wife. On the one hand he would be leaving a secure job. On the other, at the age of forty-two he should not let such an opportunity pass by because he may never get another chance. Tommy told her that the task was not going to be an easy one. He had seen the premises and had found the place extremely disorganised.

Taking up his new post he faced the greatest challenge in his working life a lot bigger than expected. Starting before seven in the morning and skipping lunch he seldom left the premises before eight in the evening, six days a week sometimes seven, ignoring the frequent nagging pain in his hip.

At home he was constantly under attack which was very unfair and hurtful.

'Oh, you have got home at last,' Maria typically greeted him upon his arrival from work or, 'You are not a husband just a lodger coming home only to eat and sleep,' or, 'The Company is more important to you than your family whom you neglect.'

Sadly, she had never asked him if he was tired or the reason for his long hours at work.

Tommy pleaded with her. 'Remember the saying, *"Behind every successful man stands a supportive woman."* Why are you dragging me down? Give me your backing. I'm not working so hard just for my own benefit.'

He asked Maria about her lack of support more than once but she never answered. Her general disposition had become increasingly unfriendly, difficult and unhelpful, making Tommy feel unwanted and unloved.

His efforts at work did bear fruit. Within two years the workforce more than doubled.

1979

Tommy suggested that instead of all three of them going to Hungary for a fortnight visiting friends and relatives, Maria and Jackie should go for four weeks giving them time to really enjoy themselves.

Jackie was seventeen and had just finished her first year of a two-year course of Catering and Hotel Management at the Colchester Institute.

She was also industrious, working as a shop assistant on Saturdays and one or two evenings a week as a waitress in the restaurant at Jacob's Hall, a 14th century building.

While they were away Tommy worked right through his fortnight's holiday, redecorating the home, painting the woodwork and had two new carpets laid replacing threadbare ones, hoping to please his wife.

Postcards arrived, Jackie describing where they had been, Maria expressing her need for his company and bemoaning the lack of it. Tommy considered her comments rather curious.

Back from holiday which they seemed to have enjoyed very much, Maria was happy. She was very pleased with the fresh look of the woodwork, the new carpets, and was full of anecdotes about the wonderful times both of them have had. She frequently recalled the many instances young men had kept eyeing her in public places like on the beach at Lake Balaton and at dance floors asking her out or asking if she would like to dance, and so on, and so on.

Tommy was mystified. Was Maria trying to make him jealous? That would be pointless and futile. Jealousy was not in his nature. By the second week following their return she had become bitter about something. Tommy leaving early morning and coming home late evening took some time to notice that his wife had turned her ire onto Jackie. She had also started going out in the evenings irregularly at first then more frequently.

On occasions when Jackie was getting ready to go out with her boyfriend Robin, Maria objected loudly. 'That dress is too tight showing too much of your figure.' 'Your skirt is too short are you offering yourself?' 'Your make-up is appropriate for a floozy.'

Tommy tried to reason with her. 'For God's sake, our daughter has turned into a young woman and Robin is beyond reproach, a real gentleman. Don't you realise that you are treating her the same way your mother treated you? Why can't you let her enjoy herself?'

'You have no idea of the dangers a young girl could be in!' Maria screamed at him. 'You are not fit to be a father!'

Maria being absent one evening Tommy asked Jackie if she knew what was going on and why. Jackie poured her heart out – she was most unhappy. Her mother was regularly checking her room with a fine-toothed comb examining the contents of the wardrobe, sideboard, her bank account, and criticising her non-stop.

'Dad, there is something else you ought to know.' Jackie said. 'On the last day of our holiday Mum had an almighty row with her mother. Grandma insisted that we return to live in Hungary and Mum disagreed. They were shouting and screaming at each other to such extent that I had to leave them and went for a walk crying my eyes out.'

Tears began to roll down from the corners of her eyes but she continued. 'Another thing. The young men in Hungary did not ask Mum for a dance or to take her out. Given that I was always in her company they asked Mum if they could dance with *me* or take *me* out.'

Tommy instantly grasped the roots of this latest problem, his wife was jealous of her own daughter who was prettier than she had been in her youth and had a very handsome boyfriend. Due to the volatile state of affairs he had no idea what he could do without inflaming the already strained and tense atmosphere even more. He hugged his daughter. 'Okay my love. Thanks for telling me. I don't know what is wrong with your mother, but something is.'

A new and disturbing feature occurred one evening. A seemingly calm Maria relaxing in an armchair suddenly called out. 'I want to be free. I want to be free!'

Tommy knelt down at her feet and holding her hand asked her what she wanted to be free from. She did not seem to comprehend the question. Her heartrending cry to free herself from something that terrified her continued to happen, yet she could not explain what she was trying to get away from despite gentle questioning by Jackie and Tommy.

Tommy visited their general practitioner, Dr Kerr, and asked him if he would be permitted to say in regard to the doctor-patient confidentiality, whether Maria was suffering from some form of paranoia. Leaning back in his chair and looking at him thoughtfully the doctor replied, 'I cannot deny the possibility of that.'

Judy, tired after a very exhausting day fell into a deep sleep. Hours had passed before the dream she had had at times recurred again, Tommy embracing her saying, 'Judy, I love you,' but in her dream she was dreadfully cold. Tommy's warm lips emphasised the coldness of hers. The dream slowly faded as it always had. The coldness persisted for a while and then it slowly ebbed away.

The situation at home was going from bad to worse. Early one morning without any grounds or provocation Maria threatened to kill herself and Digger, their seven-year-old Irish Setter dog, in an unfamiliar, strange voice. Her face displayed an expression of resentment almost permanently.

'I want a divorce. I demand a divorce!' she declared the same evening, abruptly and in a loud voice.

'Why do you want a divorce, on what grounds, what is your reason for it?'

'On any grounds, grounds do not matter but I want a divorce.'

'Have you thought of the consequences? Our home you and I had worked so hard for would have to be sold so that we could share the proceeds. That would leave both of us with financial problems and Jackie with a very difficult choice to make.'

Tommy noticed that she did not hear his words. Her eyes were glazed and staring.

The demands for a divorce multiplied and Tommy concluded that he might as well agree to it; there was no point carrying on living in an angry, destructive atmosphere. He accompanied Maria to the solicitors and gave his consent to a divorce on any grounds with the exception of adultery or physical violence.

Christmas dinner was consumed in a strained silence. Jackie also realised that saying nothing was the best option. She loved her parents with their faults and imperfections, but her life in the past few months had been an absolute hell. The perpetually tense atmosphere and the quarrels and arguments between the two people closest to her was bad enough – the incessant harassment by her mother she had to put up with lately was becoming unbearable.

After the excellent dessert Jackie had made, Tommy passed a small jewel-box over to Maria containing a gold silhouette style four-leaf clover on a gold chain.

'I hope it will bring you luck.'

Maria shoved a five-pound note across the table. 'Buy yourself what you want.'

Silence ruled once again over lunch on Boxing Day. They were about to leave the table when Maria announced in a belligerent tone, 'I'll make sure you will never see your daughter again! The Court will stop you!'

Tommy was stunned but said nothing. He had failed to notice the shocked expression on Jackie's face.

1980

Tommy engaged a solicitor to protect his interests. The solicitor told him that owing to Jacqueline's eighteenth birthday approaching fast no Court would issue an order to bar him from seeing her.

He had to wait for Maria to be in a calm, peaceful mood to explain what his solicitor had told him. Her reaction was extraordinary. She dropped onto her knees, grabbed his hand with both of hers and began to cry. Tears rolled down her face.

'Please forgive me. I know I was hurting you. I am sorry, I was unable to help it.'

Tommy pulled her to her feet dumbfounded at the sudden, incredible change. Maria promised she would have no more moods and would stop the divorce proceedings. Tommy did not believe any of it, the situation was too unreal, but he was wrong. Next day on Maria's insistence Tommy accompanied her to the solicitors and she stopped the divorce proceedings in his presence.

There was more to come. She changed into a cheerful and pleasant person and a willing and responsive lover. Tommy could neither comprehend nor believe the transformation. Why was the atmosphere at home so unhappy for so many years? Why did Maria behave the way she had for so long? Why had he had to endure a semi-celibate life for nineteen years?

For six whole weeks they enjoyed a very happy time visiting friends at weekends or some evenings, eating out, and a delightful home life. The situation was too good to be true and Tommy had a strong premonition that sooner or later it would come to an end.

Maria got up before him on a Sunday morning in February which was unusual. Tommy needed little sleep and was always first out of the bedroom. He followed as soon as she was out of the bathroom, brushed his teeth, washed and shaved. As he entered the kitchen, one foot still in the hall, Maria screamed at him, 'You are a liar and a cheat. I know you have lover and I know who that is!'

Despite her angry, contorted face Tommy could not stop himself laughing.

'What *are you* talking about? In the last six weeks we have made love at least five times each week sometimes twice a night. I am forty-five years old for heavens' sake! Who do you think I am, Superstud?'

'Don't try to deny it I know you are lying! Do you think I don't know where you are when you are not at home?'

There was no way convincing her that, apart from being at work, he was not out of her sight long enough to justify her suspicions. The illusion of tranquillity was truly dead and buried and the bad times had returned with a vengeance.

Jackie, still in bed at that time on a Sunday morning and hearing her mother's loud and appalling accusations, pulled the blanket over her head. It didn't help. The heated exchange remained clearly audible.

Tommy and Jackie consulted Dr Kerr about Maria's behaviour, asking for help and advice.

'I am afraid your wife's behaviour, its pattern, is typical of people with her condition'. The doctor explained. 'They are perfectly all right while they are taking their medication regularly. Regrettably, and almost without exception, when feeling well they cease taking the pills and that leads to an inevitable relapse. The only help or solution I can offer is sectioning her to hospital. She would only be released when she regained her stability and readmitted when necessary.'

Father and daughter exchanged glances, neither of them was prepared to do that to her.

Maria then made their lives even more difficult. First she refused to take Digger for walks which meant that Tommy had to get up and leave home half an hour earlier to take the dog to the nearby fields and from there to the company car park. Tethered on a long lead to the door handle of the car's open rear door the dog was quite content to wait for his master and for his evening walk before going home again.

Next, despite working only part-time, Maria refused to cook, wash, or even shop for them. What's more, she set up enclosures in the pantry and in the fridge for her own foodstuff.

A young female employee confided in Tommy with a personal problem and he realised he had neglected to monitor his daughter's progress to womanhood. He had no idea what she may or may not have learnt from her mother. He was accustomed to young women employees coming into his office and crying on his shoulder. It was an almost weekly occurrence. Chastity was no longer a virtue. Girls were daring each other to 'get done'. Every now and then a girl would ask him what she should do when her boyfriend wouldn't take no for an answer and saying that 'if you don't do it, you don't love me'.

Occasionally girls in their late teens fell pregnant and were terrified of their parents' reaction. Some had also found out the hard way that the boyfriend responsible refused to accept responsibility for the baby growing in their womb.

Tommy chose his moment carefully. Maria was out somewhere and he and Jackie had been chatting while preparing tea. Turning his daughter toward himself and looking at her, he gently popped the question, 'Jackie, have you made love yet?'

Jackie's face turned scarlet. 'No, Dad. Not yet.'

Tommy explained his reasons for asking such a pointed question and Jackie admitted to being teased at college as the 'last one out'.

'What would you do if you were to find yourself in a romantic situation – Robin making advances that come naturally to young people?'

'I don't know Dad,' she said still blushing.

Tommy involved her in a lengthy and frank discussion about ovulation, its cycle, the most unsafe time of it, and the eventual option of going on the Pill, hoping to build up her confidence in him. Then he explained, 'Regarding those who go for it just for the experience, bear in mind that any two people can have sex but it will amount to no more than a form of bodily function. Only people with an emotional bond enjoy the true delights of making love.'

Maria's exclamations of wanting to be free persisted but she could not explain the meaning of them. She ignored Tommy's advice and pleadings to stop persecuting their daughter. When Jackie could not find her favourite scarf she received a vicious verbal attack for being untidy.

The same had happened to an antique book Tommy had acquired: *Goethe und Schiller* printed in 1851 in gothic German and bearing a mauve-coloured library stamp on the inside cover: Bibliothek Hügel. The book disappeared without a trace. Maria had no idea where it might be. Tommy either had lost it because he was untidy or had lent it to somebody. Tommy knew he had done neither.

Living under one roof was becoming very stressful. Maria was constantly withdrawn and antagonistic, wearing her dark tinted spectacles all day long indoors and out. Only her excursions most evenings brought father and daughter some relief.

'Dad,' Jackie said one of those evenings, 'I know this is going to hurt you and I am very, very sorry but I can't take any more of this. I'm going to move out.'

Tommy begged her to consider the consequences of her planned move. She would have to give up her studies and find a job only months before gaining her diploma. He could not say any more; the thought of his daughter leaving home and ruining her future was too much. At that moment he had reached the point of the 'glass being full'. Despite trying hard to maintain his dignity as a father he broke down.

Jackie watched him with alarm. She had seen her father upset, angry, received his hard-hitting disapproval on occasions but had never seen him like this. She embraced her father and held his head to her shoulder.

'Don't cry Dad, please don't cry. Calm down Dad, calm down please. I didn't realise how much my leaving home would hurt you. I won't leave, I promise. Please Dad stop crying.'

Regaining some control over his emotions Tommy produced a hand-written letter from his pocket given to him by a young woman at the company. She had received support and guidance from him in the aftermath of a truly dreadful and horrifying experience she had endured and had to learn to live with for the rest of her life. The letter was very genuine, written from the heart, expressing her thanks and declaring her love for Tommy.

Jackie read it and said, 'I am glad someone loves you Dad, you deserve it.'

Jackie was unaware of the effect the letter from the young woman, only nineteen years old, had on Tommy. He knew the girl's letter was genuine and the temptation to receive love and loving, emotional and physical, traits he hadn't had for many years was overwhelming. Yet he had to resist and stand firm against the allure and temptation of an affair with someone only eighteen months older than his own daughter and working under his care. The happiness they could share would probably be ecstatic and delightful but very short lived. It was not to be.

The first time he found Maria in a quiet mood Tommy told her about Jackie's intentions of leaving home because of her harassment. He spoke to her gently and quietly.

'I have tried to please you. I have put up with your moods and tantrums for almost twenty years and all I've had in return was heartache. Jackie told me about the awful row you had with your mother last year but you came back as a happy woman. Since then though you have made all our lives a living hell including your own. Our daughter was planning to throw away her future because of your behaviour and that is the last straw. She will leave anyway after her final exams in four months' time and after that there will be no more purpose for us to carry on with this marriage. All your promises three months ago were broken in six weeks. There is no future in us staying married. I want you to know that I am going to start divorce proceedings against you.'

Maria did not respond and her expression did not change. She did not utter a word.

An acquaintance stopped Tommy in the street referring to a forthcoming jumble sale.

'I am rather concerned because your wife keeps turning with more and more items, some I think may be quite valuable. You ought to come and see.'

Tommy said he would rather not. Recovering items donated to a jumble sale would look mean and petty. Bringing them back home would also cause more friction.

Maria was not at home, presumably visiting someone and Jackie had gone to the restaurant at Jacob's Hall when Tommy got back from work. The first task before making tea for himself was to wash up pots and dishes left in the sink. He was drying them when Maria returned unexpectedly and flew into an immediate, vicious rage.

'So now you are trying to make me look lazy, that I leave things dirty!' she screamed and opening the cabinet flung the crockery in one-by-one smashing them and the plates and dishes inside. Tommy hung up the tea towel and walked out of the kitchen.

Lying sleeplessly in bed that night he pondered; Jackie is afraid of being in the kitchen with her mother because the knife rack on the wall is within easy reach. How do I know my wife hasn't got one under her pillow right now? He realised immediately that the prospect of dying did not frighten him at all; it would be a welcome release. For the first time his thoughts turned to suicide and to arrange it like an accident so that Jackie wouldn't realise he had opted out. Thinking of his daughter made him see sense. He could not and must not abandon her, come what may he would have to carry on.

Julia had stopped visiting long before Christmas. Maria went berserk even when she found Tommy talking to his mother on the telephone. To keep in touch he rang her regularly from his office. Julia was as authoritative as ever.

'I told you five years ago when she had left you with no explanation to divorce her. You didn't listen to me! Had you followed my advice you wouldn't be in this mess now!'

'Mum, had I followed your advice when Jackie was thirteen and I was the breadwinner at work all day, who do you think would have got custody of her?'

After a long pause Julia said in a whisper, 'I didn't think of that.'

'I know you didn't, but I did.'

Servicing their car in the garage on a Sunday morning Maria surprised him by popping in.

'Would you like a cup of coffee?' she asked cheerfully.

The offer was totally out of character and the first for many months.

'Yes please if it's no trouble.'

She returned with his mug. Tommy took a sip and the coffee tasted bitter.

'Thanks. It seems that you have been rather generous with the coffee, it tastes very strong.'

'Oh, I am really sorry. I must have put two spoonfuls in absent-mindedly.'

Tommy carried on working, taking the occasional sip. The more he drank the more he detected a bitter, tingling sensation at the outer edges of his tongue. He poured the coffee away.

When the car was ready for a test run, Jackie asked for a lift down town. Tommy dropped her off at the main square, feeling very tired which was not unusual. By the time he parked the car in the garage he was struggling to keep his eyes open. He went indoors, sat in an armchair and instantly fell into a deep sleep.

Waking up late evening his eyelids and all his limbs felt heavy. Jackie said with great concern, 'Dad, you look worn out, you are working much too hard. Shall I make you a sandwich and a cup of coffee?'

'No thanks, I'll make one myself in a few minutes.'

'By the way, Mum was out by the time I'd got back home and she is still out.'

Tommy washed his face with cold water and then made himself a cup of coffee with two heaped spoonfuls of instant coffee powder. The coffee tasted very strong but lacked the tingling bitterness he had experienced earlier. He sat down at his typewriter, fed paper into it and tapped out:

'TO WHOM IT MAY CONCERN'

– followed by the details of the strange tasting coffee and the effects of it.

Next morning he passed the document to Dr Kerr. The doctor read it and looked at him.

'Apparently your wife is trying to treat *you,* for the condition affecting *her*. She is actually transferring her illness to you. In her mind *you are the one* in need of treatment. Let me know if it happens again.'

Tommy's humour surfaced, 'I most certainly will. I'm going to haunt you from my grave.'

Jackie received her diploma and found a job in north-west London with accommodation provided. Maria immediately moved out of the main bedroom and into Jackie's. Having had no marital relations since the end of the 'honeymoon' in February, Tommy was glad to have the bedroom to himself.

The divorce declared absolute, Tommy explained to Maria that he had arranged a second mortgage on the property in order to let her have her half share. She responded screaming that the property would be hers and hers alone because the 'Court' would make it so, and refused to accept that it could not be like that because her wages would not cover the mortgage instalments and her living costs.

A letter from his solicitors at the end of July informed Tommy that:

'...the final settlement in the form of a cheque would be made available to the solicitors of the other party, subject to the other party moving out of the marital home...'

He passed the letter over to Maria. She read it with tears rolling down her face.

'Do you think we could start again?'

Clearly, the enormity of the final stage, the end of her marriage and family life had finally sunk in. Harsh reality shattered her distorted dreams and beliefs but too late by far.

'I don't think so Maria. Not after what we have been through.'

'In that case I think I might return to Hungary.'

'Are you sure? If that is what you really want I'll make enquiries at the Hungarian Embassy.'

There were no more tantrums but Maria still had her dark glasses on indoors and out and going visiting every evening. However, she did not raise her voice or cause an argument any more. About a week later she came up with a suggestion.

'You told me that to repay the second mortgage you would have to get a lodger and probably fit locks on some doors. Could I be your lodger? That would save you from having to fit locks. I'd stay in my room I won't be any bother.'

Deeply moved by the naivety of the request, Tommy gently stroked her face. 'The money I had borrowed was for you to have a home of your own. What would be the point of you paying rent helping me repay the loan if we would still be living together? How would you feel if some time in the future I would bring a woman friend home?'

'I'd lock myself in my room.'

'I couldn't do that to you.'

At the weekend Maria asked if she could take the dog for a walk.

'There is no need for you to ask, of course you can.'

Monday morning at half past seven Tommy was getting ready to leave for work and Maria was not up yet. He knocked on her door half expecting to be shouted at. Not a sound. He knocked again and getting no response entered the room.

Maria was in a deep sleep, try as he might he couldn't wake her. It had happened before. At times she was very difficult to wake. Tommy checked her pulse, breathing and pupils, all normal. He weighed up the situation. The nearest ambulance station being ten miles away and the situation not life-threatening he decided to ring the local surgery.

The early call automatically redirected alerted the new doctor in the partnership of four general practitioners. Tommy explained the situation and the doctor arrived shortly afterwards.

'Apart from being in a deep sleep, I can't find anything wrong with her. I will have to open up the Surgery and check the medication prescribed for her. Just keep an eye on her.'

The doctor departed and Tommy telephoned both his employers and Maria's to inform them of the situation.

The phone rang shortly afterwards, it was Jackie.

'Dad, I called you at your office and they told me you weren't there. That was most unusual, what's going on?' Tommy told her.

'Dad, I'm coming home!'

With time passing he rang the Surgery and asked if Dr Whitney was still there, to be told the doctor had been and gone again. He must be on his way back Tommy concluded and went to check on Maria. She seemed all right but examining her he found that her hands were getting cold. Going to the window in the front room Tommy kept his eyes on the road expecting to see the doctor's car roll up but it did not. He could have been called out to some emergency he pondered. I'll give him a bit more time.

He tried to wake Maria once more without success. Tommy telephoned the Surgery again.

'Could I speak to Dr Kerr please?'

'Dr Kerr is on holiday, I am afraid. Would another doctor do?'

'Yes, of course. Dr Whitney came to see my wife early this morning but he has not returned so far.'

Tommy explained what had taken place and his concern about the unnecessary delay.

'I am sorry but Dr Whitney is not back yet,' said the receptionist. 'As a matter of fact we are unable to contact him. I will ask one of the other partners to look into the matter.'

She rang back some ten minutes later rather agitated. 'Mr Tottis, I'm afraid it doesn't look good at all. I was told to call an ambulance at once. It should be there soon.'

Returning to Maria, Tommy found her trembling and chewing both her lips between her teeth. He dashed to the front door, opened it wide and then ran back to Maria. He prised her mouth open, wedged his thumbs in at the corners to stop the chewing action and to let her breathe freely.

The ambulance men found them like that about twenty minutes later. 'Oh dear! We are in a bad way,' said the one in front. They wrapped her in a blanket and placed her in a wheelchair. Tommy told them that he would follow as soon as his daughter had arrived.

At the hospital a nurse apparently waiting for them at the door of the ward asked if Maria was on a course of anti-depressants. Tommy explained that he had no idea what medication she had been prescribed. Had he found any medication or empty pill bottles he would have called an ambulance immediately.

Maria was lying motionless on her back, her neck and chest the colour of deep purple. Jackie held her hand at one side of the bed and Tommy at the other.

'Jackie, I am really sorry but it does not look good.'

Jackie was crying. Tommy went over to her and wrapping his arms around his daughter tried to comfort her. The nurse offered them a small room for privacy and led them there. After she had gone closing the door behind her father and daughter embraced and wept unashamedly.

Knocking on the door, the nurse entered and informed them that Maria had passed away. Jackie hugged his father and burst into tears again. When she had calmed down a little Tommy asked her if she would like to say a final farewell to her mother. Jackie, her eyes full of tears replied, 'Dad, I can't.'

'I do understand. There is no need to distress yourself but I would like to see her once more.'

'Are you sure you are up to it Mr Tottis?' the nurse asked with a very worried expression.

Tommy smiled at her. 'Thank you for your concern but I am certain I have seen more dead bodies than you have.'

Maria looked relaxed. Tommy was astonished to see a resemblance of a happy expression on her face, something he had not seen for a very long time. He said a prayer for her, kissed her forehead and drew the sign of a cross on it with his finger.

Returning to the small room he said to Jackie, 'I am glad I went to see your mum, she looks happy. I am convinced that what she wanted to free herself from was the other, evil personality inhabiting her mind.'

He started to sob. Jackie hugged him and tried to console him despite tears pouring down her cheeks.

'Dad, it's my fault,' she said and her sobbing shook her body. 'Mum took her life because I had left home. I am the one to blame'.

Tommy placed his hands on Jackie's cheeks and made her look at him. 'Stop thinking that. That is silly. You did not leave home, you have moved to Harrow to take up your new post. Don't ever blame yourself for something you are not guilty of. Your mother was ill and it was the illness that made her end her life.' He hugged her to stop her shaking.

They had been sitting silently for a long time, taking the occasional sip of tea the nurse had brought with no intention to do anything but share each other's company.

The nurse knocked and putting her head around the door asked whether Tommy would be prepared to talk to the Coroner's Investigating Officer who happened to be at the hospital, investigating another death.

'We have to notify him in cases of suicide and certain other deaths.'

'Fine, I'll talk to him.'

The nurse led the way down the corridor to another room. The uniformed officer sitting behind a small desk rose to his feet, introduced himself and offered his condolences. After asking some questions and making notes, he asked if Tommy had any objection to a visit from the local police.

'None at all, as a matter of fact I would like them to be there by the time we get back from here in about three quarters of an hour.'

They were there waiting, Sergeant Robinson from the local police station and a detective in civilian clothing. Tommy let them in and gave them the freedom of the house. He had nothing to hide. A short time later the telephone rang. It was Maria's best friend, Rachel.

'I'm sorry Rachel, she is not in.' Tommy listened to her. 'No, I am afraid she's gone away for a few days. Bye.'

'Who was that, Sir?' the sergeant asked.

'One of her best friends. I couldn't tell her right now.'

'OK Sir.'

A few minutes later the phone rang again and it was Rachel once more, audibly sobbing.

'Hello Rachel, what's the matter?' The unexpected second call took Tommy by surprise.

Sergeant Robinson came to the phone with an inquiring look. Tommy held up the receiver enabling him to listen to the conversation.

'Tommy, I know what happened. I rang Essex County Hospital and they told me.'

'What made you ring the hospital, Rachel?'

'Maria had an appointment there this morning. I thought they had kept her in.'

'An appointment? What for?'

'She told me of a growth in her throat. She was terrified it was cancer.'

'Rachel, I had no knowledge of that.'

'I know that. There was something else you didn't know. I should have told you but Maria made me promise not to.' Her sobbing forced her to stop for a while and then she said haltingly and almost in a whisper, 'Maria had two months' supply of... anti-depressants stashed away... Tommy, I am *so sorry*.'

'Calm down, Rachel. You only did what Maria asked you to do. Don't blame yourself. I promise I won't.'

'Thank you Tommy.' She hung up.

Sergeant Robinson summoned his colleague, the detective, to join him.

'I don't think we need to stay any longer, Sir. Thank you for your co-operation in these sad circumstances.'

The telephone rang in the evening. A woman with a soothing voice from the Samaritans called.

'Very kind of you to call,' Tommy said. 'How did you learn about our tragedy?'

'We have been asked by David Westropp, the Coroner's Investigating Officer to get in touch. He was concerned about you being on your own at a time like this.'

'That was nice of him. I would also like to thank you. Fortunately I have my daughter here with me.'

'Oh, that is good, but call us if you want to talk.'

Tommy realised that the officer, David Westropp, must have made quite a few inquiries in the short time since their meeting at the hospital and appreciated his thoughtfulness. He soon found out that the man was really the proverbial 'friend in need is a friend indeed', very supportive and insisted on being called by his first name. No friends or neighbours turned up for some days but David Westropp had, or telephoned asking questions and offering assistance.

The following Monday morning Tommy received a telephone call from Dr Kerr asking him to visit the Surgery as soon as possible. Tommy dropped in at evening surgery.

The first question the doctor asked him was, 'How are you coping?'

When Tommy assured him that he was all right the doctor asked whether he was going to take legal action against the Practice.

Tommy looked at the man. 'On what grounds?'

'Mr Tottis, my colleague had left you, an unqualified person, in charge of a patient for an indefinite period and he did not return!' The doctor's voice was angry.

'Dr Kerr, I had just divorced my wife. It would be the ultimate of hypocrisy if I were to sue the Practice.'

On his father's insistence Jackie returned to work and Tommy had only Digger for company in the evenings and at weekends. His suffering was not over yet. He received anonymous phone calls and letters full of venom. With the news of Maria's death spreading, some friends had rallied round. Gradually a very painful picture emerged from the few who had realised during the preceding months that the tales Maria kept telling everyone could not be true. In her troubled state of mind she had spread stories about her husband and daughter conspiring against her, that she was going to be thrown out of her home without a penny and how badly treated she had been in the meantime. Some people believed her allegations, despite having heard only her side of a very dubious story.

Father and daughter agreed that the kindest way to inform Maria's mother would be to say that Maria had died of a brain tumour. She was not on the phone but her sister Ilonka was. Tommy rang her with the sad news of his wife's passing away.

'Did she take her own life?' was the immediate question Ilonka asked, startling him.

'Ilonka, what makes you think that?'

'She had tried that once before when she was young. I expected her to succeed one day.'

'Yes, I am afraid she did take her own life. I thought it would be kinder to tell her mother that she had died of a brain tumour.'

'Oh, I agree with you. Mad as my sister is, it was her attitude that made Maria a nervous wreck. On one occasion she locked her out on a cold night just because she was late coming home from the theatre.'

'Maria told me about that,' Tommy said, greatly relieved by Ilonka's reaction. 'I wonder if you would mind throwing some light on something else that had puzzled me for a long time.'

'What is it? Tell me.'

'Maria said that she used to work as a laboratory assistant or technician. Was that true?'

'Oh no, it wasn't. A company producing household chemicals employed her as a packer. The technician bit was just one of her delusions.'

Tommy received notification of the forthcoming date of the inquest from David Westropp. He asked the investigating officer whether a solicitor should accompany him.

'There is no need for one,' the officer replied. 'You are not guilty of anything.'

The pathologist at the inquest reported the cause of death being a massive overdose of anti-depressants – the deceased had no other illness or symptoms.

The Coroner asked if Tommy had any questions.

'My wife was supposed to have suffered from arthritis of the spine and a peptic ulcer for many years.' Tommy said. 'Recently she believed she had a growth in her throat.'

The pathologist shook his head. 'Let me assure you she was in a perfect state of health. There was nothing at all wrong with her. She didn't even reach the menopause.'

Obviously it was all in her mind Tommy pondered. Her mentality had been attacked and destroyed by a dreadfully malevolent and horrible entity, a monster she could only free herself from by ending her life. He wondered about other reasons for her action:

Did she fear the future in the belief of having cancer in her throat?

Was she afraid of living on her own on a tight budget?

Was it an attempt to frighten him into taking her back and start living together again, a ploy that went wrong due to the delay of Tommy calling the surgery instead of an ambulance?

Did she comprehend the suffering she had inflicted on her husband and her daughter, just like she had shortly after Christmas and decided to spare them from having to live with the demons in her mind? Tommy realised it could be any or all of these, or even something else he was unaware of.

In the meantime the Surgery had Dr Whitney's name removed from the foyer and in due course it was also taken off from the registers of the BMA and the General Medical Council for addiction to morphine.

At the crematorium Jackie had Robin by her side, he was a great help to her in her grief.

Tommy and Jackie decided that Maria's ashes ought to be scattered in the peaceful Garden of Remembrance at the cemetery, in respect of her wanting to be free.

Tommy had 'adopted' a rose tree for her in that beautiful garden with a plaque bearing her name and the caption:

Released from pain and suffering
18th August, 1980

Weeks passed by and Tommy frequently found himself talking to the dog. 'Digger, you don't know how lucky you are. You get your food and drink served up at regular times while I have to shop and cook for myself.Your basket is cleaned at weekends but I have to wash and iron all my bed linen and my shirts myself.' 'Digger, you have nothing to worry about. You don't even have to work for a living. Do you realise that you have the life of Reilly?' 'Digger, you could help me a lot by not shedding all that hair. I am fed up with vacuum cleaning three or four times a week. I wish you could do it, you parasite.'

Sat upright looking at his master, Digger listened to every word but as he could not answer the conversations had always been rather one-sided.

Tommy's hip was getting more and more painful, stiff and troublesome. Eventually he decided to consult Dr Kerr because he had other problems as well.

'I get a sudden tremor come over me during the day and cold sweat running down my sides for no reason at all,' he told the doctor, 'and I wake up at night bathed in perspiration so much that I have to take a shower and change the bed linen. I am unable to concentrate most of the time and I have lost interest in everything including the opposite sex. I also experience frequent feelings of light-headedness and loss of balance for a few seconds. My constant desire to be dead worries me most, although I am not suicidal and I would not take my own life, I just do not enjoy living any more. There seems to be no pleasure or purpose in my existence.'

'You are suffering from depression,' said the doctor. 'Not surprising after what you have been through in the past few years. I'll prescribe something to make you feel better.'

'Are you giving me tablets to make me feel happy?'

'That is a fairly accurate description. Yes.'

'No thanks. If I have to rely on tablets to feel happy then the happiness would be artificial and the feeling of contentment false. I don't want that.'

'You are going to have a very hard time without them.'

'For how long would you say?'

'A couple of years. Maybe more.'

Tommy proffered his right hand over the desk for a handshake, 'You are on.'

He had a new and different challenge to face up to.

1981

His friends, the ones who remained as such, invited Tommy to their parties but each time he was the odd one out because all the others were married couples. He arrived on his own, nobody sat by his side and he departed on his own. They did mean well by inviting him and he appreciated the gesture but his feeling of loneliness at parties was painful. People often asked why he didn't move out of his home full of painful memories. Tommy had a standard reply: 'Wouldn't you say that if I did, I would also have to sell the furniture, the crockery and cutlery, pots and pans, in fact everything? The memories are in my head. Wherever I would go, they will go with me.'

Julia came visiting regularly. Her looks belied her age. No one would have guessed her being even seventy when actually she was well past her eighty-first birthday. Her looks concealed her growing problems with osteoarthritis. She expressed her concern about Tommy's walking, the limping had turned into a hobble. Tommy was aware of that and told her the X-ray had confirmed that the hip joint damaged in 1951 was in an advanced state of arthritis. Julia said she had suspected that and changed the subject.

'Tommy,' she said, and then hesitated... 'Katie Kéry sent me a newspaper cutting more than two years ago. You had plenty of problems at that time so I didn't pass it on. Now I think it is time for you to know.'

Tommy looked at the small article, no more than a column filler that had originally appeared in a Hungarian newspaper.

**TRAGEDY IN THE
CARPATHIANS.**
**Caught by an unexpected
frost, four members of a
party of hill walkers died of
hypothermia in their sleep.
The alarm was raised
by the only survivor.
Two of the four victims
have been identified as the
distinguished author and
academic, Judith Bodor
and her son Tamás Bodor.**

Emotionally Tommy was too numb to be shocked by the news of Judy's tragic death but the memory of their first and only kiss was still very much alive. How many more could they have had if only she had not joined the Pioneer Movement, or if only he had given Judy another chance when she was trying to make amends. If only… if only… if only…

The first anniversary of Maria's death approaching, Tommy composed a short poem and had it inserted in the local paper's 'In Memoriam' column on the day:

> **We shall not forget the tragic day
> Holding your hands as you slipped away.
> Time flies fast, goes slow when healing,
> Memories come back, keep hurting.
> You're at peace now, suffer no more
> In God's garden for ever more.**
> > **Tommy and Jackie.**

1982

Despite the economic recession biting hard, orders drying up and suppliers and customers going out of business, Tommy had plenty to do. The hardest task for him was telling young women employees, nearly all had been there since they had left school, that owing to lack of orders they were going to be laid off. He really considered them his second family and as he was living on his own the nearest.

Tommy also had his home and garden to look after and keep in shape and Digger to care for. All in all, he had little time for himself which in some way alleviated his loneliness yet he had the feeling of being surrounded by an enormous void. There was no one to talk to or share anything with, no one to care for, no one to hug and no one to love. He accepted that finding someone, a lady friend, a partner, would be extremely difficult. Being a realist he realised that a man in his late forties, short in stature and with a gammy leg couldn't be described as irresistibly attractive.

The lonely evenings made him change part of the regime at home. Digger had never been allowed to get onto the furniture and would never try. Tommy collected an old curtain from the loft, spread it across himself and the armchair while watching television and encouraged the dog to climb up. Digger obliged and Tommy helped him curl up to a comfortable position.

This then became the norm. Tommy enjoyed holding the warm body of the large dog on his lap and he received no complaints from Digger.

He enrolled with a friendship/marriage bureau and was introduced to Helen, a nice and pleasant woman.

They were quite a good match and Tommy got on well with her two daughters and her elderly and often grumpy mother. The one limitation to the friendship was the distance which meant that they could only see each other at weekends.

Jackie married Robin. Helen excelled herself as a substitute mother, her younger daughter Jennie was a bridesmaid. The young couple found employment on the Isle of Wight and they moved there. The distance troubled Jackie.

'Dad I think I have let you down and I am really sorry. Being so far away makes me feel that I have abandoned you, leaving you on your own.'

Tommy tried to put her mind at rest. 'Never mind love. This way I don't have to be invited every Sunday. You don't have to put up with my company and I don't have to suffer your cooking.'

Jackie had to laugh at the quip because she was an excellent cook.

Julia still very active, visited her son frequently at weekends just for the day. She travelled by train, Tommy picked her up at the railway station and took her back there.

1983

With time passing and seeing Helen only at weekends Tommy suffered from acute loneliness between Sundays and Saturdays and there was nothing he could do about it. Emotionally and financially he could not undertake total commitment to a whole family and eventually he gently parted from Helen giving her a chance to meet someone who could. She was badly hurt, not realising how much Tommy would miss her and her two lovely daughters.

The bureau brought him together with another rather shy woman, Gladys. During the first few weeks their only contact was by telephone because Gladys felt embarrassed by dragging her left foot slightly. Tommy told her that due to a pelvic fracture in his youth he limped rather badly, a worse plight than hers and after a while she plucked up some courage and they arranged a meeting.

The friendship flourished fast. They complemented each other in almost all aspects. Thrilled with their affair they soon began thinking of the future together. Gladys had just turned forty and told Tommy of her desire to have a baby by him, something she always wanted but never had – this being her last chance.

Level headed as he tended to be, Tommy considered it a bit late for him to be a father again but he was prepared to undertake the responsibility for her sake. He asked Jackie for her opinion and feelings. Jackie declared that she would be delighted to have a little brother or sister.

The plans made, Gladys insisted on a check-up of her problem with the lazy foot. In the following weeks she visited a hospital several times and after that she persistently declined going out with Tommy. They stayed in touch by telephone talking for an hour or two every evening for weeks, yet she could not be persuaded to carry on where they had left off.

Finally, to relieve Tommy from his torment, Gladys explained why she had had to give up her plans for a baby and a happy future. Hearing the details, Tommy thought that the ground would open up under him and he would be swallowed up in one gulp. Gladys's 'lazy foot' was the first symptom of acute multiple sclerosis and she was determined not to let him see her again. Tommy kept ringing her for weeks, begging her to let him visit her. Gladys steadfastly refused. Eventually she pleaded with Tommy to stop telephoning her.

1984–5

Tommy joined a club of divorced, separated and widowed people and attended dances, parties, and coffee evenings but made no firm attachment to anyone. On the one hand it was nice mingling with people, on the other the women Tommy would have liked to make friends with he could not, and the ones nudging up to him he found wanting.

A number of people left the venues with different partners he noticed, and clearly understood their motives. At times even a one-night stand was better than a lonely one.

At the age of nearly fourteen Digger had difficulty in walking and was as thin as a rake. Tommy had to take him to the nearby fields in his car lifting him in and out of it. As Christmas was approaching he informed Jackie that on this occasion he would have to decline the usual invitation to stay with her and her husband. The dog was too frail to travel and he would not leave him in a neighbour's care.

Despite attending a Christmas party and some invitations for drinks after Christmas, Tommy endured many lonely days during the long Christmas break, conscious of being surrounded by a still and empty space. He tried watching television but could not concentrate on any of the programmes. Reading books he realised that either he was re-reading the same page again and again because he could not remember what he had read, or he had found himself simply staring at a page with his thoughts wandering. In extreme desperation he dragged out the furniture from the main bedroom, stripped the paper from the walls and redecorated the room with leftover rolls he found in the loft.

On the last but one day of the year Digger refused all forms of coaxing to get up, he would only raise his head at Tommy calling him to go for the morning walk and then he dropped his head back on his cushion again. Tommy carried the dog to the car with great care, placed him on the back seat and covered him with a blanket.

He returned from the veterinary surgery on his own, biting his lips all the way home to stop himself crying.

In the evening he sat down in his armchair to watch TV and instantly realised that there was no need any more to cover himself with the old curtain. He got up, sat down at the kitchen table, buried his head in his arms and bawled. Now he was really and totally on his own.

1986

Tommy left work at six, earlier than usual. There was a coffee evening scheduled at the home of a lady member. He contemplated the pros and cons of going while preparing his tea. After more than two years of membership he had not formed any attachments, it seemed to be a waste of time. What was the point of shaving, showering, getting dressed, and driving ten miles just to see a group of people? He had seldom attended any gatherings lately because he always went full of expectation and then returned frustrated and disappointed.

Finishing his meal he decided that he would go, having not been to any of the venues for some weeks and also because Gillian's coffee evenings had always been very popular.

By the time he had arrived, the place was packed with people. Fellow members lined both sides of the hall and the room on the left was full. So was the kitchen at the end of the hall. He exchanged greetings with members he was acquainted with and entered the large living room squeezing past people standing in the doorway. The room was crammed all seats taken, people sitting on the floor in-between chairs.

'Hello Peter, hello Heather, hello Dot,' Tommy greeted some members. Dot was talking to a woman Tommy had not seen before, sitting next to her on the floor. She was in her early forties, small built, had a nice roundish face with hardly any make-up on and neatly trimmed salt-and-pepper hair which added to her attraction. There was a small space on the floor between her and the fireplace.

'Is this seat taken?' Tommy asked her pointing to the floor.

'No, you are welcome to it,' she answered with a bright smile.

'Tom, this is my friend Carolyn,' said Dot. 'Carolyn, this is Tom.'

The introduction over he sat down next to Carolyn and they spent over an hour in pleasant conversation.

Tommy was glad he had not stayed at home but as people started to leave he had a decision to make; should he ask Carolyn for her telephone number and risk getting the reply he had received so many times: 'I'd rather not, if you don't mind', or should he wait to see her at another venue before asking her? That would incur the possibility of him being pipped at the post by someone else. What the heck he thought, better get it over with.

'Carolyn, may I have your telephone number?'

'Yes, you may, it is 823394. I'd like to hear from you.'

That was different! For the first time he drove home with rays of hope in his heart.

The orthopaedic consultant, Mr Thomas, examined Tommy and then told him to get dressed and join him in his office. Sitting behind his desk he explained exactly like other consultants had in the previous five years that Tommy was too young for a total hip replacement although he was in need of one. The joints last twelve to fifteen years and replacing them is very difficult. Maybe in eight years' time at the age of sixty.

Tommy replied rather impatiently, 'Mr Thomas, the muscles in my thigh are contracting and despite daily exercises I can only reach my right foot with great difficulty. Pulling on trousers, socks and tying shoelaces are all problematic. Paring my toenails in agonising pain is a real struggle. I live alone and work all day. I can't ask my neighbours to dress and undress me every morning and evening or to wash my foot as the muscle contraction worsens. In eight years' time my thigh muscles will have contracted so much that even after the operation I will remain crippled for the rest of my life.'

Mr Thomas studied the man sitting at the other side of his desk thoughtfully, in silence. The patient was small in stature and about 8½–9 stone in weight. There was a chance to prevent him becoming crippled but the additional operation would exceed the limits set by the National Health Service. On the other hand he lived by the Hippocratic Oath and it had always been his guideline, '…may I long experience the joy of healing those who seek my help…'

He proffered his hand across the desk for a handshake. 'I'll do the operation within six months.'

Age had been catching up with Julia. She had endured the agonies of spinal osteoporosis for some years and now she suffered from angina attacks as well.

Tommy chided her. 'Mum, I've asked you many times over the years to move down here, telling you that when you grow old I'll be too far away from you to be of any help. You never listen to me do you?'

'Never mind Tommy, I'll be all right. I like it here, all my friends are here. You'd be at work all day.'

'I accept that but I could see you and do things for you I cannot do now because of the distance.'

'Thank you. Very nice of you but I can manage.'

Jackie asked her to move to the Isle of Wight but she declined. Telling her father about it Tommy said, 'That was very kind of you but I think that out of her environment she'd be dead in three weeks.'

Carolyn sat opposite him at a table Tommy had booked at a cosy little restaurant where all meals were prepared fresh after their order was taken. Customers had to wait for their selection but it was worth it. The lady proprietor, whose husband was the chef had already taken Tommy's order. Carolyn was still scrutinising the menu.

'I'd like the roast chicken, provided the stuffing contains no pork.'

'No madam, it does not.'

'Fine, in that case that is what I'd like.' The proprietress departed.

'Unusual request. Are you Jewish by any chance?' Tommy asked.

'I am. I also have the impression that you might be as well. Part of your attraction.'

'Ah,' Tommy said, 'not quite,' and explained, hoping that she would not be overly disappointed.

Tommy was convinced that he had a lot of love to offer to the right person but it proved incomparable to what Carolyn possessed. Love and tenderness radiated from of her. Julia perceived it instantly. To Tommy's great relief Jackie also took to her on their first meeting.

Even though Jackie had got on well with his first lady friend, Helen, Tommy was aware that he could never replace her mother with anyone else. He had tried his best to fill in for Maria and did quite well. Jackie frequently asked his opinion and advice and confided in him her most delicate and intimate thoughts and problems. Tommy was very pleased and happy about that.

For her part, Jackie greatly appreciated that her father was always there when she needed him and for visiting the rose tree at the Garden of Remembrance on birthdays and anniversaries. On Mothering Sundays Tommy placed daffodils under it, freshly cut from his garden on Jackie's behalf.

He received a beautifully worded birthday card from Jackie which he considered his greatest treasure, far beyond the values of money or possessions. Jackie must have gone to great lengths to find a card that matched her sentiment, but it was her inscription that made it so significant:

> **Dad,**
> **Thank you for being my friend and**
> **confidant and so much more**
> **Jackie xxx**

1987

Mr Thomas kept his word. Tommy received notification that he would be admitted to Black Notley Hospital on 5th February. Two days before entering hospital he informed both his mother and his daughter of his impending journey to Switzerland on company business as he had done in the past and he wouldn't be back for a week or more.

At Black Notley Hospital the Matron told him that he was due in theatre next morning at eleven o'clock. According to the information sheet handed to him, the operation would last approximately ninety minutes. After that he should be coming round about six o'clock in the evening at the latest.

Next morning he was told to go into a cubicle and change into the shapeless white gown patients have to don before an operation. Rolled up in his hand he smuggled in a post-it-note in a snap bag he had prepared at home for this occasion. The snap-bag had a large drawing pin at each of its four corners with the pin bent flat and double-sided sticky tape on the underside.

Attaching it to his abdomen, under the gown, the note in the plastic bag gave the impression of being held in place by drawing pins and read:

> *To my Surgeon:*
> *Should you let your scalpel slip,*
> *Damaging my precious bit,*
> *My curse will strike you down below,*
> *A dozen warts on yours will grow.*

Naked under the gown he was transferred on a hospital bed to a room adjacent to the operating theatre.

The anaesthetist looked at his arm and said in a good-humoured manner, 'You won't be a problem with your large veins,' and proceeded to insert a huge hypodermic needle into one.

'Where did you get that needle from,' Tommy asked, 'from the end of the fire-hose?'

'Keep your voice down', whispered the anaesthetist, smiling. 'We have to economise!'

Immediately after that everything went black.

His eyelids were heavy and he was aware of a touch of nausea. His mind quite alert, Tommy observed his surroundings. The place was dark. On the far side stood a small office, light coming through its windows and a nurse studying something behind a desk. The small blue night-light on the ceiling was also illuminated. It didn't make sense he had gone under before eleven that morning and should have regained consciousness hours ago.

'Nurse!' he heard himself croaking.

The nurse looked up and came over to his bedside.

'Hello, how d'you feel?'

Tenderly, Tommy placed his right palm on her left buttock. 'That's how I *feel*, now you know.'

'You cheeky devil,' the nurse laughed. 'You must be on the mend!'

'What's the time?'

'Quarter past one.'

'In the morning? Where have I been for so long? I went into theatre at 11 a.m.!'

'All I know is that you were in theatre for a very long time, six hours, I believe. Go back to sleep you need the rest.'

The morning after his operation Mr Thomas visited the ward and ascertained all was well with Tommy and his leg in traction, which on this occasion had not been attached to a pin through his leg but to a plaster cast wrapped round it. The surgeon said that the traction would be removed after one week and the hip joint he fitted Tommy with had a removable 'wear part'; changing it would be a relatively simple operation. Bending right over him Mr Thomas said very softly, 'We have taken great care not to cause any damage elsewhere,' and departed with a smile.

Tommy wrote a letter to Jackie explaining what had been done to him and apologising for misleading her by the tale of going to Switzerland. Jackie was to explain to Julia gently, Tommy did not want her to have a heart attack.

In due course, a nurse rolled the telephone trolley to his bed with an indignant Jackie on the line.

'Dad, how could you? You have never lied to me before! What if you had died?'

'Well, there you have it Jackie. I saved you from being worried about me dying on the operating table or hoping for an early inheritance.'

Jackie could not stop herself laughing. 'Just wait until I can lay my hands on you, you monster!

Three weeks later he was back home moving around on crutches. Contrary to instructions but in need of a good wash, Tommy manoeuvred himself into the bathtub for a good soaking. He let his legs float and could not take his eyes off them. They were the same lengths with both feet at identical angles, the first time in thirty-six years. Tears welled up in his eyes. The surgeon had gone far beyond the call of duty and spared no effort reconstructing his deformed pelvis. The operation was a masterpiece, different, but in the same class as Jenő Manninger's handiwork in 1951.

Was it just pure luck that he had been operated on in two different countries by the best surgeons available, or had Sister Zoé been right saying in 1945 that he had a guardian angel?

Carolyn lavished her inexhaustible supply of love on Tommy. She showered him with presents ignoring his pleadings not to. Tommy did not want them to finish up in the loft or in the back of a drawer. At the appearance of yet another unwanted present he told her off and she was hurt. Being very sensitive she had problems with his straightforward and blunt manner even if Tommy had no intention hurting her. Tommy demonstrated his tenderness in many ways. He was conscious of the gift fate had bequeathed on him in the form of Carolyn and he loved her. Subconsciously though he was protecting himself from being hurt again. Three times was too much, Judy, Anna, Maria. The last one had inflicted irreparable damage. Tommy had helped many people with all sorts of problems through his life but he had failed to relieve his wife from her mental anguish. He did not consider himself guilty, he had no reason to because he had tried long and hard to save the marriage yet the feeling that he had missed some sign or signal has never left him.

The Beginning of the End.

Julia's condition had deteriorated over the years. No more could she travel to visit her son. Jackie was even further away. Tommy and Carolyn travelled to London frequently to do what they could but there wasn't much to do. Despite her aching joints and angina attacks Julia carried on with shopping, going to the Post Office and keeping her home in order. She was as stubborn and resolute as one can be, Carolyn noted – just like her son.

Infrequently Julia insisted on Tommy visiting her during the week and that he would come on his own for no obvious reason. It was probably just a natural desire to be alone with her son and reminisce. She kept telling him to marry Carolyn and Tommy reminded her she wanted him to marry Helen at the time.

'That was then,' she said. 'But you are going to lose Carolyn if you are not careful.'

'What makes you think that?'

'You don't know how to treat her. If you don't marry her she will leave you.'

'Mum, don't treat me like child. I am your son, not your little boy any more.'

'You will always be my little boy!'

The statement confirmed Tommy's view that his mother's mind had become trapped in a time warp in the long distant past. She was trying to protect him from harm, unable to appreciate the fact that he was passing middle age and had a mind of his own.

At one of his visits, she made Tommy compile a list of items, mementoes to be given to her friends after her eventual demise. Having finalised the details she said in no uncertain terms, 'Tommy, when I die I want to be cremated at Golders Green. I don't want a priest or a rabbi. I want you to perform the service.' That was not a request it was more like a command.

'Mum, do you realise what you are asking of me?'

'Yes, I do. Nobody knows me better than you do. That is why I want you to do it.'

Tommy sat there in silence watching her, convinced that his mother was unable to comprehend the enormity of the task.

'Mum, people will think that I had lost touch with reality! Would you mind putting this in writing?'

He recognised his mother's handwriting on the envelope delivered a few days later. It contained her request written both in English and in Hungarian. The final request, Tommy contemplated. Will I be able to carry it out?

Talking on the telephone every evening Julia told him all her problems, physical and emotional, that she would not share with anyone else. Tommy understood her need to reveal her anguish but it was very distressing at times when she was crying in agonising pain because not even the strongest painkiller could ease her suffering any more.

She told Tommy more than once that she had no wish to go on living any longer. She suffered from incessant pain and asked him to tell her what to do.

'Mum, I appreciate how you feel. It hurts me watching you suffer. I won't condemn you whatever you decide to do. But please do not expect *me* to encourage you to end your life.'

In the middle of the night of Good Friday, 1995, Julia suffered a heart attack. Her life was saved by the red panic button she had with her all the time combined with the emergency telephone system. The attack was a mild one. By the time Tommy and Carolyn arrived at University College Hospital she was sitting up in bed.

A week later the hospital discharged Julia and she said that she felt better than ever.

In spite of this she suffered another heart attack at the end of June, again in the middle of the night. She found herself at the same hospital in the same ward and just as on the previous occasion Tommy and Carolyn were at her bedside shortly after nine in the morning. Jackie was on her way too.

Concealed by curtains all round Julia was in a pitiful state, semi-conscious. Holding her wrist Tommy could not find her pulse at first it was so weak. He counted the heart rate being over a hundred not knowing how many beats he might have missed.

He stayed outside the curtains after eleven o'clock waiting for Jackie.

They embraced when she arrived and kissed each other on the cheek.

'Jackie, your Gran is not a pretty sight don't be shocked by her appearance.'

'Dad, you and I have been through an experience like this once before. I'll be all right.'

She confirmed her words by sitting with her grandmother, holding her hand and talking to her for hours making Tommy proud of her.

'I don't think my mother will last much longer.' Tommy said to the nurse in charge.

'We are doing all we can to help her,' she replied.

'I have no doubt about that, Staff Nurse, but I can't help wondering that by prolonging her life we are prolonging her agony. In the last six or seven years she has had to endure constant, unrelenting pain. There is no cure available for her problems. She will have nothing to look forward to but more suffering.'

The telephone rang early next morning. It was the nurse in charge of the ward.

'Mr Tottis, I am sorry to inform you that your mother passed away peacefully an hour ago. She was in great discomfort last night. I gave her an injection to help her sleep better.'

'Thank you very much Staff Nurse for *everything* you have done. Would you please thank all members of your staff on my behalf.'

At Golders Green, the director of the chapel discussed the arrangements and acquainted Tommy with the general course of action and service. Most of the assembled mourners were Julia's friends, some of them he had not met before. They took their places in the pews and Tommy mounted the rostrum.

Bracing himself for the difficult task he gave a brief résumé of Julia's life from childhood onward with the trials, tribulations and happy times. He concluded by praising the courage and fortitude she had displayed during the last few years of ill health. Tommy also explained her insistence on being cremated at Golders Green with no religious ceremony, requesting him to hold the service. Taking a deep breath he continued, 'I have very good reasons to believe in God, therefore I cannot allow my mother to go exactly as she wanted to. A stray sheep is a bewildered sheep. It needs guidance back to the flock. Being a Christian I cannot say the Kaddish, the last prayer for my mother, so in a moment I will say the Lord's Prayer in Hungarian. Carolyn has kindly offered to read the Kaddish for her.' With his throat tightening, he began,

> "Mi Atyánk, ki vagy a mennyekben,
> Szenteltessék meg a Te neved..."

It was time to press the small push-button concealed in the woodwork of the rostrum. Pressing it gently with his thumb he started the machinery taking the coffin slowly out of the chapel. His throat went tight and at the line: 'Thy will be done...' Tommy had to stop.

After a short pause, fighting in vain to stop his tears coming forth as the coffin gradually moved out of sight and the curtains closed around it, Tommy finished the prayer and a tearful Carolyn joined him on the rostrum. She read the Kaddish in Hebrew and took the mandatory three steps backwards.

On the way home Tommy realised there was no one left he could reminisce with about the early part of his life. Never again could he say or be asked: 'Do you remember when...?'

However, he appreciated that that was a small price to pay considering that his mother's pain and distress had at last ended. Wherever she was, she was not suffering anymore. And the knowledge of that cheered him up.

THE END